Handing Down the Faith

Handing Down the Faith

*How Parents Pass Their Religion
on to the Next Generation*

CHRISTIAN SMITH
AND
AMY ADAMCZYK

OXFORD
UNIVERSITY PRESS

OXFORD
UNIVERSITY PRESS

Oxford University Press is a department of the University of Oxford. It furthers
the University's objective of excellence in research, scholarship, and education
by publishing worldwide. Oxford is a registered trade mark of Oxford University
Press in the UK and certain other countries.

Published in the United States of America by Oxford University Press
198 Madison Avenue, New York, NY 10016, United States of America.

Library of Congress Cataloging-in-Publication Data
Names: Smith, Christian, 1960– author. | Adamczyk, Amy, 1974– author.
Title: Handing down the faith : how parents pass their religion on to the
next generation / Christian Smith and Amy Adamczyk.
Description: New York, NY, United States of America : Oxford University Press, 2021. |
Includes bibliographical references and index.
Identifiers: LCCN 2019048266 (print) | LCCN 2019048267 (ebook) |
ISBN 9780190093327 (hardcover) | ISBN 9780190093341 (epub) |
ISBN 9780190093358
Subjects: LCSH: Christian education—Home training—United States. |
Christian education of children.—United States.
Classification: LCC BV1590.S579 2020 (print) | LCC BV1590 (ebook) |
DDC 248.8/45—dc23
LC record available at https://lccn.loc.gov/2019048266
LC ebook record available at https://lccn.loc.gov/2019048267

DOI: 10.1093/oso/9780190093327.001.0001

3 5 7 9 8 6 4 2

Printed by Sheridan Books, Inc., United States of America

For Bobby
– C.S.S.

For my mother – Carol Adamczyk (R.I.P.)
– A.L.A

Contents

Acknowledgments

WE WOULD LIKE to acknowledge first the generous funding of Lilly Endowment Inc. for supporting this study—thanks especially to Jessicah Duckworth and Christopher Coble for their interest in our research, without which this work could not have been completed. We are also grateful to the clergy of the many religious congregations whose parents we interviewed for this study, for their cooperation and assistance; and to those parents themselves who were generous enough to share such a personal and important part of their lives with us. Thanks also go to our research collaborators who, along with us, conducted interviews across the country: Justin Bartkus, Katie Comeau, Donna Frietas, Hilary Davidson, Michael Emerson, Nicolette Manglos-Weber, Daniel Matus, Heather Price, Pier Pigozzi, and Angela Williams. Rae Hoffman, Heather Price, and Sara Skiles did a great job administering the project management through the University of Notre Dame Center for the Study of Religion and Society, the institutional support of which we are also thankful. Thanks also to Jacob Felson and Tricia C. Bruce for providing comments on a few early chapters.

Introduction

THIS BOOK IS about how American religious parents approach the handing on of their religious practices and beliefs to their children. We know a lot about the importance of parents in faith transmission and factors that influence its effectiveness. But we know much less about the actual beliefs, feelings, and activities of the parents themselves when it comes to the intergenerational transmission of religious faith and practice.

To help remedy this lack of knowledge, this book uses new empirical evidence from more than 230 interviews, as well as data from three nationally representative surveys, to answer the following kinds of questions. What do American religious parents actually *assume, desire,* and say they *do* to try to pass on religion to their children? What kind of *cultural assumptions* do parents make about religious transmission to children? How do parents *view* and *relate to* their religious congregations as they seek to instill religious faith and practice into young people? How do parents' experiences in their *own larger families*—as children and spouses themselves—affect their religious parenting? How do *different* kinds of parents—in terms of religious tradition, social class, family structure, race and ethnicity, immigration status, and personal religious commitment—*vary* in the way they approach passing on religion to their children? These questions have been understudied to date. By answering them here, we hope to contribute significantly to knowledge about parenting, religion, culture, and socialization—important matters both in academic scholarship and to countless parents and communities of faith.

The Overriding Importance of Parents

Some readers might be surprised to know that the single, most powerful causal influence on the religious lives of American teenagers and young adults is the religious lives of their parents. Not their peers, not the media, not their youth group leaders or clergy, not their religious school teachers. Myriad studies show that, beyond a doubt, the parents of American youth play *the* leading role in shaping the character of their religious and spiritual lives, even well after they leave home and often for the rest of their lives[1] (about which we will have more to say later). Furthermore, this parental influence has not declined in effectiveness since the 1970s.[2] Some American parents believe that they lose most of their influence over their children around the early teen years; more than a few American teenagers act as if their parents no longer matter much in their lives. But in most cases those are cultural illusions belied by the sociological facts.

The influence of parents on children while they still live at home— including their influence on their religious identities, beliefs, and practices—is

1. Christian Smith and Melinda Denton, *Soul Searching: The Religious and Spiritual Lives of American Teenagers* (New York: Oxford University Press, 2005); Christian Smith with Patricia Snell, *Souls in Transition* (New York: Oxford University Press, 2009); Vern Bengtson, *Families and Faith: How Religion Is Passed Down across Generations* (New York: Oxford University Press, 2013); S. Myers, "An Interactive Model of Religious Inheritance: The Importance of Family Context," *American Sociological Review* 61 (1996): 858–866; Lisa Pearce and Arland Thornton, "Religious Identity and Family Ideologies in the Transition to Adulthood," *Journal of Marriage and the Family* 69 (2007): 1227–1243; Richard Petts, "Trajectories of Religious Participation from Adolescence to Young Adulthood," *Journal for the Scientific Study of Religion* 48 (2009): 552–571; Marjorie Gunnoe and K. Moore, "Predictors of Religiosity among Youth Aged 17–22," *Journal for the Scientific Study of Religion* 41 (2002): 613–622; Christopher Bader and S. Desmond, "Do as I Say and as I Do: The Effects of Consistent Parental Beliefs and Behaviors upon Religious Transmission," *Sociology of Religion* 67 (2006): 313–329; Darren Sherkat, "Religious Socialization," in *Handbook of the Sociology of Religion*, ed. Michele Dillon (New York: Cambridge University Press, 2003), 151–163; J. Kim, Michael McCullough, and D. Chicchetti, "Parents' and Children's Religiosity and Child Behavioral Adjustment among Maltreated and Non-maltreated Children," *Journal of Child and Family Studies* 18 (2009): 594–605; Vern Bengtson, C. Copen, N. Putney, and M. Silverstain, "A Longitudinal Study of Intergenerational Transmission of Religion," *International Sociology* 24 (2009): 325–345; Sarah Spilman, Tricia Neppl, Brent Donnellan, Thomas Schofield, and Rand Conger, "Incorporating Religiosity into a Developmental Model of Positive Family Functioning across Generations," *Developmental Psychology* 49 (2013): 762–774; Pamela King, J. Furrow, and N. Roth, "The Influence of Families and Peers on Adolescent Religiousness," *Journal of Psychology and Christianity* 21 (2002): 109–120; W. Bao, L. Whitbeck, D. Hoyt, and Rand Conger, "Perceived Parental Acceptance as a Moderator of Religious Transmission among Adolescent Boys and Girls," *Journal of Marriage and the Family* 61 (1999): 362–374; R. Day, H. Jones-Sanpei, J. Smith Price, D. Orthner, E. Hair, K. Moore, and K. Kaye, "Family Processes and Adolescent Religiosity and Religious Practice," *Marriage and Family Review* 45 (2009): 289–309; K. Hyde, *Religion in Childhood and Adolescence* (Birmingham, AL: Religious Education Press, 1990); E. Maccoby, "The Role of Parents in the Socialization of Children," *Developmental Psychology* 28 (1992): 1006–1017; John Wilson and Darren Sherkat, "Returning to the Fold," *Journal for the Scientific Study of Religion* 33 (1994): 148–161.

2. Bengtson, *Families and Faith*, 54–67, 185–186.

paramount, lasting for years, decades, often lifetimes. The best general predictor of what any American is like religiously, after comparing all of the other possible variables and factors, is what their parents were like religiously when they were growing up. Parents do not, of course, control or determine the religious lives of their children; and many households produce children whose religious lives vary wildly. But a large body of accumulated research consistently shows that, when viewing Americans as a whole, the influence of parents in religiousness trumps every other influence, however much parents and children may assume otherwise.

That profound influence of parents provides the premise for the importance of this book, which speaks to many audiences. Sociologists are interested in understanding processes of social reproduction, how social practices and beliefs are carried on with continuity from one generation to the next. That involves learning about the role of families and other institutions in the process of socialization.[3] Many parents are also invested in how their children turn out religiously, as are many grandparents, religious leaders, clergy, youth pastors, family friends, teachers, and mentors. Since parents are so important in shaping the religious outcomes of their children, their approach to the matter deserves to be understood and explained well.

In fact, however, social scientists have conducted surprisingly little reliable empirical research on the culture of parenting in the intergenerational transmission of religious faith and practice.[4] Sociology contains a massive literature on marriage and family, some of which engages questions of religion, since in America, family and religion are so closely tied together.[5] The sociology of religion has also enjoyed a recent burgeoning of studies on the religious lives of teenagers and emerging adults. Sociologists of religion have also long studied religious conversion from one faith (or lack thereof) to another. Some sociologists and political scientists also research institutions involved in socialization generally, including political socialization, such as families,

---

3. For a landmark and exemplary work, see Annette Lareau, *Unequal Childhoods: Class, Race, and Family Life* (Berkeley: University of California Press, 2011).

4. For example, religion as a topic merits only one sentence in Joan Grusec and Paul Hastings's 720-page *Handbook of Socialization: Theory and Research* (New York: Guilford Press, 2007). Ute Schönpflug's *Cultural Transmission: Psychological, Developmental, Social, and Methodological Aspects* (Cambridge: Cambridge University Press, 2009) includes no references to religion at all.

5. For example, Penny Edgell, *Religion and Family in a Changing Society* (Princeton, NJ: Princeton University Press, 2006); Wesley Burr, Loren Marks, and Randal Day, *Sacred Matters: Religion and Spirituality in Families* (New York: Routledge, 2012).

schools, peer groups, and the media.[6] But few have studied the perspectives and approaches of parents themselves when it comes to the religious socialization of their children—especially on a national level that includes a broad array of religious traditions and other demographic characteristics.[7] This book helps redress that deficiency.

Related Background Findings

Previous research has also established a number of related, fairly reliable findings in this general field of inquiry.[8] They include the following:

6. For reviews of the complex literature, see Joan Grusec and Maayan Davidov, "Integrating Different Perspectives on Socialization Theory and Research," *Child Development* 81, no. 3 (2010): 687–709; Joan Grusec, Jacqueline Goodnow, and Leon Kuczynski, "New Directions in Analyses of Parental Contributions to Children's Acquisition of Values," *Child Development* 71, no. 1 (2000): 205–211.

7. See, for example, the observations of S. Hardy, J. White, Z. Zhang, and J. Ruchty, "Parenting and Socialization of Religiousness and Spirituality," *Psychology of Religion and Spirituality* 3 (2011): 217–230; Kim et al., "Parents' and Children's Religiosity"; P. Heaven, J. Ciarrochi, and P. Leeson, "Parental Styles and Religious Values among Teenagers," *Journal of Genetic Psychology* 171 (2010): 93–99.

8. The following points are gleaned from Bengtson, *Families and Faith*, 71–98, 99–112, 114–119, 121–128, 145–164, 182, 186–188, 132–142, 196; H. Grovant and C. Cooper, "Individuation in Family Relationships," *Human Development* 29 (1986): 82–100; Loren Marks and David Dollahite, *Religion and Families* (New York: Routledge, 2017), 111–155; David Dollahite and Jennifer Thatcher, "Talking about Religion: How Highly Religious Youth and Parents Discuss Their Faith," *Journal of Adolescent Research* 23 (2008): 611–641; Valerie King and Glen Elder, "Are Religious Grandparents More Involved Grandparents?" *Journal of Gerontology* 54 (1999): S317–S328; Vern Bengtson, "Beyond the Nuclear Family: The Increased Importance of Multi-generational Bonds," *Journal of Marriage and Family* 63 (2001): 1–16; Holly Allen and Heidi Oschwald, "The Spiritual Influence of Grandparents," *Christian Education Journal* 5, no. 2 (2018): 346–362; Diane Garland, "Faith Narratives in Congregants and Their Families," *Review of Religious Research* 44 (2002): 69–92; M. Pinquart and R. Silbereisen, "Transmission of Values from Adolescents to Their Parents," *Adolescence* 39 (2004): 83–100; L. Kuczynski, "Beyond Bidirectionality," in *Handbook of Dynamics in Parent-Child Relations*, ed. L. Kuczynski (Thousand Oaks, CA: Sage, 2003), 3–14; W. Grolnik and R. Ryan, "Parent Styles Associated with Children's Self-Regulation and Competence in School," *Journal of Educational Psychology* 8 (1989): 143–154; R. Myan and C. Powelson, "Autonomy and Relatedness as Fundamental to Motivation and Education," *Journal of Experimental Education* 60 (1991): 49–66; J. Grusec and J. Goodnow, "Impact of Parental Discipline Methods on the Child's Internalization of Values," *Developmental Psychology* 30 (1994): 4–19; Leah Power and Cliff McKinney, "Emerging Adult Perceptions of Parental Religiosity and Parenting Practices," *Psychology of Religion and Spirituality* 5 (2012): 99–109; Holly Allen with Christa Adams, Kara Jenkins, and Jill Meek, "How Parents Nurture the Spiritual Development of Their Children," in *Understanding Children's Spirituality*, ed. Kevin Lawson (Eugene, OR: Cascade, 2012); Kara Powell and Chap Clark, *Sticky Faith* (Grand Rapids, MI: Zondervan), 71; Spilman et al., "Incorporating Religiosity into a Developmental Model"; Smith with Snell, *Souls in Transition*; Naomi Schaefer Riley, *Till Faith Do Us Part: How Interfaith Marriage Is*

- Crucial in the parental transmission of religion to children is having generally *warm, affirming relations* with them. Parents can be very invested in and intentional about religious transmission, but if they have emotionally distant and critical relationships with their children, their efforts are likely to fail or backfire. (See Chapter 2 for more on this.)
- The *quality* of conversations and interactions about religion between parents and children is more important for influencing children than the particular content that parents try to instill or teach. *How* parents and their children interact about religion has more influence on the outcomes than the particular substance that parents try to communicate. (We explore this point in greater depth in Chapters 2 and 3.)
- The most effective parent conversations about religion with children are *children-centered* rather than parent-centered. In them, children ask questions and talk more while parents mostly listen; the questions about religion are clearly related to children's lives; parents try to help children understand their religious faith and practices; the conversations are open, not rigid or highly controlled; and the larger relationship between parents and children is thereby nurtured. When parents, by contrast, talk too much, make demands without explanations, force unwanted conversations, and restrict discussions to topics that they control, faith transmission to children is likely to be ineffective or counterproductive.
- The role of *fathers* is especially important in forming children religiously. Both parents matter a lot in faith transmission, but the role of fathers appears to be particularly crucial, providing dads (when they are present) with extra influence and responsibility in the matter.[9]
- Parents who *share the same religious faith and practice* are more effective in socializing their children in that religion than parents who differ.

Transforming America (New York: Oxford University Press, 2013); Larry Nelson, "The Role of Parents in the Religious and Spiritual Development of Emerging Adults," in *Emerging Adults' Religiousness and Spirituality: Meaning-Making in an Age of Transition*, ed. Carolyn Barry and Mona Abo-Zena (New York: Oxford University Press, 2014); also see Emma Green, "It's Moms Who Get Kids to Church," *The Atlantic*, October 26, 2016. https://www.theatlantic. com/politics/archive/2016/10/its-the-moms-who-get-kids-to-church/505310/.

9. Robert Wuthnow, for example, noted in a study he conducted in the 1990s: "When fathers were absent or emotionally distant, people did not adopt a maternal image of God; religious teaching[s] that associate God with maleness were too prominent for that to happen. Instead, a wrathful, distant view of God emerged, sometimes closely resembling that of the absent father. Or, [conversely and] more interestingly, the absent father actually created a kind of psychological space in which a more loving God-father came to dwell." Robert Wuthnow, *Growing Up Religious* (Boston: Beacon Press, 1999), 62.

Religiously similar parents present to their children a "united front" that better transmits across generations than religiously different.

- *Two-parent households* are most effective in transmitting religious faith and practice to children. Parents who are never married, separated, or divorced are, on average, less likely to pass on their religion to their children.
- *Grandparents* (and sometimes other family relatives, such as aunts, uncles, and cousins) are also influential in shaping the religious lives of their grandchildren, potentially substituting for, reinforcing, moderating, or even subverting the impact of parents.
- *Too much or too little religious socialization* by parents tends to undermine the transmission of religious faith to children. Religion seems most effectively passed on to children by parents who are intentional, consistent, and actively engaged, but neither hands-off nor overbearing. Weak and sporadic religious socialization tends to produce benign apathy in children; whereas against relentless or overbearing religious socialization children tend to distance themselves or rebel against the family religion.
- *Parental consistency in word and deed, rules, and meaningful intentions* affects the success of religious transmission to children. Perceptions of hypocrisy when parents do not act in congruence with their religious teachings, or when parents follow the letter but not the meaning of the law, such as parents insisting on praying in Hebrew but unable to explain what the prayers mean reduce children's interests in carrying forward the religious faith and practices of their parents.
- *Children influence the religious lives of parents reciprocally* and are not simply the recipients of one-way parental influences. Research and theory traditionally assumed a unilateral direction of causal influence from parents to children; but more recent, sophisticated scholarship has shown that children also influence their parents' beliefs, values, and practices.
- Parental influences that strengthen the religious faith and practice of children have *long-lasting effects* on their psychological adjustment, romantic lives, and future family functioning as adults. The effects that parents have on their children's religious lives not only shape their religion and spirituality but also a host of other nonreligious outcomes.

These research findings are important and help to motivate and inform this book. But they are not our primary concern here. We want to know instead from the *parents'* own perspectives and experiences how they view and try to pass on their religious faith and practice to their children. We keep these related research findings in mind but also pursue here our own central concern: the culture of parenting for religious transmission to children.

Our Research

Our substantive findings and theoretical arguments in this book are based on a national sociological study of American religious parents that we and colleagues conducted in 2014 and 2015.[10] We conducted 215 personal, in-depth interviews with parents who belong to churches, synagogues, mosques, and temples who by affiliation are white conservative Protestant, mainline Protestant, black Protestant, white Catholic, Latino Catholic, conservative Jew, Mormon, Muslim, Hindu, and Buddhist. To compare with this primarily religious group, we also interviewed an additional sample of 20 nonreligious parents.[11] The parents we studied lived in the Chicago, Houston, Los Angeles, Albuquerque, Washington, DC, and New York City areas; and in various parts of Indiana, New Jersey, Florida, Wisconsin, Rhode Island, and Minnesota. We sometimes conducted interviews in locations that in some way typify their religious group—for example, we conducted most of our Latino Catholic interviews with parents in Albuquerque, New Mexico, and Brooklyn, New York, rather than, say, Minnesota.

We selected parents to interview using a "stratified quota" sampling method. This means that we interviewed a set number of parents (the quota) from combinations of categories (the "strata" of types) of religious tradition, social class, race and ethnicity, family structure, and parental religious commitment. So we intentionally interviewed parents in middle-class and upper-middle-class households and in poorer and working-class households. We interviewed parents in two-parent households and parents who are divorced, remarried in "blended" families, and never married. We interviewed parents who are white, black, Hispanic, Asian, and of some other race or ethnicity. Most of the parents we interviewed were heterosexual, but some were in same-sex parenting households. Many of the children of the parents we interviewed are biological, but some are step-children and others are adopted.

---

10. For details, see Appendix: Methodological References.

11. Ten of the 215 parents sampled from religious congregations also turned out to be de facto "nonreligious" parents, even if they had much to say about religious transmission to children, so our total number of actual nonreligious parents interviewed was 30. We do not include systematic comparisons of our religious parents to the nonreligious parent sample in our findings.

Our interview sample is not strictly representative of the populations of religious parents it includes. In-depth research interviews rarely are. Nor does our study include every possible religious tradition. We only studied Conservative Jews, for instance, not Reform, Orthodox, or other kinds of American Jews. Our interviews do, however, provide a large and varied enough sample of different kinds of American parents to be able to identify major themes and differences among these groups of parents in our sampled religious traditions. One purpose was to identify the primary "cultural models," which we further discuss in the next chapter, that inform the ways that many kinds of American religious parents approach the challenge of handing on faith and practice to their children. We also wanted to identify and explain apparent dissimilarities between different types of parents. The questions animating this book have received so little study by scholars that we found it enough to undertake these basic explorations. Our interview sample enables us to do that well—although future research with larger samples and including other religious groups can build upon and perhaps revise our findings here.

Our findings do also, however, include some nationally representative survey data and perspective. In addition to our personal, in-depth interviews, we also statistically analyzed four existing, nationally representative survey datasets of American parents and congregations that included questions about the transmission of faith and practice to children: the National Study of Youth and Religion survey (2002–2013), the Culture of American Families survey (2012), the Faith and Families in America survey (2005), and the US Congregational Life Survey (2008–2009). The results of these statistical analyses provide a big-picture, contextual framework that is nationally representative, within which we can set and understand the qualitative findings from our personal interviews. Our presentation thus combines qualitative and quantitative evidence from complementary sources, enabling us to benefit from the different strengths of rich interview data and nationally representative survey statistics.

The heart of our argument in this book nonetheless rests on our analysis of the 235 personal interviews we conducted. Our central purpose is to begin to identify the major themes, differences, and complexities concerning faith transmission to children among American religious parents. Our findings from the interviews, again, do not purport to represent all types of religious parents in proportion to their numbers in the population. Still, they offer great breadth and insight. Ours is a first venture into some "deep waters" on the research questions we are asking, so our findings represent something more like an initial "sounding" of major parts of the underwater terrain than a comprehensive mapping of its exact depths and contours.

Having said that, we are confident that our interviews-sampling methodology has exposed us to major swaths of different kinds of American religious parents, so that our findings really do identify the major cultural models of religious parenting in the United States. Our story will not be complete and our interview-based findings do not represent in exact proportion the full population of American religious parents. But we are assured that the themes, differences, and complexities that we present in the following chapters are real and roughly proportionate to their reality in American life. And our quantitative survey statistics provide nationally representative evidence as a framing reference and context within which to understand the qualitative findings from our interviews.

Our interview sample largely represents *religious* parents, those who have some membership connection to a church, synagogue, temple, or mosque.[12] For comparative purposes, we also interviewed a sizeable group of nonreligious parents. However, our main focus here is American parents who are religiously connected and invested enough to have a tie to a religious congregation, not the full range of all American parents. We intentionally chose to investigate the religiously "higher end" of American parents because we think they will provide more insight to better answer the research questions we are asking. Readers must keep in mind, then, that we are not discussing American parents of all levels of religious commitment—even if our sample includes some variation of religious commitment—but more highly religious American parents. If we wish after our analysis to think about the implications of our findings for less religious parents, we might be safe to assume that they are similar to those discussed here, only reflecting less religious interest, coherence, and intensity. Or perhaps they are qualitatively different. Only more research can tell. But for present purposes, readers should remember that what we describe and analyze mostly concerns American parents who are relatively more religiously active than the others.

---

12. The nonreligious parents we interviewed were a convenience sample, intended to provide some nonsystematic comparisons for our religious sample, not the basis of a study of nonreligious parents in its own right.

What Follows

We provide readers with a "pocket roadmap" of what comes in this book by closing here with summaries of what each chapter presents. Chapter 1 describes and illustrates the "cultural models" that inform what the vast majority of American religious parents assume and believe about the value and means of passing on religion to their children. Our interest there is sketching out the cognitive maps that religious parents use to make sense of the task of religious transmission to children. Chapter 2 presents the results of statistical analyses of nationally representative longitudinal survey data to examine the importance of parent religiousness, parenting styles, and religious traditions in shaping the religious outcomes of their children 10 years later. In Chapter 3, we consider why parents are—and we think increasingly have become—the central players in their children's religious socialization. We theorize historical transformations of the American religious field and of family life that are crucial for understanding intergenerational religious transmission. Chapter 4 then zooms out to explore findings from two other nationally representative surveys of American parents about their priorities for, expectations about, and practices to influence their children's religious futures. Chapter 5 focuses on parents in four different immigrant religious communities: Muslims, Buddhists, Hindus, and Hispanic Catholics. We explore there how the combinations of immigration, ethnicity, and minority religious status complicate the ways these parents try to pass on their religion to their children. Chapter 6 explores the complex ways that today's parents' personal experiences growing up as children under their own parents influence their approaches to parenting their children. In Chapter 7, we examine what parents want and expect from the religious congregations to which they belong. How do religious parents engage their churches, temples, synagogues, and mosques? Our Conclusion then draws together the various findings and arguments in this book into a final assessment of the complex, contingent, and multileveled forces that shape American parents' task today of passing on religion to their children.

I

Cultural Models of Religious Parenting

HOW DO RELIGIOUS parents in the United States approach the task of passing on their family's faith and practices to their children? What assumptions, categories, and beliefs inform their views on the question? Which desires, feelings, and concerns influence the ways they undertake the transmission of their religion to their kids? This chapter provides partial answers to those questions by summarizing the cultural models that most US parents hold about the issue. To be clear, we are not here examining parents' actual faith-transmission practices, that is, their behaviors. Our concern instead is to identify the relevant cultural models that parents hold, and which we have good reason to believe significantly influence their behaviors. In short, we are interested here in cognitive frameworks that we think shape practices rather than the practices themselves.

In another book from this same project, one of us (Smith) elaborates in detail and develops a theory about these cultural models.[1] This chapter only summarizes what that book develops at length. We cannot reproduce here the hundreds of quotes from parents that substantiate and illustrate these cultural models. Readers interested in exploring this chapter's themes in depth can read the other book. Even so, we do provide a few quotes with each cultural model simply to illustrate, rather than definitively validate, our point. And other parent interview quotes also emerge in different forms around other important topics in the chapters that follow. Meanwhile, readers should know that our findings about the cultural models outlined in this chapter

---

1. Christian Smith, Bridget Ritz, and Michael Rotolo, *Religious Parenting: Transmitting Faith and Values in Contemporary America* (Princeton, NJ: Princeton University Press, 2019).

developed out of more than 2 years of highly detailed coding and analyses of our 235 interview transcripts completed by a small army of research assistants and finished by us, the book authors.

That said, the dominant cultural model of most American religious parents for why and how they should pass on their religious faith and practices to their children can be summarized as follows:

> *Intergenerational Religious Transmission*: Parents are responsible for preparing their children for the challenging journey of life, during which they will hopefully become their best possible selves and live happy, good lives. Religion provides crucial help for navigating life's journey successfully, including moral guidance, emotional support, and a secure home base. So parents should equip their children with knowledge of their religion by routinely modeling its practices, values, and ethics, which children will then hopefully absorb and embrace for themselves.

This is the simplest, most compressed version of the culture model of intergenerational religious transmission. Unpacking this simple model, however, reveals a constellation of cultural models that hang together in parents' cognitive networks, representing and governing their approach to religious transmission. Our interest is with their cultural models of the purpose and means of passing on religion to children. But those make sense because of related cultural models about life's purpose, experience in the world, the nature of children, the task of parenting, family solidarity, religion's value and truth, and the role of religious congregations. Figure 1.1 depicts the full constellation

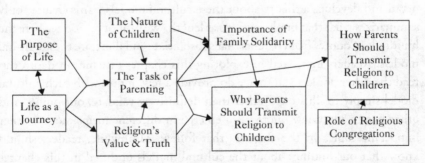

FIGURE 1.1 The constellation of cultural models defining why and how American parents should transmit religious faith and practice to children.

Source: The Intergenerational Religious Transmission Project Interviews, 2014–16 (N = 235).

of these models. This chapter describes each model from the parents' perspective, elucidating the metaphors, beliefs, and language that parents use to express themselves on the issue.

To be sure, few American parents think like philosophers. People generally do not consider or discuss life in systematic, coherent, logical terms. When people give verbal accounts of their ideas and actions, much of what they say in the moment can be pretty uncertain, inarticulate, and spotty. But that does not mean people are not reflective or do not have explicable reasons for the ways they live. They usually do. If as scholars we cannot perceive those reasons, the problem is ours, not theirs. To identify and understand people's reflective reasons motivating and making meaningful how they live, we need to listen long and analyze patiently. When we do, people's thinking can become clearer, usually taking the form of networks of clusters of beliefs, which we can represent in cultural models. Our sociological task here was reconstructing as accurately as possible from the mass of messy interview materials the cultural models that parents actually embrace but which they can have difficulty making explicit and cogent. To do that, we had to read not only on the "surface" of interview statements, as if they might only provide direct propositional "proofs" of beliefs, but also to discern and ferret out the assumptions and beliefs that stand behind and beneath the interview quotes, ideas that are latent in or must be presupposed by the surface statements and by interviews read in their entirety.

Here we focus on the "dominant" cultural models of religious transmission to children, by which we mean the models held by the majority of American religious parents across most religious traditions. We realize that our emphasis on *similarity* across religious traditions violates the current insistence, especially in the discipline of religious studies, on the detailed *particularities* of different religious traditions, subtraditions, and sub-subtraditions. The days of fitting "The World Religions" into neat analytical typologies and categories or of speaking blithely about "*the* Judeo-Christian worldview" are over, and rightly so. Nevertheless, for our purposes here, the empirical evidence in fact does point to *sameness* and *convergence* across religious traditions, which we cannot ignore, even if it does not fit the expectations of some scholarly fields. We do note when different kinds of parents accentuate different aspects of the shared dominant cultural models, as well as exceptions and contradictions when they arise. But our primary focus is on what is dominant due to its being widely shared.

The Purpose of Life

What religious parents in the United States believe about the specific issue of intergenerational religious transmission is partly driven by what they believe about the general issue of the purpose of human life. For the vast majority of American religious parents, the cultural model of the purpose of life is this:

Life's Purpose: The purpose of living is to lead a happy and good life, in the dual sense of both having life go well (enjoying success and happiness) and living life rightly (doing what is morally right). A good life is one in which self-directed individuals are happy, live ethically, work hard, enjoy family and friends, and help other people. Good lives must be self-determined and pursued in ways that are true to each unique individual self. But they should not be individual*istic* in the sense of isolated or selfish; they must always be realized and enjoyed with others, in and with communities, groups, families, and probably marriage partners. Good lives achieve a certain quality of life in this world, in the here and now; they are not primarily preparing for the hereafter, eternity, or some ultimate reality. In order to realize life's purpose of living well, one must be equipped by others with preparation, learning, and competences for the task of self-realization—without which one may become lost, compromised, or fail in life. Still, each individual must find his or her own particular way to discover their own purpose and lead a good life true to who they are as a unique self.

Among the 235 American religious parents we interviewed for this study, it is not possible to find even one who does not assume, affirm, and support these first two propositions of this cultural model. These ideas are "hegemonic," as sociologists say, among parents from every religious tradition, race, ethnicity, social class, family structure, and region of the country examined here. The other propositions in this model were also ubiquitously expressed by religious parents in the United States. Thus, to summarize, the parental task of equipping children is not to prepare them to sustain and reproduce an established inheritance, but rather to discover their own singular, authentic identity and way of life. Preparation during the period of family dependence is precisely to become individually independent. Parent training is thus not so children can carry on stable traditions, like an apprenticeship in an ancient craft. It is rather something more like sailing lessons, so that children are prepared to strike out on their own and sail unexplored waters as they wish.

The idea is not "stay on this trail" but "you must find your own path." What matters is not what parents or society wish them to do, but what they want to do, what will make them happy.

The parents we interviewed thus said things like this white Catholic father from New York City: "I want my kids to be really happy people. Happy people who like their parents, who like their family, to be independent. I want them to explore the world, to be interesting people, good people, to be kind and generous." A Muslim mother from Indiana told us: "I always want them to be safe, happy, educated. I want them to be in control of their life instead of life choosing for them. I want them to be open to everything and worldly, so that they can decide what they want to be in charge." This mainline Protestant mother from New York City disclosed that "everything" one could want has to do with life here and now: "In my life now I feel like I have everything that I want. Basically, the things I was looking for was to be married, have kids in the house, and friends. And I have those things, so for me I have everything." A conservative Protestant mother from Florida explained the importance of preparing her children for good, happy lives: "I set rules, and as long as they stay safe, safety is a key issue. I try to build their self-esteem by allowing them to feel independent—they think they're doing everything on their own, but I've already put the boundaries up, and within those boundaries they can do things. It's amazing watching and allowing them to grow and explore and figure things out 'on their own,' even though I know what the boundaries are." This Hindu father from central New Jersey summarized the outlook of most parents we interviewed when he said, "Honestly, I just want them to be happy with whatever they do. I know it sounds like such a cliché, but I'm not pushing them to be one thing. I want them to find their own path, to be able to have a future."

The Experience of Life in the World

Understanding life requires not only grasping its purpose but also knowing how it will be encountered in the living. What is the experience of life in the world like? On this question, most American religious parents also share a similar view—which gives us a second and closely related cultural model—as follows:

Life in the World: Life is a journey out in the world that each individual must venture and do their best to make go well. The world, which exists beyond the walls of the family home, "out there," offers potential for growth, achievement, and fulfillment, but also threats of instability, confusion, danger, and failure. The world presents a variety of paths to travel and options to choose—some good, some bad. "The culture" sends some bad "messages" that, if believed, threaten success on life's journey, which therefore must be recognized and resisted. Even when life's journey goes well, everyone faces trials, makes mistakes, and confronts discouragement along the way; but these can be overcome when one is properly equipped with resources to surmount them. The good and bad influences of the external world always transform people one way or another, so personal change is inevitable. Only by maintaining a solid internal "grounding," a "true sense of self," can life's travelers navigate their journey successfully and happily.

This model is clearly tied to the first concerning life's purpose, both together being mutually constitutive and reinforcing. In this, one of the most common metaphors the parents we interviewed used to describe life is of a journey, along with the closely related images of life as a path, quest, stage, road, track, rail, and walk, on which we are all travelers.[2] And the idea that "the culture" sends some bad "messages" that, if believed, threaten success on life's journey, which therefore must be recognized and resisted, was the most common response by parents when we asked about their biggest challenges as parents raising children. In the minds of nearly all religious American parents, a powerful force comprised of "the culture," "messages," "technology," and "the media" exists "out there" and makes their jobs very difficult. Partly as a result, most parents also believe and express the ideas of the need for children to have a stable grounding and a solid sense of self. And usually what parents mean by this is something like the same beliefs and values as the parents. That may seem contradictory to the idea of children choosing their own path, but parents make it work by believing that "the foundation" is laid for children early in life, whereas independent path-choosing comes later in life.

One black Protestant father told us, "I let them live their life, let them choose what they want, don't force-feed them. I just want them to be happy and successful and respectful as they journey through life." A Jewish mother from Indiana explained, "I've given my girl a road to be on and we love each other dearly. But she has also come packaged with her own goals and track in

---

2. For an analysis of the quasi-religious theme of redemption central to Americans' self-understandings, see Dan McAdams, *The Redemptive Self: Stories Americans Live By* (New York: Oxford University Press, 2006).

life she's on regardless of anybody else around her. She's on this road and just independent of us and on her own, too." An Hispanic Catholic mother from Indiana described how she reasons with her son to stay on a good path in life:

> You can get sucked into anything, alcohol, drugs, those temptations, out in the world, you can choose your path. You can choose to be successful and take you that way. But if you start doing [bad] stuff, it's gonna take you down the road you don't wanna go, a road you wish you'd never taken. I don't believe he's ever done them [drugs] again, I don't know for sure. But you just don't do drugs, because where is that gonna lead you? You've got two paths to take, down the good road or the bad road. And down the bad road, it's gonna be hard to come back to the good one.

A white Catholic mother from Indiana emphasized the messages of the "culture" that must be resisted: "The biggest challenge is being heard over the din of the crazy culture. There's so much relativism, utilitarianism, all the 'isms that influence kids. I think they do see our witness, during their formative years they need to see the authentic witness and be touched by that and value that above all the easy and crass and materialistic things in the world." And a Buddhist mother from Chicago emphasized the importance of being "grounded" to handle change well:

> Partly our kids' friends are handpicked [chuckling], but sometimes when their friends don't make the best decisions, they can see that. I told him to think how he could help his friends make better decisions. It was a learning experience. As long as they're grounded, I make sure my kids are grounded enough and know how to react to different situations. So I'm not so worried about the bad friends.

The Value of Religion

For few American parents does religion singularly determine their understanding of the ultimate purpose and expected experience of life. Instead, the latter involves clusters of largely autonomous beliefs forming their own distinct cultural models, perhaps partly shaped by religious traditions generally but not principally determined by the specific views and priorities of those traditions. Those basic cultural models being firmly in place, religion then comes in as its own distinct issue. And when parents think about religion, the primary focus is its practical value, how it helps people, what makes it important in this life. To understand the beliefs of the majority of religious parents about religious transmission, toward which this analysis is leading, we need to next understand their more basic cultural model of the importance of religion, which is this:

> *Religion's Value*: Religion is a normal, valuable, meaningful, and worthy part of life, at least in its general principles, not something deserving of skepticism or indifference. Like anything, religion can be manipulated for bad, but its central teachings are good, valuable, and practical for most people—in ways almost exclusively having to do with this life now, not eternity or an afterlife. Religion helps people to "have the right values" and to "be a good person." By providing a "bigger picture" on life, among other things, religion provides feelings of peace, comfort, protection, and belonging, which reduces anxiety and increases wellbeing. Religion also produces pragmatic, humanistic social results, like fostering good citizenship, strengthening society, and upholding morals—all desirable in the world here and now. Religion is good, too, because it can provide cohesion and solidarity in family relationships, and often helps marriages and families get through hard times. We humans have a natural tendency to stray and misbehave in self-harming ways, but religion is effective at helping "keep people in line," which is beneficial. For these reasons it is almost impossible to imagine being a family without religion (even if for others religion is not necessary for achieving the same values, morals, well-being, and good relationships that religion provides our family).

The parents we interviewed spoke positively about religion and its role in their lives, which makes sense since this was a sample of religiously affiliated parents. On occasion they questioned or criticized aspects of religions, but religion overall was for them a good and valuable part of life. The idea that religion helps people to "have the right values," to "be a good person" was one of the most commonly assumed or believed ideas in all of the cultural models. It is patently obvious to all the parents we interviewed in every religious tradition, and nobody ever doubted, questioned, or contradicted it. For most parents, helping people "be good" essentially defines what religion *is*, what religion's basic purpose in life is about. Nearly all of the parents we interviewed also agreed that religion provides feelings of peace, comfort, protection, and belonging, which reduces anxiety and increases well-being. Few spoke about religion's demands or trials or the difficulties of, say, self-mortification (some black Protestant parents being the rare exceptions). Instead, parents routinely praised religion for its therapeutic value and social, cultural, and political benefits.

For this black Protestant mother, as for most religious mothers, religion is normal and important: "It's important to grow up and become a spiritual person because you need that to sustain, just to keep your mind sane, to keep it together, you need faith, belief, that security. I can't imagine not having it, it's very important. You need it and you're absolutely ridiculous if you think you don't" [laughing]. Religion can be bad at times, but it is most fundamentally good, as this Muslim father from Indiana explained:

When you hear in the media about Islam, it's the bad Muslims are the ones who are affecting Islam. The extremists, people who understand religion the way they want it, any religion in the whole world, you can turn it the way you want. People start changing in their religion, but God never changed and the rules of God never changed. But when they try to get into God's business with your own rules, then it will become something you're adding to. So it doesn't matter if I'm Christian or Jew or a Muslim, it depend on my actions and the way I live my life under God's rules.

A Hindu father from Chicago explained how religion promotes the right values and choices for being a good person: "Religion, it's a guidance. It's up to people to decide, but for me, I have chosen that way, I need some guidance. It's a good thing to be a little bit god-fearing, so I won't do any mistakes, at least I think about god before what I'm doing, whether I'm doing right or wrong." Religion makes life better, as this Mormon mother from New York City expressed:

Even if God doesn't exist and the church isn't true, it actually really doesn't matter to me, because I'm choosing it, it's an act of faith to believe in God, who can't be proved or disproved, and it's something that makes my life better. It's a way to raise my children, talking openly. We love them and hope they find their own path, but for now it's really brought us closer together as a family to have this faith we all believe in.

So for many, including this Jewish father from Indiana, it is difficult to imagine life without religion: "I don't even think I can answer the question how
I would be without Judaism, because everything I've said, it's just who I am
deep down. It's informed me in ways some of which are probably genetic,
some cultural, and some learned through religious observance. But I mean,
I wouldn't be me at all, I just don't even really know how to answer that."

Religious Truth

The dominant view of religion held by most religious American parents is defined not only by its value for life in the world but also by a particular approach
to the validity of religious truth claims. Do religions teach authentic truths or
is objective truth not even the point of religion? And if the former (authentic
truths), how can one make sense of the diversity of truth claims made by different religions? The common operative cultural model of religious truth is as
follows.

> *Religious Truth*: All or most religions are after the truth, religions do
> teach genuine truths, and it is possible (for some parents) for a religion
> to teach *the* truth. Two religious truths are paramount for children to
> learn, one vaguely theological and existential; the second, instrumental
> and functional. First, children should learn to "believe in something"
> along the lines that "there is a greater picture" out there, "something
> bigger" going on, such as a God who is with us and answers prayers or
> the force of karma. Second, religion can help people live good lives in
> this world. However, exclusivity, superiority, and fanaticism in religions
> are bad, dangerous, and must be avoided. Even if one believes that no
> one religion has a monopoly on truth, it is still not a bad idea to belong
> to some particular religious tradition or community, to be located some-
> where specific. Beyond the two paramount truths, however, one can take
> from one's own religious tradition the parts that make sense and work
> best, and leave the parts that don't, according to "whatever seems right"
> to you; nobody needs to accept or be subject to the whole package of a
> religious tradition.

Religious parents in the United States express beliefs on this point of religious truth as we would expect according to the religious tradition to
which they belong, based on what we know already about those traditions.
Through religious socialization (and some self-selection through tradition

switching),[3] the subcultures of various religious traditions as environmental contexts shape the beliefs of parents on questions of truth. Mainline Protestant parents express a range of beliefs about religious truth, but they generally tend toward moderate and cautious positions. Most white conservative Protestants consider most or all of Protestant Christianity to teach the truth on "the essentials,"[4] their views about Catholicism vary, as some think Catholicism teaches truth and others that it is flawed with errors; and most would hesitate to say that non-Christian religions teach truth. Black Protestant parents tend to be confident about what they believe but also fairly ecumenical in downplaying the importance of religious differences. Most black Protestant parents seem comfortable keeping Christianity broadly as the center of gravity of religious truth. Most white American Catholic parents tend to express fairly relativistic and ecumenical views of religious truth. Minorities of Catholic parents do take stronger views of the truth of Christianity or of Catholicism, but not many. Hispanic Catholics in the United States are different, however, with views that are more implicit than expounded. Most expressed surprise and sometimes even shock at our very question of whether, for example, their children might switch to a non-Christian religion—especially those who are more recent immigrants. Hispanic Catholics wish for their kids to remain Catholic, and very much hope they do not become non-Christian. That suggests by implication that they think non-Catholic religions do not contain the truth that Catholicism does. Belief in the particularity of Catholic faith and practice among Hispanics more closely resembles that of white conservative Protestants than white Catholics or black Protestants.

Parents from most other religions express similar ranges of positions on religious truth. Some tend to take stronger stands on the truth of their own traditions. But most take different strategies that affirm the truth in many religions. The Jewish parents we interviewed—all Conservative, not Reform

---

3. Not all religious Americans remain for their entire lives in the religious traditions in which they were raised. In fact, many religious Americans change denominations and sometimes religious traditions at least once in their lives. Our point here is that some people may switch religious affiliations because of personal dispositions or greater comfortability with other denominations or traditions, in which case what they may say in a research interview would not reflect their early socialization in their current religious tradition but rather personal tendencies that influenced them to move into that tradition later in life.

4. Because they vary wildly about how to correctly interpret the Bible, they have to focus on "the essentials" strategically in order to avoid self-defeating truth claims amid "pervasive interpretive pluralism." See Christian Smith, *The Bible Made Impossible* (Grand Rapids, MI: Brazos Press, 2012).

or Orthodox—approached the question of religious truth with a distinctively Jewish style of explanation. All seemed uncomfortable with the idea that there exists an ultimate religious truth that people should be interested in discovering. Rather, they seemed primarily concerned with the idea that there are genuinely good ways to live, which is what people should seek out. Practices of ethical goodness trump claims to ultimate truth. At the same time, Jewish parents emphasized the historically and culturally particular nature of good ways of life. In the end, Jewish parents managed to avoid both exclusivity and relativism as they explained what in their tradition was worth sustaining. They would not say that all religions are simply different expressions of the same universal reality or truth. Nor would they take the individualistic strategy of claiming that some religion is the truth "for me." But neither would they claim that Judaism is the one or highest religious truth or way of life. In sum, among the various beliefs of the different cultural models that we are examining here, the question of religious truth gives rise to the greatest diversity of specific approaches by religious parents. Still, underlying most of them is the shared dominant view that religions are after and actually do teach ideas and ways of life that are correct, valuable, and worth following. The idea of needing to "believe in something" was also commonly expressed, perhaps especially by Catholic parents. For more than a few, it appears that what one believes in is less important than simply actually believing in *something* or other.

The cultural belief against religious exclusivity, superiority, and fanaticism is also ubiquitous and clear. Not one parent from any tradition we interviewed disagrees with it. For most parents from every tradition—not only including but actually especially Muslim parents—radical Islamist extremism is the archetypical example of what must be avoided. But violent Islamists are by no means the only concern of parents. What parents consider religious fanaticism can also be evident in aggressively proselytizing members of Christian groups, and even lamentable features of one's own religion. One of the main effects of parents' objection to religious exclusivity and fanaticism is to dampen their own religious fervor.

So to illustrate some of these points, one conservative Protestant father from Los Angeles expressed the typical (but by no means exclusive) view of his tradition about the importance of truth and the truth value of other religions: "We exposed our children to other world religions, teaching it is what someone else believes without considering it true. That's the route we take: this is what Hindus believe, what Muslims believe, what even Catholics believe. Obviously, though, they understand that we are propagating our faith that we have come to know as being the truth." But for most parents one of the most important truths is simply realizing that "there is something bigger," as said by this Mormon mother from New York City:

> Parents ought to raise kids to believe in something stronger or more powerful than themselves, because it's important to see they are not everything in life, the world does not revolve around them, there's something bigger than them that they owe their services, talents, who they are, to something bigger than them. Ideally it would be God, I believe it's God, but I don't want to say that for everyone, because this is my world, right? I love the story of Christ because Christ taught us to think about others before ourselves, what can you do for other people, not what you can get out of somebody for yourself.

That belief will help people live good lives, just as this Hispanic Catholic father from New York City suggested:

> If she wants to follow another religion, I don't mind, as long as she follows the ways God wants us to live, as long as she's doing the right thing. God is for humankind, to be good, to do the right thing. I don't think religions matter. I'm not a fanatic Catholic. I come to church because I want to learn more about God and to be a better person. To be a good Catholic, or religious person, you have to follow whatever God is telling us in the Bible. I want to be a better person.

This black Protestant mother from Houston stressed the social rewards of membership in a religious congregation: "Belonging to a church is a benefit, it makes you feel wanted, warm, that you are somebody, that you belong somewhere, there are other people like you." In the end, people just choose whatever seems to work as right for them. One white Catholic father from Indiana, for example, was self-conscious about what he thinks is the normal human tendency to use religious beliefs pragmatically: "Jesus if nothing else was a fantastic storyteller, you can always take something he said and apply it to your life, somehow, someway. I'm sure other religions claim the same thing, and us being human beings we tend to take what we want and somehow make it work for a situation. So I just choose Christianity over, say, Buddhism."

The Nature of Children

The dominant view of religious American parents about intergenerational religious transmission is also informed by a particular understanding of children's nature and potentials. This view somewhat represents the personal side of the cultural models of life's purpose and life in the world, described earlier. The cultural model is this:

> *The Nature of Children*: Every child possesses within themselves a "best self they can be," something like an inherent, unique, and inalienable ideal personality and optimal life-to-be-lived. Children are unrealized bundles of personally unique "ideal outcomes" that need to be prepared and cultivated if they are to develop, endure, and reach their full potentials. Each child's "best self" exists internally as a latent yet real potential that must be actualized and manifest through growth and experience, driven ultimately by each child's own personality and wants. Children can only realize their "best selves" by venturing upon and effectively navigating the challenging journey of life, especially the first half of life. Success means not only enjoying life's opportunities and pleasures but also effectively facing and surmounting the problems and trials in one's quest through the world, which promotes positive growth, maturity, and understanding, and reveals and progressively unfolds one's ideal personal self. The frightful but real alternative is for growing children to become compromised or wrecked by an inability to overcome the hardships, temptations, and misfortunes that assail them in life's journey, and so to fail to realize the "best selves" they could have been.

Many parents we interviewed talked explicitly about their children reaching their potential in terms of having a "best self." And children's "best selves" do not automatically happen. They must be nurtured and achieved. Nurturing is the parents' job, and achieving is the children's job. Crucial in this growth process is children learning personal independence and not becoming dependent on or influenced by others. Parents know that their children can and will make mistakes, which can be hard, but also from which they can learn, so they prepare themselves for that near inevitability. Through this kind of life experience, parents hope that children learn resilience and flexibility but also inner strength. The existentially most pressing and difficult issue for parents while their children are still living at home is learning how and when to ease their children into life's journey so they are adequately prepared but not overwhelmed. Most parents think the loose oversight and boundaries they can provide while their children still live at home will lessen the pain of learning from their mistakes later in life. Nearly every parent we interviewed was hopeful that their own children would successfully rise to the challenge of life's journey and so realize and fulfill their true selves. But pressing on that hope is also an acute awareness and fear that for many young people life does not always turn out well. Amid their optimism and confidence, parents recited a litany of failures and fears and cautionary tales about much they hope their children will manage to avoid.

One Mormon mother from Indiana represented well the idea that every child has a best self they need to attain: "You can't protect your children from difficulty, they need to learn through difficulties. But they are also God's children, their personalities, they come with fully developed personalities, they already are the person they are. And it's your responsibility to help them be the best version of that that they can be, but not to think that you can fundamentally change them." According to this mainline Protestant father from New York City, each person's best self must be nurtured and grown:

> I want my kids to develop and achieve the abilities they already have, finding and developing them and showing up, not hiding or suppressing them. That's a really great thing God gave us individually; that's profound, amazing. That's a really healthy way we grow up. My son has a lot of skills and abilities; he's quite smart. I want him to be happy, independent as much as possible, really helping other people too, and be nice to others and himself, and really develop his skills and achieve what he is able to do. I want him to do more, just a little more pushing, just a little bit, to make him more developed.

That will involve having to venture out and facing challenges, as an Hispanic Catholic father from Indiana explained: "I am not a helicopter parent; I don't hover. There's times I'm in the background, but I do believe they need to take risks and learn on their own. I'll be there if there's something's gone wrong, I'll step in, but most of the time it's up to them." And failure is always a scary possibility, as one conservative Protestant mother from Florida confessed:

> I'd hate if they did something crazy and it broke my heart, but the ball is in their court after a while. Our job is to raise productive adults, but adult kids do weird things. There are many parents who have so many sorrows over their adult kids, it's ridiculous. I just hope that doesn't

happen. But it's like rolling dice. You do all the things you felt were right, and then your adult child does crazy stuff, and what do you do? I know from too many other parents it doesn't always work out.

The Task of Parenting

American religious parents have a cultural model not only of the nature of children but also the job of parenting, which is determined by all of the preceding cultural models. Having accepted all of the aforementioned, the cultural model of the task of being a parent turns out to be clearly defined, as follows:

The Task of Parenting: The central job of parents is to prepare and equip their children not only to enjoy all that is good in life but also to successfully navigate, endure, and overcome difficulties in their personal life journeys in the world. Good parents provision their children with the grounding, learning, and resources they will need to surmount life's difficulties and come out stronger and truer on the other side. How parents do this will be shaped a lot by their own experience growing up in their families. Parents may simply enjoy their offspring as children, but the true quality of their parenting work will be tested when their children face life's trials and tribulations down the road. The demanding task of parenting is made especially difficult by two major complications: parents must never violate their children's ultimate self-determination nor trigger teenage rebellion. These demand that parents carefully navigate the narrow, difficult straits between lax and overbearing parenting.

Particularly important here, religious parents in the United States commonly believe they need to tread carefully with their children lest they provoke them to rebel and produce outcomes that backfire on their intentions. Parents generally do not think every teenager will necessarily rebel, yet rebellion remains a continual danger worth averting. And in the minds of many parents, religion is the very area of life most likely to inflame rebellion, as some parents know personally from their own youth. The key to avoiding rebellion is to "not force" religion on children. Given all they believed about children and parenting described earlier, most parents see the strait between being too slack and too strict as tight and tough to navigate. Either way, life moves inexorably forward and parents continue with more or less angst and success to wrestle with the challenges of their job.

Parents need to equip children to navigate their life's journey, as a representative black Protestant father from Houston insisted: "God says that's your duty to get your child on the straight path, you don't let him make the decision for hisself, if that was the case, then he could take care of hisself. Since he can't take care of hisself, then he do what [tapping table] *I say do*. And I'm not gonna tell him nothin' wrong." Highly influential in the way parents do that, however, is their own experience being raised by their parents. One Muslim mother from Indiana, for instance, explained: "When I grew up, I used to be against everything like my parents did. But after I had kids and family, I understand more about my parents maybe or decisions they've made in their life, and I tried not to pass on their mistakes, but learn from their mistakes and improve my life. That's how I am and how I hope my kids learn and improve themselves, hopefully." In time, the results will reveal how well parents performed, just as one conservative Protestant mother from Indiana said, "The test of how well a parent has done in the values communicated is found out as it proves itself out over time. You hope you've done a good job, but there is seeing how things work in a child's life. You want to do the best for her, but you can't do it all for them; they have to find a way too." Crucial in the process is finding the balance between too lax and too hard with children, as this mainline Protestant mother from New York City expressed: "I have a friend who is a really good parent; she gives her kids a lot of freedom and lets them be independent but she's also very strict about some things, so it's a good balance between freedom and structure. A bad parent would be someone who doesn't give their kid any attention, just uninvolved. A good parent is involved but not controlling, involved but letting them have their independence."

The Priority of Family Solidarity

Conversations with religious parents about passing on religion to children brought to the surface a distinct cultural model with its own beliefs and associated feelings, about the importance of family solidarity, which we must grasp in order to understand how parents think about the intergenerational transmission of religious faith and its relative priority among the demands of family life. It sounds like this:

The Importance of Family Solidarity: Parents desire to have warm, close relationships with and among their grown children in the future (harmony while children live at home is not necessarily to be expected). Major differences or divisive conflict with or alienation from or between adult children would be deeply saddening. Anything parents can do in the present to foster a family cohesion that will continue into the empty-nest decades—such as fostering common recreational interests like sports, political views, and basic life values—is therefore important, including working to pass on the family religion. Families that agree on the same religious beliefs, practices, and ways of talking enjoy a particularly strong basis of harmony and cohesion, because shared religion is a potent source of family solidarity. However, if religion ever gets in the way of other activities that also build family solidarity (such as league sports), then religion may have to give way, for the very same reasons. Shared religion can also be set aside in specific cases by the higher-priority imperative of family solidarity. Furthermore, if a child eventually marries someone of a different religion, that would not be ideal but also not a serious problem, as long as they shared the same "basic values" of the family.

Religion, no matter how important parents consider it, is often not as important as other priorities, especially sports and homework. This is true even among many parents in more "strict" traditions, such as Mormonism and conservative Protestantism. When they believe religion will help their kids and family, most parents will push it to some extent. But when religion itself threatens to disrupt internal family peace and unity, religion often gives way.

All the parents we interviewed want to be close to their children when they grow up and think family conflict and division would be bad. This Muslim father from New York City said, typically:

> I hope we maintain that close relationship. I always tell my wife, "I can't wait until the kids get older," and at the end of Ramadan they'll all be over at our house, kids and grandkids. That's my hope and dream. I hope my business does so well that I can pass it on to them. My dad never gave me a dime, and I want to do the opposite with my kids, like, "Here's fifty-thousand dollars each, go put a down payment on a house."

So fostering close connections with children in the present in any way is important. A Buddhist mother from Chicago reported:

> I dropped a day from my work schedule so I could be at home more with the kids. Drive them around, I feel like a chauffeur, driving them from one class to another to another. It's great. I don't have him go to preschool all week, just because I actually feel it's more important for him to have me and for me to have that bond with him. I had so much time with my daughter before he came along, he didn't ever really have alone time, just mommy or daddy time.

Shared values are also crucial, as this Jewish mother from New York City explained:

> I try to show my kids the joy and love of being Jewish, and creating a routine, being part of the larger Jewish community, and doing a lot of rituals that, even if right now don't feel touchy-feely, still gives us family experiences together and memories. It's not strict or about heaven and hell or doing the right thing, but just showing them that, with structure we're creating something, and doing it year in, year out, celebrating a holiday and creating memories, you're gonna appreciate that later on.

But for most parents, religion is secondary to other means of family bonding, as expressed by this white Catholic father from Indiana: "We try to keep track of scheduling so we don't overwhelm them, because we want to balance our home life, school, religious life, and whatever else. But we've seen it take the hit this time of year when our religious life always gets really crunched down to almost nothing." Finally, marrying someone of a different religion is not ideal, but acceptable, especially if everyone shares most of the same values. Thus, an Hispanic Catholic father from New York City reported, "If he marries a person of another religion, it is to be respected. You respect my religion, and I respect yours, put aside what's personal as a couple, and I think it will work, just like in politics. Leave political parties at the door, and enter inside only as a couple, I think it will work."

Why Parents Should Pass on Religion
to Their Children

What cultural model runs in the background of and helps to guide American religious parents' approach to handing on religious faith and practice to their children? The answer to that question is determined by the content of all of the cultural models examined earlier, as is clear here:

> *Why Parents Should Pass Religion on to Children*: Parents do good and well to pass on religious faith and practice to their offspring, because religion can help growing children successfully navigate the journey of life in the world that they will soon face. Life's journey can be a difficult one, and parents' primary job is to prepare and provision their children for safety and success on the road. Religion offers particularly valuable help in the forms of guidance, comfort, and rest stops offering rejuvenation and aid along the way. Religion also provides a "home base" or "grounding" that serves, among the vagaries and troubles of life, as a stable reference point by which to navigate life, and a foundation upon which to build a life that need not go ruinously off course or be shaken. When a child's life's journey takes the wrong path, she or he can always "return home" to and through religion, reset themselves, and start again on the right road. Shared religion also glues families together, which, besides being a desire of parents, is good for growing children. Therefore, parents instilling the right foundation of religion in their children effectively provisions them with crucial life resources that greatly enhance their chances of living good lives as they proceed on their journeys in the world.

The metaphors of religion as a "base," "foundation," "grounding," "basis," "guidance," "rooting," and "anchor"—which parents very much want for their children—was pervasive in our interviews. Religious parents in the United States also have a tremendous, though not absolute, faith in the power of religion to draw wayward children home after periods of error and confusion. Religious parents generally found themselves well motivated to pass on their religious practices and beliefs to their children.

A white Catholic mother from Indiana told us: "Life is difficult, and you need some place to turn to in difficulties. That's what religion provides. You can turn to it and find some comfort, someone to talk to and help you make the right decision, and guide you when you need guiding, to show you the path and keep you [on it] if you're trying to decide which way to go." This mainline Protestant father from Washington, DC, concurred:

> I hope they will join me in heaven but also that their faith would be part of their success and happiness in life and guide them to make good decisions and have good relationships. They'll live a richer life in a relationship with God, and be able to survive the highs and lows that they're inevitably going to experience when I'm not around, knowing that God is around to love and take care of them. I've always found my faith as a centering aspect of life, as you get distracted or the highs get too high or lows too low, coming back to having the ritual of a weekly church service or the reflection around what's right and wrong, is an important part of life.

This Muslim mother from New York City explained that religion provides a stable home base or grounding: "I wanted him to have a good religious grounding, given all the frustrations and internal identity crises I'd had growing up. I wanted to give him a strong foundation, so I started him in a Muslim school when he was in pre-K till eighth grade." And, as this black Protestant father from Houston too told us, religion gives you something to return home to: "The Bible says if you train up a child in the way he should go, he may leave but he'll come back. And really all you can do is wait till they come back, so that's what we doing."

The Proper Role of Religious Congregations

A distinct but relevant model concerns their view of the proper place and role of religious congregations in that process:

> *The Role of Religious Congregations*: The primary responsibility for passing on religious faith and practice to children rests with parents; religious congregations are secondary and primarily supportive. Religious congregations should reinforce what parents teach at home, not determine it. Reasonable parents hold only modest expectations for what congregations offer them and their children. Most helpful is when congregations provide a general sense of an inviting, comfortable community and some positive experiences for children.

Kid-appealing programs and some teaching of the moral "basics" (e.g., the Ten Commandments, the parable of the Good Samaritan) are also great. Congregations that do things to make time spent there fun for children help in getting kids to participate less of a headache, and so are particularly attractive and appreciated. But specifically "religious" aspects of congregations—like theology, liturgy, and doctrinal teachings—are not especially important when it comes to parenting.

In addition to what our other book on cultural models of religious transmission says to elaborate this model, Chapter 7 of this book explores parents' views of the role of religious congregations in greater depth. Here we provide four illustrative parent quotes. A mainline Protestant mother from Indiana exemplified the key point by explaining that parents come first, religious congregations second:

> Me teaching them as a parent is more important than the church teaching them. The church has a little bit more to offer. Everybody's going to have a different perspective as to how they interpret things, and just because I view it one way doesn't mean that you have to view it that way. The person at church is going to be able to show you something different than I will, so one of the reasons I don't want [exclusively] to teach my kids is they hear it from me all the time. I probably have the more important role, but church can reinforce and back me up.

Religious congregations can only reinforce what parents already primarily teach, as this Mormon father from Indiana told us: "I feel like it's my job to raise them religiously, so anytime their teachers at church can support what we're doing at home it's really nice. Kids might think maybe mom and dad aren't so smart, then they'll hear the same things at church that we're telling them, and I'll be so thankful. So yeah the church's responsibility is to back up what we're teaching at home." Good congregations create community and positive experiences for children. One Hindu mother from central New Jersey, for instance, expressed that she primarily appreciates the social support her temple provides for what she and her husband teach at home: "Learning in a group or community, it's a better way of learning, so kids don't feel like, 'Oh my mom and dad are just telling me stuff,' in one ear and out the other, but like, 'Oh, all these people are listening.'" But matters of religious doctrine are for most parents of all traditions of peripheral importance, as expressed by this Jewish mother from New York City: "My Jewish connections are much more practice and community-based than theological. The theology is there, but I don't examine it too closely."[5]

How Parents Should Pass on Religion to Children

The final dominant cultural model that we examine concerns the best strategies and methods that most religious parents think they should use to transmit religion to their children:

> *How to Pass on Religion to Children*: Parents have only one good and hopefully effective way to raise children to understand and carry on their family's religion (or perhaps return to it someday after a period of disaffection). That is for parents simply to practice their own personal religious faith, naturally, for its own sake and as role models for their children. If all goes well, children will over time learn, absorb, and embrace their own version of that faith, almost unconsciously. Children are observant and malleable, especially when young; the key for parents is to provide them religious practices to observe and try out, such as prayer, worship, and volunteering. Raising religious children should thus primarily be a practice-centered process, not chiefly a didactic teaching program. If along the way children ask questions about religion out of curiosity, parents should answer as well as they are able. On occasion parents might also proactively share religious ideas and observations. But parents must never "preach" or be verbally overbearing in any way. Hypocrisy is the worst, so parents must be consistent and "walk the talk" (even if there is not much talk). Parents also need not expect dramatic religious experiences from their children; passing on the faith to the next generation can and should be a gradual, natural, intuitive process. Parents will need to insist that their young children attend religious services and other religious community activities, as appropriate; but when children become teenagers,

---

5. Wuthnow has noted: "Attending [religious] services was meaningful to people who grew up religious for reasons that generally had little to do with the content of those services, at least as homileticists [theorists of preaching] and liturgists have understood them. People absorb their understanding of the sacred from staring at stained glass windows, from realizing that the altar was elevated and on one side of the church or the other, from picking garnets out of the church walls, from singing [hymns] . . . and from eating fried chicken. These activities all point to the importance of community in congregations . . . of how social relationships create that feeling of community" (*Growing Up Religious*, 86).

parents must adjust their requirements to allow them as self-directed individuals to make "informed" religious decisions for themselves.

The idea that parents should simply practice their own personal religious faith, naturally, for its own sake and as role models for their children works well for parents because, among other reasons, it does not require them to understand and explain orthodox content to their children, which most cannot. It avoids preaching or imposing religion on their children. Instead, it is seen as appropriately leading, not coercive; a semi-voluntary socialization, not direct indoctrination or social control. All parents across all traditions agree on this belief. Some actually equate the "influence" of children with "forcing" them against their will. Parents also generally believe that they can and should explain and teach their children some, but they also look to religious institutions—church, Sunday school, Hebrew school, youth group, temple classes, summer camps, and so on—to contribute the more "official" religious formation of children through the didactic teaching of religious knowledge.[6]

Furthermore, while some parents had a religious conversion or other "religious" experiences earlier in life, none we interviewed seem to expect anything like that from their children. We found this pattern across a range of different religions, including among parents from revivalist traditions that have historically emphasized the need to "make a decision for Christ," raising a hand or walking down the aisle of an evangelistic or revival meeting, or even youth at some "age of accountability" simply "becoming a Christian" and being baptized. No parent we interviewed focused on the idea of religious conversions or the need to have a "religious experience." They instead expressed confidence in their own ability, sometimes with the help of God, and often with some support from their religious congregations, to pass on religious faith and practice to their kids in an ongoing life process. But, again,

---

6. Wuthnow has observed: "The most significant challenge facing people who have grown up religious is whether their identity will carry forward with the next generation, or whether family patterns have changed so substantially that this identity will soon become a relic of the past. . . . There are many indicators, in fact, that people who have grown up religious are not subjecting their children to the same kind of upbringing. . . . Most of the people who talk about their aspirations for their children say they want them to have some exposure to religion and to share some of their own religious values. [But they do not want them to] grow up hedged in by religious rules or having religious dogma forced down [the] . . . throat. . . . If this . . . view prevails, the future of America's religious culture is likely to be characterized more by an underlying belief in God, some understanding of one's own tradition, and exposure to and tolerance toward other traditions, rather than intense, communal, and familial involvement in a single tradition" (*Growing Up Religious*, 212–213).

religion for nearly all of them is mostly about being a good person, not a dramatic enlightenment or personal encounter with God, Jesus, or any other superhuman force. So dramatic religious experiences or conversions are not considered necessary for learning to be good.

An Hispanic Catholic father from New Mexico said, "We have to be an example for them. It would be difficult to say, 'Be Catholics, go to Mass,' when I won't go. The most important thing I've done is to be consistent going to Mass, lead by example, so they can see it, or they will not believe me." "If I believe and go to temple," explained a Buddhist father from Chicago, "not even talking about such deep believing, just go to temple and take them with me, I know for sure it affects them. It's not even a choice, but now they just identify as 'I'm Buddhist,' I don't have to teach them, they just heard us say it. That's one of the values, the family values and bond, and there's no reason to change that." A Hindu father from New York City explained that practice is what most matters:

We do the festivals, fasting, she prays every day in our prayer room, goes to the temple, and from very young we did the ceremonies, washing the gods, getting new clothes for the seasons. That's how it is stamped in the brain as they grow, not only offerings but also washing and cleaning, different foods, a small piece of jewelry, everything going on in the household. That immediately puts the question in their mind, "Why is this happening?," [which you then explain]. The gods are also a part of your family, you eat, god eats, right? It's not just a piece of metal just sitting there, it's part of your family. You feed them, you bathe them, you see them every day, and in summer we have a small fan that turns on if the temperature goes up, cause the god is part of your family. It's all family based. My mother-in-law was a very practicing religious Hindu; she knew all the verses to explain their meaning. We are from Brahmin family, so we have all this in our family traditions.

This conservative Protestant father from Florida: "A lot of our family life revolves around church, so as I continue to make that a part of our lifestyle, things naturally fall in place. That's sort of my idea." In the end, of course, children will have to decide for themselves. "Certain things they're forced to do because they're children," explained a Jewish mother from New York City, "but then when they're adults, they have the knowledge to say, this speaks to me or this doesn't speak to me, and whatever they choose, at least they'll know, they will be making an informed choice."

Conclusion

The preceding summary of the constellation of cultural models representing and informing religious American parents' approaches to religious transmission to their children is a mere sketch of the richer and more complex views of parents and what we as analysts can say about them. It does, however, provide a big-picture cultural context for the analyses in the chapters that follow. As the exposition of our findings in the following chapters unfold, these cultural models held by the majority of religious American parents can serve as a larger framework to help interpret them.

2

Parent Religiousness, Parenting Styles, and Intergenerational Religious Transmission

IN THIS CHAPTER we address the question whether and how different parenting styles and parenting religiousness influence parents' success in passing on their religion to children. We already know from previous research that the religious commitments and practices of parents are in most cases the most powerful shapers of the religious lives of their children later in life. That fact we confirm here. But we also interact the parent religiousness factor with the question of parenting styles. Previous research and common sense suggest that we have reason to believe that parenting style does matter for child life and religious outcomes. Most scholars believe that parents who combine high expectations of and involvement with their children along with emotional warmth and good communication (the "authoritative" style) are the more effective at socialization, including transmitting religious belief and practices. Yet the issue may not be fully settled. Some other research calls the importance of parenting styles into question. In this chapter we show direct, independent effects of parents' religiousness and to some extent parenting styles on the religious outcomes of children 10 years later. We also present evidence that some parenting styles, namely an authoritative style, moderate the relationship between parents' religious importance and adult children's religious attendance and importance of faith. Having explored those issues, finally, we shift focus and present findings on the role of religion in strengthening the relationship between parents, as well as the relationship between corporal punishment and religion.

The Influence of Parent Religiousness

The more important religion is to parents and the more parents attend religious services, the more important religion becomes for their children and the more their children attend religious services, even years after they no longer live with their parents. Parents are major forces shaping the religious lives of their children, whether they fully realize that or not. Previous research has established this finding, and we find it again here. Consider, for example, the middle bars in Figure 2.1, which show the differences that parents' religiousness during their children's teenage years makes in the probability their children will report that religious faith is "extremely important" in their lives 10 years later (net of the influence of many demographic control variables). There we see that children whose parents report that religious faith is "extremely" important in their (parents') lives are significantly more likely to also

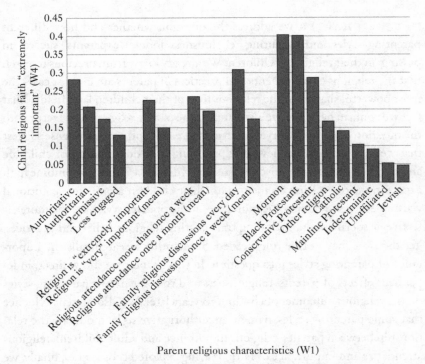

Parent religious characteristics (W1)

FIGURE 2.1 Marginal probabilities (standardized) of religious faith being "extremely important" to children 10 years later (W4) by teenage-years' parent characteristics (W1).

Note: Estimates based on Model 1 of Table 2 of Appendix C in this chapter. All other variables have been held constant.

Source: National Study of Youth and Religion (W1 & W4).

say religion is extremely important in their own (children's) lives a decade later, compared even to the average parent report that faith is "very" important (the difference would obviously be much larger compared to parents who reported that religion is less important in their lives). The same kind of relationship holds for religious service attendance: emerging adult[1] children will significantly attend more 10 years later whose parents attended more frequently when they were teenagers, compared to the average level of parental religious service attendance. (We discuss the effects of the other parent influence reported in Figure 2.1—namely, families having religious discussions during the week—later in this chapter.)

The religious tradition of parents matters, too. The cluster of bars on the right side of Figure 2.1 shows that Mormon and black Protestant parents are particularly likely to have emerging adult children who 10 years later say that religion is "extremely important" in their lives (even net of the eight demographic control variables). The marginal probability of those adult children reporting that religious faith is "extremely important" in their lives is .40, which is double the average (.20). Parents who are conservative Protestants are also much more likely (at a marginal probability of nearly .30) to produce children who say religion is extremely important a decade after their teenage years.

We find the same general patterns of results when we consider the variations that parent religiousness makes on the different levels of religious service attendance of their children 10 years after their teenage years, the results for which are reported in Figure 2.2. Appendix B at the end of this chapter provides regression models for estimating the influence of parents' religious characteristics on religious importance and attendance 10 years into adulthood. On average, 52 percent of adult children say that they *never* attend religious services. But parents' religious characteristics can change this. Parents who say that religious faith is "extremely" important in their lives and who attend religious services more frequently are significantly less likely to have children who report never attending religious services a decade later, compared even to average levels of parent religiousness. The same holds true for parents who belonged during their children's teenage years to the religious traditions of Mormonism, black Protestantism, and conservative Protestantism.

The influence of parent religiousness on the religious outcomes of their children is by now quite well known, because it has been studied by many

---

1. For an explanation of the meaning of "emerging adult" and "emerging adulthood," see Smith with Snell, *Souls in Transition*.

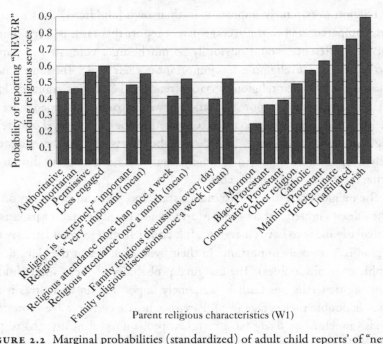

Parent religious characteristics (W1)

FIGURE 2.2 Marginal probabilities (standardized) of adult child reports' of "never" attending religious services 10 years later (W4) by teenage-years' parent characteristics (W1).

Note: Estimates based on Model 3 of Table 2 of Appendix C in this chapter. All other variables have been held constant.

Source: National Study of Youth and Religion (W1 & W4).

scholars for decades. The possible influence of different parenting styles on children's religious lives, however, is less well understood. We now turn to that topic.

Dimensions of Parenting Styles

One major area of research on parenting and childhood outcomes concerns different styles of parenting. Scholars normally divide parenting styles into four types: authoritative, authoritarian, permissive, and less engaged.[2]

---

2. Diana Baumrind, "Authoritarian vs. Authoritative Parental Control," *Adolescence* 3, no. 11 (1968): 255–272; Diana Baumrind, "Parental Disciplinary Patterns and Social Competence in Children," *Youth & Society* 9, no. 3 (1978): 239–276; Diana Baumrind, "A Blanket Injunction against Disciplinary Use of Spanking Is Not Warranted by the Data," *Pediatrics* 98, no. 4 (1996): 828–831.

Authoritative parents tend to be demanding and hold high standards of their children, but they also express high levels of warmth and communication with them. These parents are active in their children's lives, provide a lot of guidance and supervision, and adequately adjust rules and requirements to fit situations and their child's personality. Authoritarian parents, by comparison, are demanding, rigid, and strict, expecting their children to obey their orders. They are not very receptive to two-way discussions, are less likely to adjust rules and standards according to their child's needs, and are not very emotionally warm and expressive with their children. Permissive parents tend to be emotionally responsive and warm, but they do not hold many expectations or make many demands of their children. They are more lenient, flexible, and try to avoid conflict. Finally, what we are calling "less engaged" parents—which others sometimes call "uninvolved"—are more disconnected if not withdrawn from their children. They may not know the names of their children's friends or teachers, for example, and are generally minimally involved in their children's lives outside of the home. Of these four, research consistently finds that the authoritative parenting style is the most effective and beneficial for the healthy development of children generally.[3]

Although we did not directly and systematically explore parenting styles in our interviews, we found that differences were fairly randomly distributed and did not closely align with parents' religious traditions or personal devotion in any obvious way. Black Protestant, conservative Protestant, and Mormon parents—those from relatively "strict" religious traditions—seemed perhaps to be stricter in their parenting styles than, say, mainline Protestants. But there are always exceptions and complications. And, if anything, these were modest tendencies, not strong correlations. But to provide a sense of the way parents talked that seemed related to parenting styles, we explore some comparisons here before moving on to more focused analyses.

One key dimension of parenting style is the degree to which parents set and stick to clear and demanding expectations of their children's behaviors and attitudes. That often shows up when it comes to religion. Some parents set and enforce demanding standards for their kids. For example, one Hispanic Catholic father told us about an incident where his daughter was late coming to Mass after a sleepover at a friend's house:

---

3. For example, Baumrind, "Parental Disciplinary Patterns and Social Competence in Children"; Marjorie Lindner Gunnoe, E. Mavis Hetherington, and David Reiss, "Parental Religiosity, Parenting Style, and Adolescent Social Responsibility," *The Journal of Early Adolescence* 19, no. 2 (1999): 199–225.

It upset me, and I grounded her for a whole week. You're not going anywhere. No computer. No Kindle. Nothing. And she's crying, like I'm
too strict, why didn't I call her to remind her?

A Jewish mother told us that on the Sabbath her kids "know that if their
friends call, 'Can we go to a movie after lunch?' No! You know you're not
doing that." Another Jewish mother explained, "When they were young and
went to synagogue, all the other families let their kids run wild after lunch.
I never did, and they were like, 'But the other kids are all doing it.' I'd be like, 'I
don't care, that's not appropriate behavior in the synagogue, you're not going
to do it, stay here.'" A black Catholic mother reported, "I don't have big fights
or arguments with them because my rule is: you live in my house you do what
I say. You don't like it [laughs], there's the door!"

Other parents had a harder time maintaining their standards and demands.
A black Protestant mother, for instance, lamented:

> It's a requirement that we go to church. But my son started, "I'm not
> going." I'm like, "Yes, you are." But you get to arguing with your chil-
> dren, trying to tell them that they are going to go, and he's like, "I'm
> not going." That's when you just let God step in. You just go ahead and
> go to church [yourself] and pray whether or not he is there.

A Hispanic Catholic mother anticipated the same sort of difficulty: "Right
now it's easy [because she is young]. But I don't know if when she is 13 years
old, and I tell her, 'We are going to church,' what is she going to tell me?
Because she is going to enter an age when they think they can say no." And
this Muslim father explained simply that "we can't burden them too much
with religion, like let them be kids. So I don't like to push it." More generally,
a white Catholic mother confessed, "I say that I am going to punish them, and
I don't punish them, nothing."

Parenting style also expressed itself through differences among parents
about whether to influence their children religiously through "osmosis" and
passive exposure or with more direct intentionality. One Hispanic Catholic
mother, for example, exemplified the osmosis approach: "I don't force her to
be Catholic, even though that is my desire. Whatever she feels, she wants to
follow another religion, I don't mind, as long as she follows the ways that
God wants us to be." A Hispanic Catholic father explained, "I have much
to grow in my religion, but I think I can be ready to talk to her. But I do not
know if it is the right time, so I try to limit myself to what I'm going to say.

Small things only, like, 'trust in God', 'God will take care of you', 'You are not alone', 'God is with you', such small things only." At the far extreme, just a few parents said they could not think of anything they did to model or promote religion to their children. When asked whether she talks with her children about religious matters, one Hispanic Catholic mother said simply, "No, not very much."

By contrast, conservative Protestant, Mormon, and Muslim parents seemed somewhat more likely to say that they were intentionally and directly trying to transmit religious faith to their children, rather than relying on osmosis. Many of these discussions focused on getting their children to pray regularly, read religious scripture, and attend religious services and classes. One Muslim father, for instance, explained that, back in his home country the extended family is able to teach values, but that in the United States, "It's the parents' responsibility really. And parents really cannot instill any values in children if they are not involved. So we made the decision that every Sunday, we will be with our children and we'll stay in the school the whole day." A conservative Protestant mother told us, "I talk to them about worship and why we worship and about meeting God in worship, rather than going to church. I'm quite hot on that distinction at the moment, and so I talk to them about that." When asked whether he simply models good religious behaviors or is more explicit, a conservative Protestant father told us, "There is the active aspect to it, where we are reading scriptures with our kids, reading the Bible with our children. Having them read the Bible, having them create a devotional time for themselves." Likewise, a black Protestant mother told us, "We watch religious television, and we always bless our food, and we say prayer. I teach them and let each one of them have their voice, so they can learn how to pray."

Another key dimension of parenting styles is openness, warmth, and mutuality in communication. Some parents seem to have developed an effective communication style with their child, including this mainline Protestant father, who said, "We try and work things out by just communicating. I would say we were pretty easygoing parents, yet the kids know that, since there's no yelling in the family, when our voice would rise and be firm, they knew this is as far as they can push mom and dad." A black Protestant father, who described himself as strict, took a different approach: "I talk to them a lot, because my daddy used to whoop a lot. Sometimes, when it's necessary [whooping], it's necessary. But then sometimes I think that it's not necessary [and you just talk]." A Mormon mother explained how she handled her son's use of the word "shit" by talking calmly with him:

He said, "I'm feeling frustrated," and I said, "You've been saying that a lot lately. What do you mean when you say frustrated?" He said, "I think I narrowed it down to two things. One, I really need to share my emotions more [and two] I just feel like saying a swear word." I said go ahead, say it. "Shitty," he said, and then he laughed.

A black Protestant mother related a similar incident in which her daughter uncharacteristically spoke some profanity, "So I just kind of talk to her. A lot of times I don't always just go for that hard force, because I know sometimes talking you can get your way through." And this mainline Protestant mother told us about a time when her daughter was not doing her math homework: "We couldn't think of a punishment, so we're like, 'You tell us how you're going to make this happen.' So, she wrote a contract, like this is what's going to happen if I do it, get rewarded, this is what happens if I don't, I get punished. We signed it and actually had the math teacher sign it too."

Other parents have not managed to establish such functional, peaceful forms of communication. A mainline Protestant mother, for example, reported, "I'm still learning. Like the other night she didn't like something I said, she screamed and slammed the door. I don't think she went as far as calling me a name, but I'm really tired of being screamed at." When we asked if her daughter accepts her parental authority, she replied, "Yes, she does, and these therapists keep telling me that's what she's hungering for: 'She wants you to discipline her.'" But discipline does not seem forthcoming in this permissive parenting case.

Do Parenting Styles Influence Religious Socialization of Children?

Some previous studies have suggested that different parenting styles shape levels of religious engagement and strength of religious beliefs.[4] The most

---

4. Most research in this area suggests that parents' religious characteristics precede parenting style (see, for example, Blake Snider, Clements, and Vazsonyi, "Late Adolescent Perceptions of Parent Religiosity and Parenting Processes"; Scott Myers, "An Interactive Model of Religiosity Inheritance: The Importance of Family Context," *American Sociological Review* 61, no. 5 (1996): 858–866; Duriez et al., "Is Religiosity Related to Better Parenting?"). This assumption about temporal ordering usually makes sense, since Americans tend to remain in the religion in which they were raised, so that religious affiliation and strength of religious belief are set before most people become parents and establish parenting styles. A relatively small proportion of people switch to a completely different religion later in life.

comprehensive, recent research on the factors shaping the successful transmission of religion from parents to children is Vern Bengtson's book-length examination of four generations of families studied over time.[5] He found that parents who have warm and kind relationships with their children were more likely than others to pass on their religion and transmit similar levels of religious belief. He also found that parents who engaged in religious activities with their children when they were young were more likely to have adult children who were similarly religious. When religious parents have a close and warm relationship with children, Bengtson found, they enjoy being with their parents and learn to like and do many of the same things they enjoy.

At the same time, other research has suggested that parenting style may not be as important an influence on children's religious outcomes as parents' religious affiliation and religiousness.[6] Different kinds of data, measurements, and analytical techniques often make it difficult to compare and assess various studies on this topic. Since the issue does not appear to be settled, we investigated the parenting-style question ourselves in this project. Our findings are not definitive but make a contribution toward a fuller understanding of an important and interesting matter. Parenting style seems to matter for the importance of faith of children, net of parenting religiousness. We find only small differences in parenting styles across different religious traditions. We also find that parent religiousness and religious tradition are more strongly associated with children attending religious services regularly than parenting style, though the combination between parents' religious importance and an authoritative parenting style is meaningful.

First, does parenting style vary by religious tradition? The answer is not drastically so, according to our analysis. Using data from National Study of Youth and Religion, Table 2.1 displays the percentage of American parents who fall into each of the four parenting styles types, according to our measures and analysis, and differences between different religious types. There we see (to the right) that 37 percent of parents in this sample embody the authoritative parenting style (i.e., high expectations/involvement and high warmth/responsiveness). Twenty-one percent are authoritarian (high expectations/

---

5. Bengtson, *Families and Faith: How Religion Is Passed Down across Generations* (New York: Oxford University Press, 2013); also see Roger Dudley and Randall Wisbey, "The Relationship of Parenting Styles to Commitment to the Church among Young Adults," *Religious Education* 95, no. 1 (2000): 38–50.

6. For example, Stephen Armet, "Religious Socialization and Identity Formation of Adolescents in High Tension Religions," *Review of Religious Research* (2009): 277–297.

Table 2.1 Relationship between Parent's Religious Affiliation and Parenting Style

	Conservative Protestant	Mainline Protestant	Black Protestant	Catholic	Jewish	Mormon	Unaffiliated	Other religion	Indeterminate	Total
Authoritative %	44.9	32	40.4	33.4	40	40	25	34.6	22.2	37.31
Authoritative N	291	105	69	152	14	22	30	19	8	710
Less engaged %	19.9	27.1	26.3	27	22.9	18.18	32.5	23.6	38.9	24.7
Less engaged N	129	89	45	123	8	10	39	13	14	470
Authoritarian %	21.9	20.7	21.6	19.3	11.4	21.82	20.8	23.6	25	20.91
Authoritarian N	142	68	37	88	4	12	25	13	9	398
Permissive %	13.3	20.1	11.7	20.2	25.7	20	21.7	18.2	13.9	17.08
Permissive N	86	66	20	92	9	11	26	10	5	325
Total %	100	100	100	100	100	100	100	100	100	100
Total N	648	328	171	455	35	55	120	55	36	1,903

Note: Parents included in Figures 2.1 and 2.2 are included here.

Source: National Study of Youth and Religion (W1).

involvement, low warmth/responsiveness), 17 percent are permissive (warm/responsive, low expectations/involvement), and another 25 percent are less engaged (low expectations/involvement and low warmth/responsiveness).

More important for our purposes, we also see in Table 2.1 that the distribution of parenting styles across religious traditions does not vary radically. Compared to the national average, conservative Protestant parents, as well as Jewish and Mormon parents, appear to have a slightly more authoritative parenting style than others. Parents who are unaffiliated and those who are undetermined about their religion appear more likely to have a less engaged parenting style. Unaffiliated and Jewish parents are also more likely to have a permissive style. Finally, there are only 36 Jewish parents in this sample, but very few of them (only 11 percent) report having an authoritarian style when the average for this parenting style is 21 percent. But these differences are not especially large.

Parenting Style and Emerging Adult Children's Religious Outcomes

A more direct way to examine the relationship between parenting style and the transmission of religious belief and engagement is to measure what difference parenting style makes, after controlling for other factors, for explaining adult children's religious importance and attendance. That is what we do next, using data from Waves 1 and 4 of the National Study of Youth and Religion (NSYR). During the first wave of NSYR data collection, both parents and teenagers were surveyed. Parents reported on their religious importance, engagement, and affiliation. Teenagers provided information on their parents' parenting style, as well as how much their families talked about religion. Ten years later—once they were now in their mid- to late 20s—adult children were asked about the importance they place on religion, as well as frequency of religious attendance. Figure 2.1 presents the marginal probabilities of adult children's religious faith being "extremely important" 10 years later by parent characteristics, as reported during the first wave of interviews. These estimates are derived from the regression models presented in Appendix Table B at the end of this chapter. The figure's estimates are all standardized so that the most important factors (i.e., largest effect sizes) are clear.[7]

---

7. We were curious whether parenting style, parent religiousness, and other parent practices, such as talking with children about religion, are really separate items or rather indicators of an underlying latent orientation or variable on which they all load statistically. We ran a factor analysis to explore this possibility, which showed that these variables did not load on a single

Looking at the left side of Figure 2.1, we see apparent differences in parenting styles. There we notice that the emerging adult children of authoritative parents are more likely than the other groups to say that religious faith is "extremely important." Stated conversely, compared to parents with an authoritative style (i.e., demanding and strict with lots of warmth), those categorized as having an authoritarian, permissive, or less engaged style appear less likely to have adult children who say that religious faith is "extremely important." Moreover, as shown in the regression models that produced these marginal probabilities, the difference between authoritative and permissive and less engaged parenting styles is statistically significant, even after accounting for differences in parents' religious characteristics (see the chapter Appendix) and a range of demographic controls. Adult children who had at least one parent with an authoritative parenting style (relative to permissive and less engaged styles) are more likely to report that religion is "extremely important."

After controlling for other characteristics, which of all the parenting factors in Figure 2.1 is the most powerful? Aside from parents affiliating at either Mormon or with the traditional Black church, the effect sizes of the other parenting variables are fairly similar. Perhaps what is most noteworthy is that they all explain unique variation in the outcome. An increase in any of the parent religion-related variables is associated with higher odds that adult children will say that religion is "extremely" important. Along with demographic controls, like family income, parents' marital status, and child's educational attainment, parenting style and parents' religious characteristics explain only about 13 percent of the total variation in the likelihood that their adult children will report that religious faith is "extremely important" (see the pseudo R^2). Parents are important for shaping religious importance of their emerging adult children (and their characteristics may be relatively easy to measure), but so apparently are a lot of other things.

What about the *interaction* between the importance of parents' religion and their parenting styles? We looked at how parenting style moderates the relationship between parents' religious importance and the odds of adult children reporting that religion is important. We found that for explaining children's religious importance 10 years later the interaction was only barely significant comparing authoritative to authoritarian parents—not a major

---

dimension. Rather, the parenting variables loaded separately from the religion variables, and none of them had a high enough correlation to warrant combining them into one measure. Furthermore, within the same statistical models they appear to explain unique variations in the outcomes.

difference. However, we found some differences for explaining religious attendance (see estimates in Appendix Table B, Models 1 and 2 at the end of this chapter). Figure 2.3 presents the marginal probabilities for the moderating effect of parenting style on the relationship between parent's religious importance and adult child reports of never attending religious services. Since about 50 percent of adult children report never attending religious services, here we focus on how parenting style and religious importance shape the likelihood of adult children landing in this group. We find that relative to authoritarian and less engaged parenting styles, an authoritative style significantly moderates the relationship between parents' religious importance and the odds that adult children will report never attending religious services. The marginal probability for an adult child who had at least one parent who was

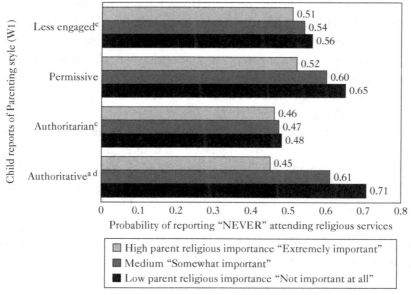

FIGURE 2.3 Marginal probabilities for the moderating effect of parenting style (W1) on the relationship between the interviewed parent's religious importance (W1) and adult child reports of "Never" attending religious services 10 years later (W4).

Notes: Estimates based on Model 4 of Table 2 of Appendix C in this chapter. All other variables have been held constant.

[a] Statistically different ($p < .05$) from authoritarian.

[b] Statistically different ($p < .05$) from permissive.

[c] Statistically different ($p < .05$) from authoritative.

[d] Statistically different ($p < .05$) from less engaged.

Source: National Study of Youth and Religion (W1 & W4).

authoritative and said that religion is extremely important of never attending religious services appears to be the lowest at .45. If the parenting style remains authoritative, but the parent did not think religion was important, adult children have a marginal probability of .71 of reporting that they never attend religious services, which is the highest probability. In other words, kids who had an authoritative parent (relative to authoritarian and less engaged parents) appear more likely to follow their religious lead, regardless of whether it is high or low on religion. Hence, if these parents are more religious, then the children grew up to be more religious. But if these parents are not very religious, the children follow and they too are not very religious.

These marginal probabilities are merely estimates that provide insight into effect sizes and the direction of the relationships. But Model 4 in Appendix Table B at the end of this chapter makes clear that relative to less engaged and authoritarian parents, authoritative parenting has a greater statistically significant moderating effect on the relationship between parents' religious importance and the odds that adult children will attend religious services. The model does not show statistically significant differences between authoritative and permissive parents in moderating the relationship between parents and adult children's religious importance. Figure 2.3 also shows that the estimates for permissive and authoritative parenting styles are more similar to each other than the others.

The finding for religious attendance suggests that there is some power of an authoritative parenting style (demanding with high standards, warmth, and two-way communication) to moderate the effect of parents' religious importance on adult children's religious attendance and importance into their mid-20s. Finally, when the parenting style is combined with religious importance, other parent religious characteristics, including parents' religious service attendance and regular discussion about religion, as well as some religious affiliations, continue to matter independently.[8]

---

8. In separate analyses we examined interactions between (1) parent's gender and parenting style; (2) parent's gender and parent's religious importance; and (3) parent's gender and parenting style and parent's religious importance. Parent's gender did not moderate the effect of parent's religious importance for either of the outcomes. For explaining children's religious importance, relative to permissive fathers, permissive mothers were more likely to have children who said religion was important. Likewise, relative to authoritative fathers, authoritative mothers were more likely to have children who said religion was important. We did not find these results for explaining children's religious attendance. Since we were primarily concerned with parent-religion-related effects and we did not get consistent effects across our two outcomes, we do not go into depth about these findings. Finally, only for explaining children's religious importance, we found a three-way interaction between gender, parenting style (authoritarian vs. less engaged), and religious importance, but the results were not robust and did

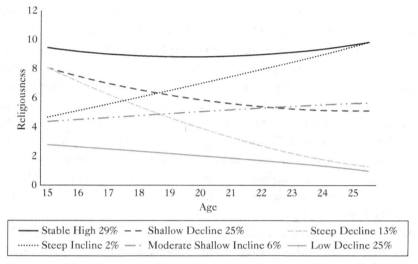

FIGURE 2.4 Growth curve modeling of the six most common religious trajectories between mid-adolescence and emerging adulthood.

Source: National Study of Youth and Religion, 2002–13.

Ten-Year Religious Trajectories

So far we have focused on understanding adult children's religious importance and attendance 10 years after they left their parents' homes. We also wanted to understand how parent religious characteristics shaped children's religious trajectories into adulthood. Do children start out with relatively high levels of religiosity and remain that way, decline steeply after they leave their parents' home, or something else? We used a statistical method called growth curve modeling to group children's 10-year religious trajectories into six most common types—stable high, shallow decline, steep decline, steep increase, moderate increase, and low declining—based on how they developed over the decade-long period for which we have data. Those trajectories are presented in Figure 2.4. We then examined how parents' religiousness at the beginning of the 10 years shaped the trajectories, after accounting for the

---

not appear for our religious attendance outcome or any of the other categories for parenting style. In a separate analysis we found that neither parents' religious attendance nor parents' religious importance significantly moderated the relationship between parenting style and children's religious importance or attendance 10 years later. Finally, there was no significant interaction between parents' religious attendance and parenting style for explaining children's religious attendance or importance 10 years later.

possible confounding influence of many control variables. The full statistical model is presented in Appendix Table C at the end of this chapter.

Figure 2.5 presents the marginal predicated probabilities (range 0 to 1) of being in each religious trajectory by high levels on three parent religiousness measures: families talking daily (the highest category) about religion in the home, parents attending religious services at least once a week, and parents reporting that their religious faith is extremely important, all three during the children's teenage years. The percentages to the left of the bars present the average proportion of people who fell into each category. The largest categories are (1) stable high; (2) shallow decline; (3) steep decline; and (4) stable low. The longer bars show that adult children who grew up in homes where their parents attended religious services at least once a week, whose parents reported that their religious faith was extremely important, and who talked daily in their home about religious matters were most likely to have a stable high religious trajectory. The same are less likely to have a stable low religious trajectory.

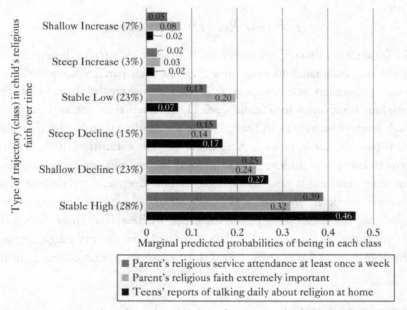

FIGURE 2.5 Marginal predicated probabilities (range 0 to 1) of being in each religious trajectory by the interviewed parent attending religious services at least once a week, parent reports of religious faith being extremely important, and families talking daily about religion in the home during the teenage years (W1).

Notes: Percentages indicate the portion of the sample in each category. Due to rounding, percentages may not add up to 100%. Estimates are based on Model 1 in Table 2.1.

On the Importance of Parents Talking
with Children about Religious Matters

This chapter has so far focused primarily on the relationship between parent religiousness, parenting styles, and emerging adult children's importance of religious faith and religious service attendance. However, we also wish to draw more attention to another key variable in our analyses that also showed up in the findings we just presented: parents talking with their teenage children about religious matters at home during the week. Other research has suggested that parents regularly talking with teenage children about religious matters appears to be strongly associated with children's religious outcomes 10 years later.[9] So we also explored that relationship in our analysis here. Our findings reported in Figures 2.1 and 2.2 confirm the importance of parents having religious conversations with their children. The more sophisticated findings reported in Appendix Table B of this chapter confirm that parents talking with teenage children about religious matters during the week is indeed a significant and powerful factor associated with emerging adult children's greater importance of faith and religious service attendance reported a decade later.

In fact, parents talking is *even more strongly* associated with religious importance than either increased parents' importance of faith or more frequent religious service attendance, both of which we already know to be major influences. In a separate analysis we standardized the three parent religiosity variables.[10] We found that a one standard deviation increase in parents talking with their teenage children about religion increases the odds of those children having the highest level of religious importance (versus the combined middle and lower levels) 10 years later by 66 percent (1.667). By comparison, a one standard deviation increase in parent religious faith increases the odds of adult children reporting the highest level of religious importance by 29 percent (1.292), and for more frequent parent religious service attendance the increase in odds is only 24 percent (1.238). All of these associations are statistically significant as independent effects. But, for explaining religious

---

9. For example, Christian Smith and Kyle Longest, "Parent Religiousness Effects on Emerging Adult Children's Religious Outcomes 10 Years Later: A Longitudinal Analysis of NSYR Data," working paper; also see the religious transmission literature reference in note 8 of the Introduction.

10. Appendix Table B at the end of this chapter shows results for all of these variables together, but the metrics are not standardized so direct comparison between them is more complicated than what follows here.

importance 10 years later, the strongest association is with parents regularly talking with their children about religious matters as part of ordinary life.

For explaining adult children's religious attendance, parents' religious attendance and parents talking with their teenage children about religion compete closely with each other. Specifically, a one standard deviation increase in parents talking with their teenage children about religion increases the odds of those children reporting the highest level of religious engagement 10 years later by 43 percent (1.429), relative to the other combined categories. Similarly, a one standard deviation increase in parent religious service attendance is associated with a 46 percent (1.458) increase in the odds that adult children will have the highest level of religious attendance relative to the other combined categories. Conversely, a one standard deviation increase in parent religious importance is associated with just a 16 percent (1.157) increase in the odds.

Most studies of intergenerational transmission of religious faith miss this important finding because the survey data on which they are based do not contain variables for parents talking with children about religion. Fortunately, the NSYR does contain this variable and its inclusion in analyses offers striking findings. Scholars need to give more attention to theorizing the causal mechanisms by which parents talking regularly with their children about religion influences their religiousness many years later. To that end, we pick up this discussion in Chapter 3, exploring the matter in greater depth. For the time being, it is simply important to note this statistically significant association.

Religion and the Quality of Parents' Partner Relationships

Religion can also influence parenting indirectly by shaping parents' relationships with each other. Most American parents do not raise their children alone, but with partners in couples. Parents' relationships with their partners, while not directly related to parenting styles, influence what they bring to parenting their children. Many studies have found that more religious American parents tend to have lower rates of marital discord, infidelity, and divorce—all of which can affect their ability to be effective parents.[11] True,

---

11. Mahoney et al., "Religion in the Home in the 1980s and 1990s"; Christopher G. Ellison, Amy M. Burdette, and W. Bradford Wilcox, "The Couple That Prays Together: Race and Ethnicity, Religion, and Relationship Quality among Working-Age Adults," *Journal of Marriage and Family* 72, no. 4 (2010): 963–975; Amy M. Burdette et al., "Are There Religious Variations in Marital Infidelity?," *Journal of Family Issues* 28, no. 12 (December 2007): 1553–1581; Annette

parents who get divorced tend to become less interested in religious participation for various reasons, which partly helps explain the negative relationship between religious engagement and marital dissolution. Nevertheless, longitudinal research that can account for most of those dynamics has found that more religiously engaged parents still tend to have better marital outcomes.[12] And that affects the likelihood that parents' children will grow up to be religious.[13]

Our interviews with religiously affiliated parents also suggest that more religious involvement contributes positively to relationships between partners. Of the parents we interviewed who discussed how religion affects the quality of their relationships with their co-parents, nearly two-thirds of the most highly religious of them said that religion positively influenced their relationships, while parents with low to moderate levels of religious involvement said the same at only one-half that amount. One highly religious white Catholic mother, for example, said, "I think the structure of the Church and the community really helps to keep us on the same page." When asked how things in her family would be different without religion, a very involved conservative Protestant mother explained, "Well honestly, we probably would not be married. You know, because in every marriage there are issues." A number of parents told us similarly that religion is the reason that they are still with their partner. When asked what helped to stabilize his marital relationship, a conservative Protestant father explained, "I would say us coming together in God's eyes and going to church as a family, and interacting with the Lord that way. Like I said, it's night and day."

Viewed from another angle, many parents also talked about how the shared task of passing on religion to their children strengthened their relationship. Numerous parents, especially those who were more religiously committed, described how their partners supporting them in the religious transmission process. For example, one Jewish mother in a same-sex relationship said about Shabbat dinner: "The Friday night thing is just fabulous, you

Mahoney, "Religion in Families, 1999–2009: A Relational Spirituality Framework," *Journal of Marriage and Family* 72, no. 4 (July 9, 2010): 805–827.

12. Timothy Clydesdale, "Family Behaviors among Early U.S. Baby Boomers: Exploring the Effects of Religion and Income Change, 1965–1982," *Social Forces* 76, no. 2 (December 1997): 605.

13. Christopher Ellison et al., "The Effects of Parental Marital Discord and Divorce on the Religious and Spiritual Lives of Young Adults," *Social Science Research* 40, no. 2 (March 2011): 538–551.

know, everybody sits down, you have a table full of friends, you drink a little bit of wine, everybody knows it's a good dinner. It's a really centering thing, growing up [for the children], and it's been incredible for our marriage." A black Protestant parent noted that religion is "very important, not anything we would do without. Always praying, we always pray for each other, it's just number one in the household." Thus, the shared task of raising children religiously itself seems to strengthen parents' relationships, which in turn we have reason to believe enhances their effectiveness in religious transmission.

Addendum: Corporal Punishment

One final aspect of parenting practices that is not an explicit dimension of the parenting styles theory discussed earlier but that is socially important and has been researched by sociologists of religion is the question of corporal punishment of children. There is no reason to equate religion and corporal punishment and violence generally, but specific variations in their associations suggest an empirical question. Conservative and black Protestants stand out as more amenable to corporal punishment. First, numerous studies have found that parents in conservative Protestant denominations or who have conservative theological beliefs are somewhat more likely than others to approve of corporal punishment and to use it to discipline their children.[14] One 2014 study, for example, showed 84 percent as the predicted percentage of conservative Protestants with a high school education who agreed or strongly agreed that corporal punishment is sometimes necessary, compared to 71 percent of people who were not conservative Protestant but also had a high school education—a 13 point difference.[15]

Why this variation? Compared to other American Christian groups, conservative Protestants are more likely to view the Bible as inerrant and interpret it literally. Several biblical passages instruct children to honor and obey

---

14. Christopher Ellison and Darren Sherkat, "Conservative Protestantism and Support for Corporal Punishment," *American Sociological Review* 59, no. 1 (1993): 131–144; Christopher Ellison, John Bartkowski, and Michelle Segal, "Conservative Protestantism and the Parental Use of Corporal Punishment," *Social Forces* 74, no. 3 (March 1996): 1003; Annette Mahoney et al., "Religion in the Home in the 1980s and 1990s: A Meta-Analytic Review and Conceptual Analysis of Links between Religion, Marriage, and Parenting," *Psychology of Religion and Spirituality* 15, no. 4 (2008): 63–101.

15. John Hoffmann, Christopher Ellison, and John Bartkowski, "Conservative Protestantism and Attitudes toward Corporal Punishment, 1986–2014," *Social Science Research* 63 (March 2017): 81–94.

their parents, and parents are told that they will be held accountable to God for teaching religious values.[16] For some, these passages legitimate corporal punishment with the aim of teaching obedience and promoting moral development. As we learned in Chapter 1, most parents see a primary purpose of religion as providing their children with moral instruction. Conservative Protestant theology also tends to view human nature as tending toward sin, which parental discipline needs to confront and root out.[17] Many conservative Protestant bookstores and online retailers sell parenting how-to books that claim that corporal punishment of children is theologically mandated.[18] Research suggests that parents who obtain parenting advice from conservative Protestant religious leaders—such as James Dobson, the evangelical author and founder of the global ministry, Focus on the Family, whose parenting books, with titles like *Dare to Discipline* and *The Strong-Willed Child*, were extremely popular for decades—are more likely to condone physical discipline of children.[19] Conservative Protestants on average have lower levels of education than the general public and are less trusting of academic elites who oppose corporal punishment for leading to poorer child outcomes.[20] Conservative Protestant support for corporal punishment has declined since the 1980s, but more among college-educated parents—and even these

---

16. For example, Deuteronomy 6:6–7; Deuteronomy 21:18–21, 27:16; Proverbs 29:15, 30:17; Proverbs 22:6.

17. Christopher Ellison, "Conservative Protestantism and the Corporal Punishment of Children: Clarifying the Issues," *Journal for the Scientific Study of Religion* 35, no. 1 (March 1996): 1, https://doi.org/10.2307/1386391; John Bartkowski, "Spare the Rod . . . , or Spare the Child? Divergent Perspectives on Conservative Protestant Child Discipline," *Review of Religious Research* 37, no. 2 (December 1995): 97.

18. John Hoffmann, Christopher Ellison, and John Bartkowski, "Conservative Protestantism and Attitudes toward Corporal Punishment, 1986–2014," *Social Science Research* 63 (March 2017): 81–94.

19. Catherine Taylor et al., "Parents' Primary Professional Sources of Parenting Advice Moderate Predictors of Parental Attitudes toward Corporal Punishment," *Journal of Child and Family Studies* 26, no. 2 (February 2017): 652–663.

20. Darren Sherkat, "Religion and Verbal Ability," *Social Science Research* 39, no. 1 (January 2010): 2–13; Murray Straus and Julie Stewart, "Corporal Punishment by American Parents: National Data on Prevalence, Chronicity, Severity, and Duration, in Relation to Child and Family Characteristics," *Clinical Child and Family Psychology Review* 2, no. 2 (1999): 55–70; Elizabeth Gershoff and Andrew Grogan-Kaylor, "Spanking and Child Outcomes: Old Controversies and New Meta-Analyses," *Journal of Family Psychology* 30, no. 4 (2016): 453–469.

conservative Protestants support corporal punishment more than their other college-educated peers.[21]

In our interviews, we too found that conservative Protestants were more likely than parents from most other religious traditions to say they use corporal punishment with their children. One conservative Protestant mother, for instance, explained, "There's this huge thing if you spank kids. But after mine were age three, it was just a little tap was all it would take. But after that time, we never had to, it wasn't necessary because they knew we would." A conservative Protestant single father said that with his daughter he can simply raise his voice, but with his son he has to do more, "Sometimes I may just hit him in the chest and be like, you know, stop."

For many of the same reasons, black Protestant parents are also more likely than others to endorse corporal punishment.[22] Additionally, our black Protestant interviews were conducted in the American South, a population generally more likely to support physical discipline of children.[23] Our interviews with them included a lot of discussions about "whooping" kids, some of which directly referencing the Bible. One black Protestant mother, for instance, reported, "I'm a very strict disciplinarian, old-school, 'spare the rod you spoil the child', but with love, never ever go over into abuse. I tell my kids, and one of my little grandsons asked me, 'Why do you have to pop me with that ruler?' I say, 'Well, that's what my book [the Bible] tells me.'" Another mother lamented, "Parenting in general, I would have done a lot differently, like at the beginning. I wouldn't have started spanking them so early in general, because Sam was getting whoopings when he was one."

In our interviews, Hispanic Catholic also seemed more amenable to corporal punishment than others, probably in part because much of our sample was less educated and drawn from the rural South, both of which are associated with greater approval of physical discipline.[24] These parents sometimes explained their physical discipline using religious justifications.

---

21. Hoffmann, Ellison, and Bartkowski, "Conservative Protestantism and Attitudes toward Corporal Punishment, 1986–2014," March 2017.

22. Straus and Stewart, "Corporal Punishment by American Parents."

23. Straus and Stewart, "Corporal Punishment by American Parents." Christopher G. Ellison and Matt Bradshaw, "Religious Beliefs, Sociopolitical Ideology, and Attitudes Toward Corporal Punishment," *Journal of Family Issues* 30, no. 3 (March 2009): 320–340.

24. Straus and Stewart, "Corporal Punishment by American Parents"; Hoffmann, Ellison, and Bartkowski, "Conservative Protestantism and Attitudes toward Corporal Punishment, 1986–2014," March 2017.

One Hispanic Catholic father, for instance, told us about a debate with his wife: "[My parents] spanked me and it worked. And she says: 'They never spanked me.' But the Bible says the rod of discipline, we should have done it." A Hispanic Catholic mother told us about the consequences of her 12-year-old son leaving without telling her where he was going: "Of course, when he came home he had his *tate quieto* [spanking] [laughs]."

But many parents from all religious traditions seemed to wrestle with the issue of corporal punishment. One Mormon mother, for instance, told us that her children have "gotten a couple of spankings. You know, the Bible says 'spare the rod, spoil the child,' and I'm not sure what that really meant [pause], don't spare the rod, save the child, whatever. In other words, it gives you permission to spank and I just don't agree with it." Some parents we interviewed were not opposed to corporal punishment in theory but simply believed that their kids were either not disobedient enough to need physical punishment or that it did not work. One Hispanic Catholic father said, "I wasn't that type [to spank]. It's not for no reason, maybe it sounds weird, but my kids weren't problematic." A white Catholic father told us his kids questioned him, " 'Hey Dad, why did we never get hit?' I said, 'You never gave me reason.' " When asked if she spanked her kids, a conservative Protestant mother said, "Not too much. It didn't really seem to work and it seemed to cause more anger and frustration with them, so you have to find what works. I mean, it can work for some parents but it didn't really do that much for me."

Other parents told us that for principled reasons they never hit their children. One mainline Protestant mother explained, "Because that's a person. You wouldn't want anyone hitting you." A Jewish mother said simply: "Hitting them is not loving." A few, such as this white Catholic mother, extended her concern about physical hitting to yelling: "Our generation has turned into a yelling generation. Instead of hitting the kids, it's more yelling at the kids. I see it and speak with my friends about it as well. Like I wish I could just stop yelling at my kids." Yet other parents offered personal reasons for not practicing corporal punishment. One mainline Protestant mother of an adopted daughter did not spank her because "her birth mother beat her, so we're not beaters." A Hispanic Catholic mother told us that she and her husband never hit their children "because as a child he [my husband] was hit, which he did not want with our children."

The larger issue of corporal punishment is complicated by a few wrinkles, however. True, research has shown that conservative and black Protestant parents are more likely than others to approve of and use corporal punishment. But research has not found that these parents are more likely to use severe physical discipline (e.g., hitting with a fist, or using a hard object to strike body parts other than one's bottom) or nonphysical harsh behaviors (e.g., threats, yelling, or ignoring).[25] Too, some studies suggest that conservative Protestant and highly religious parents may have more positive parenting qualities and practices.[26] For example, one study found that parents who hold theologically conservative views of the Bible report more frequent hugging and praising their children.[27] Other research has found that more religious parents are more likely to express a parenting style that adapts well to their children's needs, are more involved, and have kids who perceive them as more supportive.[28] Studies of African Americans, who are more religious than the average American, have found that black parents tend to have more consistent parenting styles and that their children are better at self-regulating and less likely to internalize (e.g., feel sadness) or externalize (e.g., start fights, quarrels) problems.[29] In short, these matters, like parenting itself, are complicated. Endorsing or opposing corporal punishment specifically does not correlate with what are generally considered good and bad parenting practices.

Conclusion

Any examination of religious parenting for passing on religion to children has to consider not only parenting religiousness but also parenting styles. We found evidence that varying parenting styles made a difference in religious

---

25. Elizabeth Thompson Gershoff, Pamela C. Miller, and George W. Holden, "Parenting Influences from the Pulpit: Religious Affiliation as a Determinant of Parental Corporal Punishment," *Journal of Family Psychology* 13, no. 3 (1999): 307.

26. Bart Duriez et al., "Is Religiosity Related to Better Parenting?: Disentangling Religiosity from Religious Cognitive Style," *Journal of Family Issues* 30, no. 9 (September 2009): 1287–1307; Mahoney et al., "Religion in the Home in the 1980s and 1990s"; Annette Mahoney, "Religion in Families, 1999–2009: A Relational Spirituality Framework," *Journal of Marriage and Family* 72, no. 4 (July 9, 2010): 805–827.

27. W. Bradford Wilcox, "Conservative Protestant Childrearing: Authoritarian or Authoritative?," *American Sociological Review* (1998): 796–809.

28. J. Blake Snider, Andrea Clements, and Alexander T. Vazsonyi, "Late Adolescent Perceptions of Parent Religiosity and Parenting Processes," *Family Process* 43, no. 4 (2004): 489–502; Valarie King, "The Influence of Religion on Fathers' Relationships with Their Children," *Journal of Marriage and Family* 65, no. 2 (2003): 382–395; Mahoney et al., "Religion in the Home in the 1980s and 1990s."

29. Gene H. Brody, Zolinda Stoneman, and Douglas Flor, "Parental Religiosity, Family Processes, and Youth Competence in Rural, Two-Parent African American Families," *Developmental Psychology* 32, no. 4 (1996): 696–706; Gene H. Brody et al., "Religion's Role in Organizing Family Relationships: Family Process in Rural, Two-Parent African American Families," *Journal of Marriage and the Family* 56, no. 4 (November 1994): 878.

transmission to children. But so does religious intensity and the demands of parents' religious traditions, and their personal religious commitments and practices. Moreover, parenting styles appear to moderate the relationship between parents' religious importance and children's religious importance and attendance 10 years later. Issues such as the interaction of religion and corporal punishment also relate to parenting strategies generally, but exactly how that works seems to be complex and deserving of more research. Finally, religion itself generally and the specific task of together raising children religiously seems to strengthen the relationships of parents with each other, which then tends to enhance their parenting abilities. Our data here are admittedly limited and imperfect, so we offer our findings only as a modest contribution to ongoing debates. But taken together, our evidence does add to previous work finding that parenting styles and parents' religious characteristics are important for raising children to carry on the family's religion.

Chapter 2 Appendix: Variables and Methodology

Our statistical analyses in this chapter test for significant associations between parenting styles reported on the first wave of the National Study of Youth and Religion panel survey and children's religious outcomes 10 years later (for a detailed description of the NSYR methodology, see the appendix at the end of book). We also look at the influence of these factors in shaping children's religious trajectories over time. Our first research question is whether certain parenting styles and parent religious characteristics expressed during the teenage years (ages 13–17) associate with higher levels of religious importance and attendance during emerging adulthood a decade later (ages 23–27). We tested two different religious outcomes as dependent variables measured at NSYR Wave 4: (1) professed importance of religious faith ("How important or unimportant is religious faith in shaping how you live your daily life?," with the answer categories: extremely important, very important, somewhat important, very unimportant, and not at all important); and (2) frequency of religious service attendance ("About how often do you usually attend religious services?," with the answer categories: more than once a week, once a week, 2–3 times a month, once a month, many times a year, and a few times a year). The first question measures a subjective feature of religiousness; and the second measures a public religious behavior. Both of these variables have ordinal answer categories, making ordered logistic regression the appropriate statistical method of analysis. (Table Appendix A lists and describes all of the variables we use in this chapter.) We also look at the influence of parents' religious importance and attendance on children's religious trajectories over a 10-year period. We focus on explaining six different trajectories—stable low, stable high, shallow decline, steep decline, steep increase, and shallow increase—using multinomial logistic analysis techniques.

The parenting-styles theory[30] we test in this chapter specifies our main independent variables, conceptualizing four categorical types of key parenting styles determined by the combination of two distinct, characteristic parenting differences. The first difference concerns the degree of parental warmth, supportiveness, and responsiveness toward their children ("warmth" for short)—varying between parents who are very warm, affectionate, and responsive, on one hand, versus those who are colder, more detached, and inaccessible to their children, on the other hand. The second key different parenting characteristic concerns the strength of parental expectations, standards, and strictness for and with their children ("expectations" for short)—varying between parents who hold and assert clear and high standards and expectations and monitor their children accordingly, on the one hand, versus parents who are more lenient, passive, indulgent, and nondirective, on the other hand. These key differences in parental characteristics are conceptually distinct from each other, so they can be combined to create four distinct parenting-style types.

Parents who are *high* on *both* warmth and expectations embody an "authoritative" parenting style; they combine warmth, closeness, and accessibility with definite and firm expectations and monitoring of their children. Their motto might be characterized as "I'm the authority here to help you mature," "Let's talk this out," or "Love holds expectations." Such parents tend to explain their reasons for their expectations to their children, are moderately flexible in their requirements of their kids, and seek to work things out *with* their children rather than to dictate commands. By comparison, parents who are *low* on warmth but *high* on expectations reflect an "authoritarian" parenting style; they combine emotional distance and unidirectional communication with high assertions of control, structure, autocracy, and rules over their children. The motto of authoritarian style parents is something like "I'm in charge here" and "Because I said so." Often authoritarian parents emphasize their power over their children and discipline them through punishment. As a third type, parents who are *low* on *both* warmth and expectations embody a "less engaged" parenting style (sometimes also labeled "less engaged" or neglecting/rejecting"); they combine emotional and communication distance with a lack of interest in and monitoring of their children's activities in life. The motto of less engaged parents would be something like "Whatever is fine" or "You're on your own." Such parents are often absent, distracted by other priorities, or simply have or devote little time for parenting. Finally, parents who are *high* on warmth but *low* on expectations dimensions represent a "permissive" parenting style; they are emotionally close and open to, but indulgent, nondirective, and nonmonitoring of their children. Their motto might be "Let's just be friends," "You're the boss," or "No hassles from me." These parents are often very "laid back," radical egalitarians, or simply averse to family conflict.

---

30. Diana Baumrind, "Effects of Authoritative Parental Control on Child Behavior," *Child Development* 37 (1966): 887–907; Diana Baumrind, "Authoritarian vs. Authoritative Parental Control," *Adolescence* 3 (1968): 255–272; Diana Baumrind, "Parental Disciplinary Patterns and Social Competence in Children," *Youth & Society* 9 (1978): 239–276; Diana Baumrind, "The Discipline Controversy Revisited," *Family Relations* 45 (1996): 405–414.

Appendix Table A Descriptive Statistics for Variables Included in the Analysis (N = 1,903)

Variable	Mean	Std. Dev.	Min.	Max.
Child importance of faith (W4)	3.045	1.393	1	5
Child religious service attendance (W4)	2.677	2.123	1	7
Child's religious trajectory (between W1 and W4)				
Stable high	0.284	0.451	0	1
Shallow decline	0.231	0.422	0	1
Steep decline	0.153	0.361	0	1
Steep increase	0.027	0.163	0	1
Shallow increase	0.075	0.263	0	1
Stable low	0.230	0.421	0	1
Child reports of parenting style for interviewed parent (W1)				
Authoritative	0.373	0.484	0	1
Less engaged (reference)	0.247	0.431	0	1
Authoritarian	0.209	0.407	0	1
Permissive	0.171	0.376	0	1
Interviewed parent importance of religious faith (W1)	4.936	1.299	1	6
Interviewed parent religious service attendance (W1)	4.313	2.198	1	7
Parents talking to their kids about religious matters (W1)	3.232	1.718	1	6
Interviewed parent religious affiliation (W1)				
Conservative Protestant (reference)	0.341	0.474	0	1
Mainline Protestant	0.172	0.378	0	1
Black Protestant	0.090	0.286	0	1
Catholic	0.239	0.427	0	1
Jewish	0.018	0.134	0	1
Mormon	0.029	0.168	0	1
Unaffiliated	0.063	0.243	0	1
Other religion	0.029	0.168	0	1
Indeterminate	0.019	0.136	0	1
Child gender (female)	0.530	0.499	0	1
Child educational attainment (W4)	2.968	1.098	1	5
Child married	0.267	0.443	0	1
Child white (reference)	0.725	0.447	0	1

(*continued*)

Appendix Table A Continued

Variable	Mean	Std. Dev.	Min.	Max.
Child other race	0.061	0.239	0	1
Child Black	0.121	0.326	0	1
Child Latino	0.093	0.291	0	1
Parent's political leanings, liberal to conservative (W1)	3.231	1.015	1	5
Parents(s) educational attainment (W1)	3.154	1.013	1	5
Family income (W1)	6.350	2.882	1	11
Parents married (W1)	0.724	0.447	0	1
Parent gender (female)	0.815	0.388	0	1
Family lived in South (W1)	0.385	0.487	0	1

Source: National Study of Youth and Religion (W1 & W4).

In order to construct those four categorical dummy variables, we used and combined multiple questions available in the NSYR survey (Wave 1). This survey asked similar questions about parenting behaviors and parent–child relations of both parent and teenage respondents (parent self-reports and child reports on parents). Since our dependent variables concerned teenagers' religious outcomes 10 years after the baseline survey (Wave 4), we expected teens' Wave 1 reports to be more useful for testing possible parent style effects—since parents' responses would more likely be distorted by a social desirability bias (their wanting to seem to themselves and survey researchers to be "good" parents) than teenagers' reports; and because teenagers' perceptions of parental styles would matter more for their own outcomes than parents' self-evaluations. Hence, all results reported in this chapter rely on variables constructed using teenagers', not parents', survey responses to questions related to parenting styles.

Few social surveys are capable of asking the extensive batteries of questions that would fully measure all of the dimensions of the complex concepts involved in sociological theories, such as the parenting-style theory tested here. In many cases, however, a more limited number of questions imperfectly but adequately captures enough of the characteristics and differences involved in those concepts to make reliable analyses feasible. The questions provided by the NSYR Wave 1 survey enable us to construct the variables and run the statistics needed to test the parenting styles theory under consideration, as follows.

We constructed a *warmth* variable (used to then construct our categorical parenting style variables) by combining answers from four different teenager reports about their parents' emotional expressiveness and communicational engagement: (1) "How often does your mother/father say she/he loves you?," (2) "How often does your mother/father encourage you?," (3) "How close to do you feel to your mother/father?," and (4) "How often does your mother/father hug you?" The answer categories for all four questions were: very often, fairly often, sometimes, rarely, and never; respondents were also able to refuse to answer the question or to say that they did not know. This created an additive scale of parental warmth ranging from 1 to 19, representing the least (all "never") to the most (all "very often") warm parents. In the absence of more direct measures, we assumed that these four questions about parent–teen closeness and warmth also positively associate with and adequately indirectly capture other dimensions of the warmth concept, namely open communication, reciprocity, and moderate flexibility with children.

We constructed an *expectations* variable used in our analysis by combining answers from three different teenager reports about their parents' monitoring of media consumption, friends, and activities: "How much do(es) your [parent figure(s)—either mother, father, or parents] monitor your music, television, and movie watching?," "How much do(es) your [parent figure(s)] monitor who you hang out with?," and "In general, how often do(es) your [parent figure(s)] know what you are actually doing when you're not at home?" (the correct parent figure wording was skip-patterned in, depending on household composition). The answer categories for all three questions were as follows: always, usually, sometimes, rarely, and never; respondents were also able to refuse to answer the question or to say they did not know. This created an additive scale of parental monitoring ranging from 1 to 13, representing the least (all "never") to the most (all "always") frequently monitoring parents. In the absence of more direct measures, we assumed that these measures of parental monitoring also positively associate with and adequately indirectly capture other dimensions of the expectations concept, namely established and enforced standards and expectations.

We created parenting-style categorical dummy variables by combining the warmth and expectations variables just described into a set of four dummy variables, representing the four parenting styles and including everyone in our dataset. We categorized parents as "authoritative" if their score on the warmth scale was 16 or greater (46 percent of respondents had a score of 15 or less and 54 percent had a score that was 16 or higher) *and* if their score on the expectations scale was 9 or greater (43 percent of respondents had a score of 8 or less and 57 percent had a score that was 9 or higher). We categorized parents as "less engaged" if their score on the warmth scale was 15 or lower *and* if their score on the expectations scale was 8 or lower. Parents were categorized as "permissive" if their score on the warmth scale was 16 or greater *and* if their score on the expectations scale was 8 or lower. Finally, we categorized parents as "authoritarian" if their score on the warmth scale was 15 or lower *and* if their score on the expectations scale was 9 or greater.

In addition to the variables described earlier and reported in this chapter's tables, we also explored other variables that did not prove useful. As we noted earlier, measures of parenting warmth and expectations based on parent reports provided few statistically significant results. Had the teenage reports also provided statistically insignificant results, we would have concluded either that parenting styles make little difference for later-life child religiousness outcomes or that our survey data inadequately measured parenting styles. But the teenage-report parenting style variables did prove highly significant in theoretically sensible ways. So we concluded that teenage-reported parenting style characteristics are more valid than parent reports of the same, probably for reasons of social desirability biases operating among parents. We also explored a handful of other survey measures that seemed arguably related to parenting styles, including teenager reports that their parents pay enough attention to them, the frequency with which they talk with their mother/father about difficult, personal subjects, the frequency that they hang out with their mother/father, and the extent of freedom their parents give them to develop and express their own views on important issues (questions y23c, y3, y9, y12, y18, and y27 in the NSYR Wave 1 survey). None of these measures produced significant results, however, probably because they cut across multiple parenting-style categories in ways that confound important differences—for instance, teenagers can talk frequently about personal issues with and may be given the freedom to develop and express their own views by both authoritative and permissive parents; and they can hang out frequently with all types of parents except the less engaged. Hence, we concluded that these measures are less appropriate than those we used for measuring the intended differences in parenting styles.

Our models also examine the frequency of parental religious service attendance, parental importance of religious faith, and the extent which the family discusses religion, as assessed at Wave 1. The exact question wording for these two measures was as follows: "In the last 12 months, how often have you been attending religious services, not including weddings, baptisms, and funerals?," with answer categories: more than once a week, once a week, 2–3 times a month, once a month, many times a year, a few times a year, and never; and "How important is your religious faith in providing guidance in your own day-to-day living?," with answer categories: extremely important, very important, fairly important, somewhat important, not very important, and not important at all. During Wave 1 surveys children were also asked, "How often does your family talk about religion?" The response categories were as follows: never, a few times a year, a few times a month, about once a week, a few times a week, and every day.

Finally, in addition to the parenting-styles independent variables described earlier, all of our statistical models controlled for a range of demographic variables in order to reduce the chances of spurious associations. Descriptive statistics for these variables can be found in this chapter's Appendix Table A. We also ran models for boys and girls separately to test for possible differing associations for mothers/sons, mothers/daughters, fathers/sons, and fathers/daughters, but found no consistent patterns of significance and so did not report those uninteresting findings. We also looked at the influence of age, but the sample had just a few different ages, it was not significant in any of our models, and we therefore excluded it.

Appendix Table B in this chapter presents the regression findings for all four statistical models described in the chapter. And Appendix Table C in this chapter presents our multinomial logistic analysis of the six different trajectories—stable low, stable high, shallow decline, steep decline, steep increase, and shallow increase.

Appendix Table B Analysis of Parenting Style and Parent Religiousness Factors (W1) Associated with Child's Importance of Faith and Religious Service Attendance 10 Years Later (W4) (Ordered Logistic Regression with Odds Reported)

	Model 1	Model 2	Model 3	Model 4
	Importance of Religious Faith (W4)		Religious Service Attendance (W4)	
Authoritative (Reference = less engaged)	1.487** [b]	0.652 [a,b]	1.120	0.364+ [a]
Authoritarian	1.184	2.132 [c]	1.272 [a]	1.552 [c]
Permissive	1.098 [c]	0.631 [c]	0.859 [a]	0.575
Parent importance of religious faith (W1)	1.222***	1.172*	1.121+	1.054
Parent's religious importance × authoritative		1.181+ [a]		1.244* [a]
Parent's religious importance × authoritarian		0.894 [c]		0.967 [c]
Parent's religious importance × permissive		1.122		1.086
Parent's religious service attendance (W1)	1.103**	1.103**	1.188***	1.189***
Parents talking to kids about religious matters (W1)	1.338***	1.333***	1.229***	1.222***
Mainline Protestant (Reference = conservative Protestant)	0.650**	0.638**	0.691*	0.681*
Black Protestant	0.950	0.976	0.949	0.972
Catholic	0.778+	0.769+	0.727*	0.720*
Jewish	0.578	0.585	0.287*	0.295*
LDS	1.251	1.247	1.423	1.431
Unaffiliated	0.705	0.699	0.866	0.844
Other religion	1.028	1.055	1.818	1.870
Indeterminate	0.587	0.581	0.479	0.475
Parent gender (female)	1.014	1.010	0.927	0.918
Child gender (female)	1.750***	1.738***	1.210+	1.206+
Child educational attainment (W4)	1.124*	1.118*	1.306***	1.298***
Child married	1.778***	1.756***	2.213***	2.171***
Child black	2.615***	2.542***	1.677+	1.640+
Child Latino	1.444*	1.462*	1.536*	1.556*
Child other race	1.252	1.227	1.000	0.978
Parent's political leanings liberal to conservative (W1)	1.320***	1.313***	1.370***	1.361***
Parents(s) educational attainment (W1)	0.922	0.919	0.889+	0.885+
Family income (W1)	0.955+	0.957+	1.019	1.022
Parents married (W1)	1.158	1.140	0.881	0.869
Family lived in South (W1)	1.231+	1.218+	1.202	1.194
Cut 1	9.130***	6.980***	46.621***	31.879***
Cut 2	16.501***	12.634***	79.640***	54.512***
Cut 3	92.790***	71.295***	120.547***	82.542***
Cut 4	303.337***	234.126***	163.018***	111.667***
Cut 5			297.871***	204.357***
Cut 6			1,436.246***	989.465***
Observations	1,903	1,903	1,903	1,903
Pseudo R^2	0.135	0.136	0.103	0.104

*** $p < 0.001$, ** $p < 0.01$, * $p < 0.05$, + $p < 0.10$.

[a] Statistically different ($p < .05$) from authoritarian.

[b] Statistically different ($p < .05$) from permissive.

[c] Statistically different ($p < .05$) from authoritative.

Source: National Study of Youth and Religion (W1 & W4).

Appendix Table C Multinomial Logistic Regression (Odds Reported) Examining the Influence of Families Talking about Religion in the Home, Parents Attending Religious Services at Least Once a Week, and Parents' Reporting Their Religious Faith as Extremely Important (W1) for Children Belonging in a Trajectory

	Model 1 (Reference = Stable low)				
	Stable High	Shallow Decline	Steep Decline	Steep Increase	Shallow Increase
Authoritative (Reference = less engaged)	3.483***	3.087***	3.235***	1.475	1.862*
Authoritarian	2.303*	1.967*	2.179*	0.766	1.144
Permissive	1.476	1.873*	2.289**	0.809	1.401
Parent importance of religious faith (W1)	1.441***	1.126	1.023	1.259	1.060
Parent's religious service attendance (W1)	1.456***	1.390***	1.504***	0.986	1.101
Parents talking to kids about religious matters (W1)	2.265***	1.721***	1.640***	1.338*	0.936
Mainline Protestant (Reference = conservative Protestant)	0.567+	0.583+	1.006	0.604	0.574
Black Protestant	0.346	0.318	0.209+	3.687	0.879
Catholic	0.510*	0.722	0.717	0.491	1.015
Jewish	0.062*	0.064*	0.231+	0.000***	0.496
LDS	0.215*	0.074**	0.176*	0.703	0.250
Unaffiliated	0.499	0.251*	1.060	1.297	0.564
Other religion	0.276*	0.103***	0.342+	0.970	1.737
Indeterminate	0.382	0.979	0.948	1.015	0.443
Parent gender (female)	1.226	1.361	0.955	1.670	0.930
Child gender (female)	4.408***	3.757***	2.643***	3.841***	2.774***
Child educational attainment (W4)	1.394**	1.291**	0.967	0.806	0.881
Child married	2.553***	0.937	1.082	2.110+	0.945
Child black	4.959**	3.334+	1.865	1.163	2.763*
Child Latino	3.332**	2.103*	2.904**	4.446*	2.492*
Child other race	2.545*	1.978+	2.912*	1.149	2.359+
Parent's political leanings, liberal to conservative (W1)	1.299**	1.135	1.047	1.275	1.372*
Parents(s) educational attainment (W1)	0.917	0.833	1.031	0.768	0.986
Family income (W1)	1.015	0.956	1.078	1.051	0.976
Parents married (W1)	0.645	0.802	0.591+	0.568	0.899
Family lived in South (W1)	2.130**	1.695*	1.681*	1.413	1.358
Constant	0.000***	0.011***	0.010***	0.010**	0.081**
Observations	1,903	1,903	1,903	1,903	1,903
Pseudo R^2	0.230	0.230	0.230	0.230	0.230

*** $p < 0.001$, ** $p < 0.01$, * $p < 0.05$, + $p < 0.10$.

Source: National Study of Youth and Religion (W1 & W4).

3

Why Are Parents the Crucial Players?

WHY ARE PARENTS *the* most important figures shaping the religious lives and futures of their children in the United States? The primary and powerful role of parents in religious socialization may seem obvious to readers today. But that is because we are familiar with our current system, not because it is historically normal or inevitable. Some older readers may remember times and religious subcultures that worked differently. People from other eras and places in history and the world could also tell about different means of religious transmission across generations. Yet all research in the United States today shows clearly that parents are by far the most important factor influencing their children's religion, not only as youth but also after they leave home. Not clergy, religious schools, youth ministers, neighborhoods, Sunday school, mission trips, service projects, summer camp, peers, or the media. Parents. That is who matters here and now. Parents define for their children the role that religious faith and practice ought to play in life, whether important or not, which most children roughly adopt. Parents set a "glass ceiling" of religious commitment above which their children rarely rise. Parental religious investment and involvement is in almost all cases the necessary and even sometimes sufficient condition for children's religious investment and involvement.

This parental primacy in religious transmission is significant because, even though most parents do realize it when they think about it, their crucial role often runs in the background of their often busy lives; it is not a conscious, daily, strategic matter.[1] Furthermore, many children do not recognize the power that their parents have in shaping their religious lives, but instead view themselves as autonomous information processors making independent, self-directing decisions.[2] Widespread cultural scripts also consistently say that the

---

1. Smith, Ritz, and Rotolo, *Religious Parenting*.

2. Smith with Denton, *Soul Searching*.

influence of parents over their children recedes starting with the onset of pu-
berty, while the influence of peers, music, and social media takes over. Other
common and influential cultural scripts operate to disempower parents by
telling them that they are not qualified to care for their children in many ways,
so they should turn their children over to experts. Further, the perceptions of
at least some (frustrated) staff at religious congregations is that more than a
few parents assume that others besides themselves (the staff) are responsible
for forming their children religiously (in Sunday school, youth group, confirmation, CCD, etc.).

Yet all empirical data tell us that, for intergenerational religious transmission today, the key agents are parents, not clergy or other religious
professionals. The key location is the home, not religious congregations.
And the key mechanisms of socialization are the formation of ordinary life
practices and identities, not programs, preaching, or formal rites of passage.
Why and how, in the face of all pressures and perceptions to the contrary,
have ordinary parents become the key agents in the socialization of their children in religion, whether successfully or not?

Time Spent and Cultural Buy-In

Some starting-point answers seem obvious. One is that most parents have
much more access to and time spent with their children than any other
people in socialization (with the possible exception of teachers and schools
for some children).[3] If we consider youth as bundles of time, attention, energy, and activity in long-term formation, the question is: who has the most
access to shape their formation? In nearly all cases, the answer is parents—
especially during the early years of socialization when basic reality, identities,
and practices are formed. Parents normally have a massive advantage of access to youth in the life-formation process.[4] Certainly more so than religious
congregations and youth groups. The latter are lucky to get an hour or two per
week of youth's lives.

A second apparent reason why parents are key players in religious socialization is that few American youth today are as rebellious as, say, Baby Boomer
youth were reputed to have been. American culture in the mid-twentieth

---

3. Most of which, however, are not in the business of religious instruction and may not be much
liked, respected, or appreciated by students.

4. Anna Rönkä and Pirjo Korvela, "Everyday Family Life: Dimensions, Approaches, and
Current Challenges," *Journal of Family Theory and Review* 1, no. 2 (2009): 87–102.

century took for granted the "Sturm-und-Drang" model of adolescence (received from early twentieth-century psychodynamic theory, such as the writings of Anna Freud), which assumed that the normal teenage years were nearly inevitably fraught with turmoil and rebellion. That model came to a peak of expression in the 1960s "youth rebellion" and its idea of an unbridgeable "generation gap." However common or genuine those experiences were half a century ago, the reality today is far different and the stereotype of an adolescent generation gap is baseless (except for some when it comes to familiarity with social media). In fact, most youth today have entirely bought into adult values and goals. The vast majority of teenagers and parents today get along reasonably well. The rates of mental and emotional troubles among youth are no higher than among adults. And most teenagers still look primarily to parents for guidance and help in life. With those kinds of relationships in play, it is not surprising that parents exert a big influence on their children today, including religious matters.

The Crucial Practice of Talking about Religion

We found in Chapter 2 that parents regularly talking to their children about religious matters during the week has a very powerful association with the children growing up to be religiously committed and involved—sometimes stronger than even parent religiousness variables. Why might that be? We think there are various, complex reasons. But one we mention here concerns language learning. Religious beliefs and practices are not only embodied but also linguistically constituted and meaningful. Language and related symbols are central to religion, and they must be learned. Yet religious language is not mainstream Americans' first language; it is a second language at best.[5] So learning to believe and practice a religion requires essentially learning a second language, and that always requires practice talking, even when one is surrounded by native speakers. So when parents regularly talk with children about religious matters in ordinary conversational settings, that provides children with exactly the kind of sustained practice in learning the second language that is necessary for religion to be sensible and possibly interesting.

When families that attend religious services even weekly do not converse together about religious things in the time between, their children only hear religion talked about by mostly others 1 or 2 hours a week. That is like sending

---

5. American culture's first language is one of liberal individualism and mass-consumer capitalism.

one's child to a weekly meeting about some foreign land where parents once lived, in which the child merely listens to others speak its foreign language. After even many years of that, most children will still not be able to speak more than a few words of the language. And we should not be surprised if they prove uninterested in extended visits there with their parents. The language would remain incomprehensible and the land still foreign, in large measure because the child was not given opportunities to learn it by practicing to speak the language himself or herself. By contrast, parents who routinely converse with their kids during the week about religious issues of interest are like those who send their children to regular classes in which everyone speaks a second language from day one and learns through practice to converse in it. Such a child is not guaranteed to want later to visit the foreign land of that language, but the chances are greater and the trip would prove more rewarding.[6]

These and other explanations of why parents matter so much today in religious socialization make intuitive sense. But we suspect that there is more of a story to be told about the larger meaning and sociocultural significance of parents' key influence. We have a hunch that, above and beyond the reasons listed earlier, the centrality of parents in intergenerational religious transmission is part of and reflects larger social changes in American society and religion. What follows is a somewhat speculative thesis lacking hard, immediate data to substantiate it.[7] But we think something like it is true and worth considering. Again, we ask: Why parents? Why at home? Why the power of talking?

---

6. Robert Wuthnow notes that, for one of his research subjects, "the basic religious principles were ones he learned at home and . . . these were simply reinforced at church, not the other way around. . . . Effective religious socialization comes about through embedded practices; that is, through specific, deliberate religious activities that are firmly intertwined with the daily habits of family routines, of eating and sleeping, of having conversations, of adorning the spaces in which people live, of celebrating holidays, and of being part of a community. Compared with these practices, the formal teachings of religious leaders often pale in significance. Yet when such practices are present, formal teachings also become more important." Wuthnow reiterates: "Religion, like charity, begins at home. The daily round of family activities must somehow be brought into the presence of God. Parents praying, families eating together, conversations focusing on what is proper and improper, and sacred artifacts are all important ways in which family space is sacralized. They come together, forming an almost imperceptible mirage of experience." Robert Wuthnow, *Growing Up Religious* (Boston: Beacon Press, 1999), 8, xxiii, xxxi–xxxii.

7. Many prior works of scholarship, however, contribute to its plausibility, including Robert Wuthnow, *After Heaven: Spirituality in America Since the 1950s* (Berkeley: University of California Press, 1998); Wade Clark Roof, *Spiritual Marketplace: Baby Boomers and the Remaking of American Religion* (Princeton, NJ: Princeton University Press, 1999); Patrick H. McNamara, *Conscience First, Tradition Second: A Study of Young American Catholics* (Albany: SUNY Press, 1992).

Religion: From Communal Solidarity Project to Personal Identity Accessory

Our thesis is this: The centrality of parents in intergenerational religious transmission indicates a long-term transformation of the character of the mainstream American religious field vis-à-vis its sociocultural context. There are many ways to try to describe this transformation. But here we offer a model involving an extended shift from religion lived as a "communal solidarity project" to religion as a "personal identity accessory." Immediately we acknowledge that our model greatly simplifies a complex process; flirts with old, simplistic sociological dichotomies; and could (wrongly) be read as a "good old days" lament. But all models simplify by nature, and good ones do so helpfully. Sometimes dichotomies are good starting points of insight. And we mean nothing of the following as a nostalgic lament, but rather as straightforward description and analysis. Our models should be read not as capturing an exact narration of historical change but as two "ideal types" (in the sense advocated by Max Weber) that seek to capture the broad features and essential spirits of religious modes of being in major eras of American history.

What do we mean by religion as a "communal solidarity project?" Table 3.1 describes key features of this constitution of religion and compares it to

Table 3.1 Comparison of Defining Traits of Religion as Community Solidarity Project versus Personal Identity Accessory Ideal Types

	Community Solidarity Project	Personal Identity Accessory
Religion's practical purpose	Right living grounded in true beliefs and right practices	Therapeutic coping practices, "good choices"
The self's needs	Formation in the good	Authentic life concerns
Religious congregations	Centers of faith's local community life	Supportive associational resources
Religious epistemology	Revelation, tradition, reason, experience, conditional trust in religious authorities	Individual personal "opinion," subjectively felt preferences, "thine own self"
Social ontology of religion	Authoritative carrier of a tradition	Optional lifestyle accessory
Home, family Mode of growth	Crucial anchor institution Participation, solidarity, practices	"Incubator of possibilities" Self-reflexivity, self-assessment, self-expression

religion as a "personal identity accessory." In religion as a communal solidarity project, the practical purpose of religion is to promote and sustain right living grounded in true beliefs and right practices. Religion exists to shape people's view of what is good and desirable, and to help govern their behaviors. This model embodies a particular view of what the human self needs, which is to be conformed to what is the good. The background assumption is that individual humans on their own do not naturally or automatically know what is good for themselves, so the religion as a tradition embedded in the larger community serves the task of shaping, inculcating, forming people to know and follow what its tradition teaches to be good. The tradition passes it on, and the members learn and follow in a life process. In this model, religious congregations serve as centers of local religious community life. Religion is fundamentally social, communal, collective, and so when important religious things happen, they do so in the communal centers of religious meetings and assemblies.

In the model of religion as community solidarity project, the way people, institutions, and traditions know what is good is through some combination of revelation and received teachings (tradition), mediated through reason and interpretive commentary. Followers of the religion proceed with a conditional trust in their religious authorities, which are normally presumed to be faithful and reliable unless proven otherwise, which is rarely expected to be seen. Religion's "social ontology" in this model—that is, the way its understood essential being is constituted in human cultures—is an authoritative carrier of a tradition. Religion is what it is and carries the social weight it does by passing forward with an authority unique to its domain and historical tradition what is believed to be very important to maintain. In this model, home and family are important, but they are not the center. Rather, they are crucial anchoring institutions that follow and reinforce what the community inculcates and enacts. Finally, people, families, and communities grow in such a religious model through participation, solidarity, and engagement in the practices, rituals, and celebrations stipulated by the religion.

We are suggesting that for much of American history, religion existed and functioned as a communal solidarity project. This was especially but not exclusively in rural areas, in small towns, and in urban neighborhoods with strong religio-ethnic subcultures, which was much of America during most of its history. This was also true in significant religious minority communities, such as in Mormonism, black Protestantism, and various branches of Judaism. There were notable exceptions, of course. But, by our thesis, most of the religious field in the United States was constituted in this way up until the early twentieth century. The last century then, we suggest, saw a basic transformation in the nature of religion away from being a community solidarity project into something else: religion as personal identity accessory. The change was gradual and did not become clearly apparent until the last quarter of the twentieth century. The "seeker church" and mega-church movements that flowered in the 1980s and after both exemplified and propelled this transformation. So what do we mean by personal identity accessory?

When religion is reconstituted as a personal identity accessory, its practical purpose is not to promote right living grounded in good beliefs, but to offer practices and techniques that promote coping with life and the making of "good choices." Religious people may not recognize this core function and may even deny it, but essentially that is what religion in this model mostly does. The human self in this version of religion is not an object with a nature in need of formation in the good, but a subject of self-development seeking to identify, affirm, and enact "authentic" life concerns. These may take various forms, as the individual decides upon them, but authenticity and good personal "fit" are essential elements. Religious congregations do not disappear in this model, but their function is transformed. Congregations are no longer centers of local community life but rather more like supportive associational resources aiding members in pursuing their authentic life concerns, coping with life, and making good choices. Membership is not determined by a mix of ascription and chosen association conditioned heavily by geographic and social limits, as with the communal solidarity project. Membership is instead a matter of personal preference dependent on how well the various options on offer meet one's felt needs. Community solidarity is replaced by consumer selection.

The basis for the acceptance of religious teachings and observances (religious epistemology) when religion is a personal identity accessory is not revelation and tradition, but each individual's personal "opinion" about what is helpful and right, that is, his or her subjectively felt preferences. "Scripture says . . . " is replaced with "Well, I feel that . . . ," "To me . . . ," and "I just don't think I can get on board with . . . " Religion's social ontology is not as an authoritative carrier of a tradition but an optional lifestyle accoutrement. It carries little weight as a self-authenticating institutional force, but it can be a valued aspect of a person's way of life. Religious congregations are decentered in the personal identity accessory model, and families and the home become central (and here we return to the question about the centrality of parents). Home and family, however, are no longer institutions that support the community. They become instead something like "incubators of possibilities." The private sphere of family is where identities are most profoundly formed, where authentic life concerns are worked out, where "values" and "good choices" are taught, where "lifestyles" are developed and expressed, and where opinions, subjectivity, and preferences are shaped.

All of this involves a shift from the faith reinforcements of complex religious cultures of "institutional closure" to a hub-and-spoke model of people relating to religious congregations instead as "commuter plug-ins." Religious congregations join a list of other potential activities that individuals and families might opt into if they work well for them—the "Y," bowling league, traveling football, swimming club, dance lessons. Finally, people and religions develop not through participation, solidarity, and the engagement of communal practices, but through self-reflexivity, self-growth, and self-expression.

Not incidental to this argument, the American family too has undergone a parallel transformation. Scholars of marriage and family life have shown that, from the nineteenth to the mid-twentieth century, the American marriage and family were redefined from being an institutional fact and something like a communal solidarity project to instead being a "companionate" arrangement centered in the privacy of the home and intending ideally to meet the felt emotional and consumer needs and desires of its members.[8] Since then, marriage and family have further transformed into personal identity and lifestyle options that adult individuals choose to enter, configure, and possibly exit.[9] This two-step reconstruction of marriage and family has thus been from the image of community *social institution* to home-based *companionate relations* and then to individual *lifestyle options*.[10] Many scholars talk about this transformation as the "deinstitutionalization" of American marriage and

8. Ernest Burgess and Harvey Locke, *The Family: From Institution to Companionship* (New York: American Book Company, 1945). Also see Allison Pugh, *Longing and Belonging: Parents, Children, and Consumer Culture* (Berkeley: University of California Press, 2009).

9. Paul Amato, "Tension between Institutional and Individual Views of Marriage," *Journal of Marriage and the Family* 66, no. 4 (2004): 959–965; Anthony Giddens, *The Transformations of Intimacy: Sexuality, Love and Eroticism in Modern Societies* (Stanford, CA: Stanford University Press, 1992); Milton Regan, *Family Law and the Pursuit of Intimacy* (New York: New York University Press, 1993); Steven Mintz and Susan Kellogg, *Domestic Revolutions: A Social History of American Family Life* (New York: Free Press, 1998); Robert Griswold, *Fatherhood in America: A History* (New York: Basic Books, 1993), 143–269.

10. Paul Amato, "Institutional, Companionate, and Individualistic Marriages: Change over Time and Implications for Marital Quality," in *Marriage at the Crossroads: Law, Policy, and the Brave New World of Twenty-First-Century Families*, ed. M. Garrison and E. Scott (New York: Cambridge University Press, 2012), 107–125. Paul Amato, "Tension between

family.[11] The new emphasis on choice means, for example, that those who want a "traditional" marriage and family must now make an intentional decision to do that and so "have tradition" rather than simply by default be traditional.[12] Along the way, normative beliefs about good parenting changed, too.[13] These parallel transformations of family and religion are not disconnected.[14]

Institutional and Individual Views of Marriage," *Journal of Marriage and the Family* 66, no. 4 (2004): 959–965.

11. Andrew Cherlin, "The Deinstitutionalization of American Marriage," *Journal of Marriage and Family* 66, no. 4 (2004): 848–861. All of this is of course shaped too by social class positions—see, for instance, Kathryn Edin and Timothy Nelson, *Doing the Best I Can: Fatherhood in the Inner City* (Berkeley: University of California Press, 2013); Rachel Sherman, "Conflicted Cultivation: Parenting, Privilege, and Moral Worth in Wealthy New York Families," *American Journal of Cultural Sociology* 5 (2017): 1–33.

12. Jane Collier, *From Duty to Desire: Remaking Families in a Spanish Village* (Princeton, NJ: Princeton University Press, 1997).

13. See, for instance, Rebecca Jo Plant, *Mom: The Transformation of Motherhood in Modern America* (Chicago: University of Chicago Press, 2010); Jack Westman, ed., *Parenthood in America: Undervalued, Underpaid, under Siege* (Madison: University of Wisconsin Press, 2001); Paula Fass, *The End of American Childhood: A History of Parenting from Life on the Frontier to the Managed Child* (Princeton, NJ: Princeton University Press, 2016). For a comparative study set in the context of the larger animal world, see Susan Allport, *A Natural History of Parenting* (New York: Harmony Books, 1997).

14. Andrew Cherlin astutely observes the connections between this type of family and Wuthnow's "spirituality of dwelling": "The spirituality of dwelling fit with a family- and home-centered decade in which marriage and children were a central part of almost every adult's life. 'Homes and congregations,' Wuthnow writes, 'acquired special spiritual significance because they were the places where children were being raised.' Much of the growth in religious involvement occurred in the suburbs, as married couples bought homes, had children, and sought churches to join. The suburban churches offered a standard package of family-related programs: Sunday schools, teen groups, Scouting, women's and men's groups, and so forth. Following the male-breadwinner ideal, these activities often presumed a two-parent family with a mother who did not work outside the home. Women's groups, for example, often met during the day so that homemakers could attend and still have their evenings free for their families. The 1950s family and the 1950s church supported each other" (74–75). Andrew Cherlin, *The Marriage-Go-Round: The State of Marriage and the Family in America Today* (New York: Knopf, 2009). Family changes also connect to American religion's subsequent reconstruction that Wuthnow describes as a "spirituality of seeking": "As American society and culture changed after the 1950s, so did American religion. . . . Across all of these denominations, American religion had moved from the spirituality of dwelling that characterized the 1950s to what Robert Wuthnow calls a 'spirituality of seeking.' Rather than relying on a religious home that provides security, stability, and familiar beliefs and rituals, individuals sought information on a variety of faiths. 'Spirituality,' writes Wuthnow, 'has become a vastly complex quest in which each person seeks in his or her own way.' A spirituality of seeking is less secure than a spirituality of dwelling but also less constraining. You are free to decide which rewards are most important to you and then to choose the faith that best provides them" (2009, 105–106). Cherlin continues: "The individualized marriage was not about rules and traditions but rather about finding a style of family life that gave you the greatest personal rewards. Religion became a site for self-development—a place where you could continually 'learn and grow'. . . . Rather

Children also throw a curve ball into this model of family, since they do not choose their parents and family, which itself has implications for the role of parents in this model.[15] As we suggest later, these transformations of the family also tend to situate parents, more than community and public institutions, as the key agents of socialization in their children's lives.[16]

Obviously, the contrasting models of the American religious field described earlier are painted with a very broad brush. Yet we do believe that something like this transformation has occurred historically. Of course, we can observe much variance within and across these models by religious tradition, race and ethnicity, social class, and other variables. The way the shift from communal solidarity project to personal identity accessory plays out among American mainline Protestants and Catholics versus, say, Mormons and evangelicals is different. But that variance does not weaken our thesis; it

---

than inheriting your faith from your forefathers, you were free to choose your own through a process that might involve exploring several churches. Similarly, you were free to choose your spouse through a process that might involve living with more than one partner in order to make that choice. And should you become personally dissatisfied with your church, you could leave in search of another, more fulfilling one. So, too, could you leave your marriage if you became dissatisfied with it. Both the spirituality of seeking and the individualized marriage became part of the larger project of developing your self-identity, a quest that became the focus of personal life for more and more Americans during the last several decades of the twentieth century" (2009, 108); also see Margaret Bendroth, *Growing Up Protestant: Parents, Children, and Mainline Churches* (New Brunswick, NJ: Rutgers University Press, 2002). Nonetheless, many scholars of parenting either completely ignore religion as a significant part of parents' concerns and family life (e.g., Plant, *Mom*; Westman, *Parenthood in America*; Senior, *All Joy and No Fun*; Ochs and Kremer-Sadlik, *Fast-Forward Family*; Pugh, *Longing and Belonging*) or treat religion only as an historical artifact of bygone days (e.g., Hulbert, 2003; Griswold, *Fatherhood in America*; Stearns, *Anxious Parents*). Rebecca Jo Plant, *Mom: The Transformation of Motherhood in Modern America* (Chicago: University of Chicago Press, 2012); Jack Westman, *Parenthood in America* (Madison: University of Wisconsin Press, 2001); Jennifer Senior, *All Joy and No Fun: The Paradox of Modern Parenthood* (New York: Ecco, 2015); Elinor Ochs Tamar Kremer-Sadlik (eds.), *Fast-Forward Family: Home, Work, and Relationships in Middle-Class America* (Berkeley: University of California Press, 2013); Allison Pugh, *Longing and Belonging: Parents, Children, and Consumer Culture* (Berkeley: University of California Press, 2009); Ann Hulbert, *Raising America* (New York: Vintage, 2004); Robert Griswold, *Fatherhood in America* (New York: Basic Books, 1994); Peter Stearns, *Anxious Parents* (New York: NYU Press, 2003).

15. In general, liberal individualism has never been able to make good sense of children as dependent, nonautonomous members of society, given that the ideal human being for those like Kant, Locke, and J. S. Mill is a well-formed, rational, self-directing adult.

16. Also see Jennifer Senior, *All Joy and No Fun: The Paradox of Modern Parenting* (New York: Harper Collins, 2014); Elinor Ochs and Tamara Kremer-Sadlik, eds., *Fast-Forward Family: Home, Work, and Relationships in Middle-Class America* (Berkeley: University of California Press, 2013).

merely adds complexity, texture, and interest to it. Viewed from a big-picture perspective over long stretches, our case holds true, we believe.

Our thesis also maps onto a variety of existing big-picture models of social and religious change. It parallels, for example, the transformation from Peter Berger's idea of a "sacred cosmos" and "sacred canopies" as concerned with broad institutional religious plausibility to Smith's idea of "sacred umbrellas" as focused on individual belief commitments in a pluralistic world.[17] It connects to Robert Wuthnow's observations about the shift of spirituality in American religious culture from "dwelling" to "seeking," and to Wade Clark Roof's analysis of the "spiritual marketplace" that the Baby Boomer generation created.[18] Our thesis also maps onto Phillip Hammond's case for a "third disestablishment" of religion in America involving the prioritizing of personal autonomy.[19] It links to Arnold Gehlen and James D. Hunter's arguments about the removal of normative questions from a presupposed "background" and their placement for open examination and choices among alternatives in the social "foreground."[20] It maps onto the idea of a transition from the acceptance of received traditions to modernity's "self-reflexive imperative," as described by Margaret Archer and Anthony Giddens (discussed later), among others.[21] Ronald Inglehart's work about the shift from "materialist" to "postmaterialist" culture resonates with our thesis as well,[22] as does Jürgen Habermas's argument about the changing relations between meaningful and humane "lifeworlds" and an inauthentic "system."[23]

---

17. Peter L. Berger, *The Sacred Canopy: Elements of a Sociological Theory of Religion* (New York: Anchor Books, 1990 [1967]). Christian Smith et al., *American Evangelicalism: Embattled and Thriving* (Chicago: University of Chicago Press, 1998).

18. Wuthnow, *After Heaven*; Roof, *Spiritual Marketplace*.

19. Phillip Hammond, *Religion and Personal Autonomy: The Third Disestablishment in America* (Columbia: University of South Carolina Press, 1992).

20. Arnold Gehlen, *Man* (New York: Columbia University Press, 1988); James D. Hunter, "The New Religions: Demodernization and the Protest against Modernity," in *The Social Impact of New Religious Movements*, ed. Bryan Wilson (New York: Rose of Sharon Press, Inc. 1983), 1–19.

21. Margaret Archer, *Making Our Way through the World: Human Reflexivity and Social Mobility* (Cambridge: Cambridge University Press, 2007); Margaret Archer, *The Reflexive Imperative in Late Modernity* (Cambridge: Cambridge University Press, 2012); Anthony Giddens, *Modernity and Self-Identity: Self and Society in the Late Modern Age* (Stanford, CA: Stanford University Press, 1991).

22. Ronald Inglehart, *Culture Shift in Advanced Industrial Society* (Princeton, NJ: Princeton University Press, 1989).

23. Jürgen Habermas, *The Theory of Communicative Action, Volume 1: Reason and the Rationalization of Society* (Boston: Beacon Press, 1985).

Some of the social changes during the twentieth century that helped cause the broad shift from religion as a communal solidarity project to being a personal identity accessory include the mass production of and popular access to automobiles in the early century; the massive expansion of advertising-driven, mass-consumer capitalism; rapid postwar suburbanization; the triumph of therapeutic culture; the decline in religious denominational loyalties; the cultural mainstreaming of American Catholicism since the 1960s; the growing distrust by Americans of all formal social institutions since the 1960s; the rapid rise of two-income households since the 1970s (that is, the decline of the midcentury ideal of one male breadwinner + a stay-at-home housewife); the decline and emptying of town and city downtown commercial and community areas since the 1970s resulting from the rise of shopping centers, malls, and big box store commerce; the increase in work hours and decrease in leisure time in the late twentieth century; the digital revolution and rise of social media since the 1990s; and the diffuse cultural influence of postmodern suspicion, skepticism, and identity fluidity since the 1990s, among other influences.[24]

On "Privatization"

How should we understand the meaning and consequences of this proposed transformation of the character of the religious field in the United States? We think it is helpful to return for starters to some ideas of Peter Berger in his classic book, *The Sacred Canopy*, in which he wrote, "Different religious groups seek, by different means, to maintain their particular sub-worlds in the face of a plurality of competing sub-worlds. Concomitantly, this plurality of religious legitimations is internalized in consciousness as a plurality of possibilities between which one may choose." One need not be a traditional secularization theorist as Berger was at the time to see that sociocultural pluralism imposes profound influences on religions. One of those influences, about which Berger was largely correct, is in transforming religion from something like a given in a social order, whether of a nation or a bounded minority subculture, to a choice that individuals have no choice but to make. The imperative of religious choice becomes inescapable. Whether or not

24. See, for example, Robert Wuthnow, *The Restructuring of American Religion* (Princeton, NJ: Princeton University Press, 1990); Juliet Schor, *The Overworked American* (New York: Basic Books, 1993); Philip Rieff, *The Triumph of the Therapeutic* (Wilmington, DE: Intercollegiate Studies Institute, 2006).

that ultimately corrodes religious belief plausibility or authority, it certainly alters the internal character of religions and relocates the bases of religious authority and formation. How does that relate to the centrality of parents in intergenerational religious transmission? Berger again: "In the sphere of the family . . . religion continues to have considerable 'reality' potential . . . [it] continues to be relevant in terms of the motives and self-interpretations of people in this [private] sphere of everyday social activity."[25] In short, whatever happens to religion in the public sphere—which here we leave as an open question—religion does retain the capacity to be "real," meaningful, and influential within the personal household spaces of families.

This has theoretical implications for our understanding of the meaning of the process of "privatization" as a feature of secularization, if and when secularization happens. One thing we learned about secularization in the academic theoretical battles in the 1980s and 1990s was that the one term "secularization" was too capacious in overgeneralizing and encompassing many different possible processes operating at distinct levels. These include macro institutional differentiation, religious institutional decline, belief implausibility, the growth of the nonreligious sector and atheists in a population, and the privatization of religion, among other concepts. Following that insight, our argument here suggests the need to differentiate the meaning of the specific term "privatization." That is generally meant to denote the removal of religious relevance and authority out of the public sphere into the private sphere. For example, the efforts of advocates of liberal political theory to remove religious arguments from public policy debates counts as privatization in this sense. Religion is not extinguished, but simply sequestered to personal beliefs and practices in the private realm. Yet important works in the 1990s and since have shown that this privatization expected by traditional secularization theory has not consistently occurred in the macro public sphere.[26]

Our observation here, however, is that that lack of privatization at the macro level is entirely compatible with powerful privatization at the micro level. Religion may visibly assert itself in social movements and political policy debates on the macro plane, yet simultaneously reconstitute itself in

25. Peter Berger, *The Sacred Canopy* (New York: Anchor Books, 1967), 152, 133; Max Weber observed in 1918, "The ultimate and most sublime values have retreated from public life . . . into the brotherliness of direct and personal human relations" ("Science as a Vocation," in *From Max Weber: Essays in Sociology*, ed. H. Gerth and C. Wright Mills [Oxford: Oxford University Press, 1970], 155).

26. A key text was Jose Casanova, *Public Religions in the Modern World* (Chicago: University of Chicago Press, 1994).

psychologized, therapeutic, and domesticated terms as a "personal lifestyle accessory" at the private, personal, and family levels. If so, the term "privatization" needs to be further clarified and conceptually disaggregated. Perhaps we should reserve the term "privatization" for religion becoming psychologized and domesticated, as described earlier, and denote the older meaning of religion's removal from politics and public deliberation with the term "depoliticization." We suspect such a distinction would add clarity to our understanding of secularization, when and where that does occur.[27]

Returning to our question about parents, here is our punchline. Religion morphing across the twentieth century from being a "communal solidarity project" to a "personal identity accessory" creates a sociocultural context in which, among other things, the "burden" of religious socialization becomes laid primarily on the shoulders of parents. Individuals, not communities, are the agents of action and focal point of value. "Private" households, not religious congregations, are the centers of identity and value formation. Parents at home rather than public communities become the ones who "own" matters of socialization of personal identity and choice. Parents are the only ones who possess the authority in such a social order to make religious beliefs and commitments possibly "take" and stick with children, even though that is far from guaranteed. Clergy, traditions, and denominational institutions lose that authority. So if religious transmission is to happen with any chance of success, it must be accomplished by parents.

Religion's appeal in this context shifts from being the place where one learns revealed and traditional truths that shape persons to live good lives as defined by the religion. Instead, its appeal is in promising to improve people's quality of life here and now by providing a "foundation" for individuals, a "grounding" for values, good choices, emotional coping, and improved personal relationships. Religious communities in this scenario become no longer authoritative centers of communal solidarity but associational resources from which parents may draw help in their task, if desired (although, as we see later and elsewhere, most religious parents hold relatively low expectations of their religious congregations and leaders). Success for most parents in their job as prime actors in religious socialization means their children more or

---

27. See Smith and Longest, "Parent Religiousness Effects." Of course, family life too has undergone both de-politization and privatization (see, for example, Jeffrey Alexander, *Differentiation Theory and Social Change: Comparative and Historical Perspectives* (New York: Columbia University Press, 1990); Christopher Lasch, *Haven in a Heartless World* (New York: Basic Books, 1979).

less embrace the family religion as a chosen feature of their own personal identity.[28] For a minority of more liberal parents, success means providing the education and orientation necessary for their children to choose well whatever religion or no religion they decide is personally well-suited for them as individuals. In either case, the responsibility of religious transmission (or orienting education) falls squarely on parents' shoulders, the question at stake concerns authentic personal identity and the benefits of adopting a religious one, and the outcome is ultimately determined by the autonomous choices of children.

More on Talking with Children

Having laid out our larger thesis, let us return to the more specific question of why parents routinely conversing with children about religious matters during the week exerts such a crucial influence on successful religious transmission. What we explained earlier about learning religion as a second language is crucial. But there is more to it than just that. For one thing, especially in the context of religion as a personal identity accessory, parents conversing with children about religion is a powerful signal to children of religion's personal importance. People usually talk about what they care about, whether it be sports, politics, music, or romantic relationships. Some people are indeed very private about religion, and others are reserved in their speech generally. But normally talk about something indicates that it matters to the talker. When all parents say about religion to children during a week is something like "Okay, everyone, leaving for church in thirty minutes," that is telling. When conversations immediately turn after religious worship services to nonreligious interests, that is telling, too. The messages may be subliminal, but their accumulated socialization effects are powerful. By contrast, when parents talk naturally and substantively about religion and its place in life throughout the week, that effectively indicates to children that, in the mix of life's many priorities and values, this stuff matters a lot. And that raises the stakes for children's decisions about their own future religious commitments.[29]

---

28. Smith, Ritz, and Rotolo, *Religious Parenting*.

29. All of this has implications for our understanding of micro influences on religious transmission and on secularization as a macro phenomenon. Might cultural differences between different societies in their expectations and practices of parenting with regard to oral interactions with children affect dynamics of religious persistence and decline? Further research is needed to sort out these kinds of issues. See David Dollahite and Loren Marks, "Introduction to the

Parents talking with children about religious matters also helps relate religion to the rest of life. Religion in modern, liberal societies tends to be differentiated off as one personal or private sphere or sector. Religion can easily come to feel like a discreet compartment, easily disconnected from other areas of life that seem to really matter: school, sports, friends, romance, sex, jobs, money, music, movies, digital media, and so on. When the religious field socially constructs religion as a personal identity accessory, that segregation becomes the default. Parents not talking about religion other than during scheduled "religious times" reinforces that compartmentalization. But when parents discuss religion with children during the week, it decompartmentalizes and desegregates religion. And the more naturally and regularly religion is talked about, the more normally it becomes a significant part of the world of the conversation participants. In religious socialization, talk about religion that unaffectedly flows in and out of larger discussions is much more powerful than discussions that begin with "Okay, children, now we are going to talk about religion" (not that many parents do the latter). As one 20-something Mormon told us about the family discussions in his household growing up, "Discussions about God usually did not start out talking about religion, but they usually ended up talking about religion." That summarizes well the kind of parent–child conversations that we have good sociological reason to believe work best in religious enculturation.

Parents who know how to raise and guide such conversations effectively not only teach their children the second language of faith and signal how personally important religion is to them. They also teach their children during the ordinariness of life how and why religion matters for the rest of life and the world outside of the religious compartment. What does our religion have to say about school, learning, education? What are its implications for romance and sex? What does it teach about life callings, careers, and money? How might it tell us to think about music, movies, the Internet, and social media? When done with authenticity and intelligence, this can bring religion alive for children, showing why and how religion matters not only as a sliver of the family schedule but something that can inform and color much of living. Religion then can be integrated into the rest of life, becoming three dimensional, a question that really matters. That then poses a greater challenge to children to decide whether they will make religion a part of their personal lives. Religion cannot gradually or suddenly diminish and disappear among

Special Issue: Exploring Strengths in American Families of Faith," *Marriage & Family Review* 54, no. 7 (2018): 617–634.

children as they grow into later adolescence without that being noticed and having consequences. Having been for years connected by parents in conversations to the rest of life, living cannot go on absent religion's connection to it without that becoming an issue. Children who, by contrast, embrace their parents' religion are also then much advantaged in already knowing how and why religion matters for the rest of their lives. They have been cultivated to understand its larger significance. Religion then becomes more meaningful. That can solidify the importance of religion in children's personal identity accessory profiles. But it can also push religion beyond a thin version of that, potentially to be established as a center of living, the orienting feature or lens that interprets most of the rest of life.[30]

The Self-Reflexive Imperative

Finally, we believe it is also critical to understand in this larger process that in modern, postmodern, and postmaterialist[31] social worlds, discursive *self-reflexivity becomes an imperative.* It becomes nearly impossible not to be continually self-reflexive.[32] Self-reflexivity means making oneself the object of conscious scrutiny and evaluation, asking questions like, "How am I doing? What do I care about? Am I being my true self? Why am I feeling this way? Should I be making different choices? Is there something important that I'm missing?" Self-reflexivity involves the continual "bending back" of the influences of one's actions and practices upon oneself. It heightens the reflective awareness of persons about how they are living, enabling and prompting them to intervene to make desired changes in their lives. Self-reflexivity is not narcissism, although it can become self-centered, depending on how the self relates to others. Yet it can also be self-judging and berating just as easily. In any case, self-reflexivity is a mode of being in which one recurrently makes oneself the reference of inspection and assessment. Self-reflexivity is profoundly personal and subjective. Still, in practicing self-reflexivity, people always

---

30. The religious traditions that most self-consciously attempt to accomplish that—Mormonism, intellectually engaged sectors of evangelicalism, black Protestantism, and some minority non-Christian religions—are not surprisingly those that perform relatively best at intergenerational religious transmission.

31. Inglehart, *Culture Shift.*

32. Paul Sweetman, "Twenty-First Century Dis-ease? Habitual Reflexivity or the Reflexive Habitus," *The Sociological Review* 51, no. 4 (2003): 528–549.

draw upon their cultural resources and histories.[33] By one account, human reflexivity is a key mediating mechanism between people's social structural contexts and their personal, ultimate concerns and actions.[34] Self-reflexivity helps people navigate the space between their highest interior values and the unalterable exterior world.

What specific features and forces in modern life make self-reflexivity an imperative? First, *rapid social change makes traditional standards and norms received from older generations unreliable if not obsolete*. Reflexivity increasingly replaces habitual action, since mere routines and conventions are experienced as ineffective in dealing with the complexities of the modern life course.[35] "The imperative to engage in reflexive deliberations . . . derives . . . from the absence of social guidelines indicating what to do in novel situations. . . . Exercising personal reflexivity in order to make choices in uncharted territory means the previous guidelines . . . are fast vanishing as they become increasingly misleading."[36] This inadequacy of received, traditional guidelines Archer calls "contextual discontinuity," which, she observes, "intensifies throughout modernity, and especially during the transition to nascent globalization, with the consequence that routine or habitual action becomes decreasingly appropriate for all. . . . These changes mean that personal reflexivity acquires an unprecedented importance in determining how we make our way through the world."[37] Therefore, "for the first time in human history the imperative to be reflexive is becoming categorical for all. . . . Increasingly all have to draw upon their socially dependent but nonetheless personal powers of reflexivity in order to define their course(s) of action in relation to the novelty of their circumstances. Habits and *habitus* are no longer reliable guides."

Partly as a result of this increasing obsolescence of specific, traditional guides to life, and partly as the constitutive meaning of modernity itself, the human experience and condition in modern society increasingly become that of *individual self-determination*. The self-reflexive imperative reflects in part the massively increased autonomy that most modern individuals face,

---

33. Julius Elster, "The Temporal Dimension of Reflexivity: Linking Reflexive Orientations to the Stock of Knowledge," *Distinktion: Journal of Social Theory* 18, no. 3 (2017): 274–293.

34. Reflexivity "mediat[es] deliberatively between the objective structural opportunities confronted by different groups and the nature of people's subjectively defined concerns." Archer, *Making Our Way through the World*, 61.

35. Archer, *The Reflexive Imperative in Late Modernity*.

36. Archer, *The Reflexive Imperative in Late Modernity*, 1–2, 64.

37. Archer, *Making Our Way through the World*, 61.

compared to that of premodern human history. Most modern people (at least believe they) are not stuck where they are in life—they can self-transform and in the process alter their station and experience in the world. Self-reflexivity is the crucial self-work that people engage in to make that self-guided transformation happen. Harvie Ferguson writes: "The fundamental insight of modernity can be stated simply in the notion of human self-determination. . . . The whole development of modernity . . . can be grasped as the continuous unfolding of the fundamental postulate of human self-autonomy. This demands a radical transformation in people's orientations to the world, to each other, and to themselves."[38]

In such a situation—where "modernity comes to itself . . . as a continuous process of restless self-production . . . [and] human autonomy . . . is actualized in dynamic self-transformation . . . [and] modernity is an endless project of human self-realization"[39]—the existential touchstone guiding the way people navigate their lives is *what they personally care about*. The self-reflexive imperative, Archer points out, is necessary, given "the opportunity for subjects to pursue what they care about the most in the social order. In fact, their personal concerns become their compasses."[40] That moves to the center of life whatever happens to be "meaningful" to individuals, and that meaning itself must come to be known and enjoyed through personal subjective experience. Harvey again: "Modernity [is] . . . consciousness of the human world as a self-generating and autonomous realm of meaningful experience. . . . Modernity makes central to its reality the category of experience itself and might justifiably be thought of as the sovereignty of experience. For the modern world, there is no higher authority than experience."[41]

Self-reflexivity also reflects modernity's *intensification of individual subjectivity*. Humans have always had the capacity for subjective awareness and reflection. One only need read Augustine's late fourth-century autobiographical reflection, *Confessions*, for example, to see that. Yet the sociocultural conditions of modernity dramatically heighten the intensity of human

---

38. Harvie Ferguson, *Modernity and Subjectivity: Body, Soul, Spirit* (Charlottesville: University of Virginia Press, 2000), 8, 198.

39. Ferguson, *Modernity and Subjectivity*, 3.

40. Archer, *The Reflexive Imperative in Late Modernity*, 1.

41. Ferguson, *Modernity and Subjectivity*, 2.

subjective experience, of what Charles Taylor calls our "inwardness."[42] As stable, predictable structures of meaning and direction external to persons recede, individuals come to rely increasingly on their own interior subjectivities as guides to life. "Increasingly, agents navigate by the compass of their own personal concerns. This growing reliance on their personal powers . . . has as its counterparts the demise of the generalized other and the diminution of socialization as a quasi-unilateral process."[43] Some theorists argue that subjectivity is in fact *the* crucially defining feature of modernity.[44] "Although reflexive deliberation is . . . indispensable to the existence of any society, its scope has also been growing from the advent of modernity onwards. In the third millennium, the fast-changing social world makes it incumbent on everyone to exercise more and more reflexivity in increasingly greater tracts of their lives."[45]

As a result of all of these factors, self-reflexivity has in our day become an *imperative*. People today essentially have *no choice* but to engage in its form of self-referential examination and appraisal. This is even more intensely so for young people. To be a legitimate self in the contemporary social context *requires* self-reflexivity. Lacking self-reflexivity in today's culture means not only being clueless and shallow, but also in some sense being an inferior and incapable human being.

Back to Parents

So how does all of this affect the task of socializing children? In contemporary modernity, the job of socialization becomes no longer about imprinting upon children knowledge of who they are and how they are to live. Socialization rather becomes about providing children with the cognitive and emotional skills to figure out for themselves who they want to be and how they wish among the available options to live their lives as self-determining individuals. That task for both parents and children is made all the more complicated by the fact that nobody faces simple categorical options and guides. Archer

---

42. Charles Taylor, *Sources of the Self* (Cambridge, MA: Harvard University Press, 1989), 111–210; reflected too in the emergence of the novel as a new literary form (see, for example, Ian Watt, *The Rise of the Novel* [Berkeley: University of California Press, 2001]).

43. Archer, *The Reflexive Imperative in Late Modernity*, 64.

44. Ferguson, *Modernity and Subjectivity*; also see Peter Zima, *Subjectivity and Identity: Between Modernity and Postmodernity* (London: Bloomsbury Publishing Academic, 2015).

45. Archer, *Making Our Way through the World*, 5.

observes: "Contemporary socialization is not viewed as a passive [receptive] process, partly because the messages received from 'socializers' are increasingly 'mixed' rather than those traditionally held to stem from consensual 'norm circles' in the past. Therefore, the reflexive imperative is confronted in the form of the necessity of selection, requiring an active 'socializant' who is a 'strong evaluator' about his or her concerns. Partly, too, this is because . . . all agents have to work at establishing a complementarity between these concerns."[46]

Consequently, as raising children has traditionally been understood, the family seems in certain ways to have become a weaker, less important agent of socialization. "Over the last quarter of a century, socialization has been decreasingly able to 'prepare' for occupational and lifestyle opportunities that had not existed for the parental generation. . . . The family unit of socialization increasingly fails normatively as a transmitter of values that underpin the concerns adopted and endorsed by their children. Today, more and more families transmit mixed messages, which are themselves incongruous, and thus confront their children with the additional problem of normatively evaluating and arbitrating upon this mélange before they can crystallize their personal concerns."[47] Yet in its new role the family has become *all the more crucial.* Most important, personal cares, subjective meanings, and skills of self-reflexivity are formed at home. But, again, what it now means to be a good parent, however, is not to fit children into a received society, but to equip them with the tools needed for their self-development and self-direction in a future that is unpredictable and will itself be ever changing. This is what we mean in Table 3.1 by calling home and family "incubators of possibilities."

In a culture and society centered on individual choice—rather than institutional and community belonging or even permanent companionate relations—the job of parents is to turn their newborns into autonomous adults that can navigate their own authentic family and religious lives. In the dependent relations between parents and children, the parents' ideal goal is to "work themselves out of their job," and the more quickly and effectively, the better. A crucial feature for succeeding in that task is to cultivate self-reflexivity in children.[48] This (temporary) tension between parental direction

---

46. Archer, *The Reflexive Imperative in Late Modernity*, 124.

47. Archer, *The Reflexive Imperative in Late Modernity*, 82.

48. See Jan Dizard and Howard Gadlin, *The Minimal Family* (Amherst: University of Massachusetts Press, 1990).

and child self-reflexivity, between dependence and autonomy, helps to explain why parents and home are both crucial in forming the religious lives of their children and yet simultaneously lack the authority simply to imprint upon or ascribe to their children their religion through teaching and inheritance—and why religious communities, institutions, and traditions lack much influence to do either of those. It also helps to explain the high-anxiety, high-wire balancing act that most religious parents perform during their children's teenage years between trying authoritatively to socialize their children into their own religion, on the one side, and fearing all along the way that they may thereby provoke rebellion and backlash against religion by being too forceful.[49]

Here then is the key point from this discussion for our purposes. When religion becomes a personal identity accessory, the individual self moves to the center of significance and authority. That self is understood as an ever-developing identity project. And in order to pull off a successful, authentic life within that cultural reality generally, people must master and practice the skills of self-reflexivity. Without them, persons exist as the mere reactive objects of the surrounding forces impinging upon them, operating on sheer learned habitual routines. But that is a socially unacceptable and practically ineffective way to live, according to the ideal norms of contemporary culture. So a crucial job of "good" parents is to help tune their children into their own inward subjectivity and to train them in self-reflexivity, through modeling and conversational engagement. Imparting that aptitude provides children with the capacities for the self-awareness, life evaluation, and personal agency necessary to successfully "make their way through the world."[50] And one of the most effective ways that parents can do that is to talk regularly with their children about concerns that matter, what they feel and believe, and how they relate them to their own lives.

Now consider parents who are religious and want their children to continue identifying with and practicing their family religion. In such cases, cultivating their children as religiously developing agents of their own self-examination, evaluation, and decision making is crucial. Passively absorbed religious identities and lives that are ascribed or imposed are simply unacceptable in contemporary culture. Individuals must actively, personally choose

---

49. See Kathryn Lofton, "Religion and the Authority in American Parenting," *Journal for the American Academy of Religion* 84, no. 3 (2016): 806–841; for a larger context into which to set this anxiety, see Peter Stearns, *Anxious Parents: A History of Modern Childrearing in America* (New York: New York University Press, 2003).

50. Archer, *Making Our Way through the World*.

such identities and lives for themselves in order for them to be considered authentic. So religious parents in effect need strategically to arrange family life, routines, and relationships in ways that *both* maximize their parental influence on their children's religious development and choices *and* cultivate their children's independence of religious self-identity, reflection, and choice. These may seem to be contradictory purposes.

But one available practice in which parents can engage that promises effectively to achieve both outcomes is to regularly converse with their children about religious issues and questions. By initiating and guiding such conversations, parents can communicate clearly what matters to them religiously, what they think and believe, and how they wish their children to turn out. And at the same time, because such talking at its best is conversational, not lecturing in monologue, parents can through them also create spaces for their children to sort out and express what they think, feel, believe, and desire for themselves. By engaging such natural, recurrent, interactive conversations, parents can be both proactive and receptive, simultaneously directing and asking for responses from their children, and teaching them how to direct themselves and practice self-reflexivity. When that works well, such self-reflexive children are the most likely of American youth to embrace their parents' religion with personal authenticity and carry it forward within the cultural order of religion as a personal identity accessory.

Conclusion

In modern American society, the most important factor for understanding the intergenerational transmission of religion to children is their parents. Parents practicing their own religion in ways that demonstrate its importance in life to children is crucial. Just as powerful is their talking with their children about religious matters during the week, outside of designated "officially religious" times and settings. Doing so sends powerful messages about religion's importance and helps to equip children with the skills and dispositions needed to sustain their religious and spiritual lives on their own. These are the micro-level interaction processes that seem most powerful in passing on religion to children. Yet all of this also points to larger features of modernity that we must understand to comprehend the broader context of religion in modern societies. One is the historical transformation of religion's social ontology from being in essence a communal solidarity project to instead being a personal identity accessory—which parallels the transformation of family from being institutional to companionate to individualistic.

Another is modernity's self-reflexive imperative required to achieve individual self-creative self-determination and navigating the larger, unalterable world of social structures. These are related yet distinct processes. Both dramatically transform what it means to be(come) religious. And both have profound consequences for the task of parenting to pass on religion to children.

4

The Big Picture of American Religious Parenting

WHAT ARE THE priorities and practices of American parents as a whole when it comes to passing on their religion to their children? In this chapter we examine the results of two nationally representative surveys of American parents that include questions focused on intergenerational religious transmission. The first is the Culture of American Families survey of 3,000 US parents of school-age children conducted in 2012 by the Institute for the Advanced Study of Culture at the University of Virginia.[1] The second is the Faith and Family in America survey of 1,131 US adults conducted in 2005 for *Religion and Ethics Newsweekly* by Greenberg Quinlan Rosner Research, Inc.[2] The findings of these two surveys—which studied all American parents, not only more religious parents—enhance our big-picture understanding of the concerns and activities of parents in the United States on the matter of passing on their religion to their children.

American Parents' Religiousness

Table 4.1 shows the religious affiliations of American parents, which closely matches the affiliations of all Americans. About one-quarter are Catholic and

---

1. For methodological details, see Carl Desportes Bowman, *Culture of American Families: A National Survey* (Charlottesville: Institute for Advanced Studies in Culture, 2012), 72–108. https://s3.amazonaws.com/iasc-prod/uploads/pdf/4a18126c1a07680e4fbe.pdf.

2. For methodological information, see https://www-tc.pbs.org/wnet/religionandethics/ files/2005/10/ReligionAndFamily_Methodology.pdf and https://www.pbs.org/wnet/ religionandethics/2005/10/19/october-19-2005-faith-and-family-in-america/11465/.

Table 4.1 Parents' Religious Characteristics (Weighted Percentages)

Religious Tradition

Catholic	26
Mainline Protestant	11
Episcopalian	2
Lutheran	4
Methodist	3
Presbyterian	1
Others	1
Conservative Protestant	28
Baptist	11
Just Christian	6
Nondenominational	3
Pentecostal	4
Others	4
Black Protestant	10
Mormon	2
Jewish	1
Unitarian	1
Buddhist	1
Other religions	4
No religious affiliation	15

Born-again identity — 36

Importance of Faith

The most important thing in life	17
Very important	34
Somewhat important	22
Not very or not at all important	26

Religious Service Attendance

Attends services at least weekly	35
Attends services less than weekly	65

Religious Affiliation History

Never religiously affiliated	6
Dropped out	9
Stayed in tradition	58
Switched traditions	21
Became religiously affiliated	7

Religious Similarity of Spouse/Partner

Partner more religious	18
Partner same level	42
Partner less religious	20
Not asked-unmarried/not partnered	20

Note: Coding of religious history is based on answers to the question of what religious tradition parents were raised in compared to the tradition with which they affiliate at the time of the survey. Percentages may not add to 100 due to rounding to the nearest whole number.

Source: Culture of American Families Survey, 2012.

conservative Protestant each,[3] about one in ten is mainline Protestant and black Protestant each, minority religions represent 1–3 percent of Americans each, and those with no religious affiliation are 15 percent. One-third of American parents (36 percent) identify as "born again." Parents in the United States are spread broadly across the spectrum of how important faith is in their lives. Seventeen percent report that faith is the most important thing. (This report is easily exaggerated by social desirability bias, however.) One-quarter (26 percent) say it is not very or at all important. In the middle, 34 percent say faith is very important, and 22 percent say faith is somewhat important. About one-third of parents (35 percent) report attending religious services at least weekly (although other research has shown that Americans overreport their religious service attendance by about one-third or possibly double their actual attendance, so this number should be assumed to tilt to the high side).[4]

Comparing their current religious tradition with the one in which they reported being raised, we estimate that nearly six in ten (58 percent) parents have remained in the same tradition of their youth, 21 percent have switched traditions, and of the 15 percent of parents who are not religious, 9 percent dropped out of the religion of their youth and 6 percent were never religious. Seven percent of American parents were not raised in a religion but later became religious. Finally, 42 percent report sharing a similar level of religiousness with their spouse, about one in five each report being more (18 percent) or less (20 percent) religious than their spouse, while 20 percent of parents do not have a spouse. The first thing we learn from nationally representative statistics, then, is that American parents are massively diverse when it comes to religious identities, practices, histories, and family relationships. On these religious features, we cannot easily generalize about American parents, other than to say that parents are religiously highly varied.

Parents' Personal Religious Activities

What kinds of religious activities do American parents report practicing? Looking at the bottom of the far left column of Table 4.2, we see that one

---

3. A general category including evangelicals, fundamentalists, Pentecostals, and most religious charismatics.

4. See Kirk Hadaway, Penny Long Marler, and Mark Chaves, "What the Polls Don't Show: A Closer Look at U.S. Church Attendance," *American Sociological Review* 58, no. 6 (1993): 741–752; Robert Woodberry, "When Surveys Lie and People Tell the Truth: How Surveys Over-Sample Church Attenders," *American Sociological Review* 63, no. 1 (1998): 119–122.

Table 4.2 Parent Religious Behaviors by Religious Tradition, Importance
of Faith, Service Attendance, Born-Again Identity (Weighted Percentages)

	Prayer or Informal Religious Group Attendance Weekly+	Talk about Religion Informally with Friends Weekly+	Read One's Holy Book Weekly+
Religious Importance			
Not very or at all	3	8	2
Somewhat	6	20	11
Very	41	62	62
Religious Service Attendance			
Never	0	7	0
Hardly ever	5	15	5
Several times a year	5	18	12
Once or twice a month	9	35	21
Once a week	41	59	68
More than once a week	66	88	83
Religious Affiliation			
Mainline Protestant	23	42	48
Conservative Protestant	32	52	61
Black Protestant	38	67	82
Catholic	15	26	22
LDS	50	60	60
Jewish	30	50	30
Other non-Christian	39	52	16
Nonreligious	11	27	0
Born-again identity	42	67	82
Full parent sample (N = 522)	26	43	39

Note: Percentages may not add to 100 due to rounding to the nearest whole number.
Source: Faith and Family in America, 2005.

in four (26 percent) of all American parents say that they attend a prayer
or informal religious group at least weekly. Those who report that religion
is very important in their lives and who attend religious services weekly or
more are (not surprisingly) the most likely to do so, at 41 percent, 41 percent, and 66 percent, respectively. Mormons, other non-Christians, and
black Protestants are the most likely to attend such religious meetings (50, 39,
and 38 percent, respectively), while mainline Protestants, Catholics, and the

nonreligious are the least likely (23, 15, and 11 percent, respectively). Parents who identify as born again are also more likely than the average to report attending prayer or other informal religious meetings (42 percent).

The numbers in the next column to the right, the center column, tell us a similar story about parents talking informally with friends about religious matters at least once a week, another indicator of religion's importance in life. More than four in ten (43 percent) of all American parents report this activity. Those for whom faith is very important, who attend religious services more frequently, and who say they are born again are much more likely than the average to talk with friends about religion at least weekly. And again, black Protestants, Mormons, and other non-Christians, as well as conservative Protestants talk weekly with friends informally about religion at higher rates, while Catholics and the nonreligious do so at much lower rates.

Continuing our analysis of Table 4.2, about four in ten American parents (39 percent) report that they read religious scripture (the Bible, Torah, Book of Mormon, Koran, etc.) at least once a week. Differences in scripture reading across the religious types and variables follow the same pattern as those observed earlier, being more common among those with greater importance of faith, religious service attendance, and born-again identity. Black Protestants, conservative Protestants, and Mormons are also especially likely to read scripture weekly or more often (at 82, 61, and 60 percent, respectively).[5]

Stepping back and assessing, Table 4.2 tells us that a substantial minority of American parents say that they are fairly actively engaged in a variety of relatively informal religious activities. As we might expect, parents who are more religious by other measures are more likely to participate in these activities, as are those who belong to religious traditions that tend to expect more and support these activities (black Protestants, conservative Protestants, Mormons, and other non-Christians).

Parents' Religious Priorities for Children

One survey question asked American parents how important it was to them that their children grow up to be people of strong religious faith. Another asked parents to rank the relative importance of raising children "whose lives

---

5. Considered from the opposite and noteworthy perspective, however, given common stereotypes, four out of ten conservative Protestant and Mormon parents do *not* read the Bible or Book of Mormon on a weekly basis.

will reflect God's will and purpose" relative to four other possible priorities.[6] (Readers should note that this question wording is somewhat biased toward the discourse of some religious traditions [e.g., "God's will" toward conservative Protestantism] and would feel alien to others, which likely somewhat affected the results that follow). The results of their answers are shown in Table 4.3. There we see that about three in ten American parents (29 percent) say that raising children of strong religious faith is essential or very important to them. A significant majority of American parents (71 percent) thus do not consider raising children of strong religious faith to be very important. Once again, black Protestants, Mormons, and conservative Protestants were much more likely than the average to value raising children of strong religious faith (at 58, 54, and 48 percent, respectively). Catholic, mainline Protestant, and Jewish parents were less likely than average to value this (at 17, 17, and 13 percent, respectively).

What do parents report when asked to rank religion against other values and priorities? The rankings of parents on religion for children was polarized or "bimodal." Thirty-four percent ranked it first of five priorities, while 31 percent ranked it last. Those extremes account for two-thirds (64 percent) of all American parents' views. The remaining one-third was evenly distributed across the second, third, and fourth rankings (12, 10, and 12 percent, respectively). In short, about one in three American parents reports seeing their children growing up to live lives that reflect God's will and purpose to be a highest priority, one-third place that somewhere in the middle, and one-third rank it last. Once again we see much diversity among American parents.

The religious tradition differences observed earlier are reflected in these rankings, too. Mormons, black Protestants, and conservative Protestants rank the religious priority higher. Catholics and mainline Protestant parents tend to rank it in the middle. And parents from the non-Christian religious traditions we analyzed rank it the lowest (again, some of this could be due to the particular question wording noted earlier, so that if different language had been used here, the results might be somewhat, though unlikely very, different). Those religious tradition differences remain statistically significant after

---

6. The five offered parenting priorities were as follows: "1. I seek to raise children whose lives will reflect God's will and purpose. 2. I seek to raise children who will make positive contributions to their communities and to the world around them. 3. I seek to provide every material advantage and educational opportunity so my children will have the best chance of achieving their goals in life. 4. I seek to offer the kind of love and affection that will nurture happiness, positive feelings about themselves, and warm relationships with others. 5. I seek to raise children who are true to their family roots and pass on the cultural traditions of their heritage."

Table 4.3　Parent's Priorities for Children's Religious Lives by Parents' Religious Tradition (Weighted Percentages)

Religious Tradition	Children Being of Strong Religious Faith Is Very Important or Essential	Ranked Priority Given to Children's Lives Reflecting God's Will and Purpose				
		First	Second	Third	Fourth	Last
Religious Tradition						
Catholic	17	24	15	13	18	30
Mainline Protestant	17	22	16	16	17	29
Episcopalian	15	21	14	12	9	44
Lutheran	9	12	13	25	21	28
Methodist	17	20	9	26	21	23
Presbyterian	15	25	4	17	14	41
Conservative Protestant	48	55	12	8	8	17
Baptist	66	68	8	6	5	13
Christian only	53	52	9	8	7	25
Nondenominational	72	79	13	0	3	5
Pentecostal	72	69	19	0	6	5
Black Protestant	58	56	14	11	5	14
Mormon	54	61	18	8	6	7
Jewish	13	16	4	0	6	74
Unitarian	0	9	0	5	9	78
Buddhist	6	2	3	0	14	81
Other religion	33	10	7	7	15	61
No religious affiliation	4	26	10	3	11	51
Full sample (N = 2,904)	29	34	12	0	12	31

Note: Percentages may not add to 100 due to rounding to the nearest whole number.

Source: Culture of American Families Survey, 2012.

accounting for standard demographic control variables.[7] Additional analyses (results not presented here[8]) show predictably that parents are more likely to prioritize religion for their children who themselves are more religious (in

7. Such as parent sex, age, race/ethnicity, household income, educational attainment, and region of residence.

8. Additional tables of statistical findings referenced later are available upon request from the authors.

reported frequency of religious service attendance and importance of faith) and who identify as born again. Demographically, black parents (compared to white, non-Hispanic), lower income parents (compared to those earning $150,000 or more), parents with college degrees (compared to high school or less), and parents who reside in the South (compared to the Northeast) are more likely to want their children to grow up to live according to God's will and purpose, after statistically controlling for other factors (the negative income effect being the strongest and most robust). Results from our multivariate statistical analysis for reporting a strong religious faith as very important or essential for their children is similarly positively associated.

Expectations of Children's Religious Outcomes

How do American parents anticipate their children will turn out religiously when they grow up? How likely, for example, do parents think it is their children will retain the same religious tradition (or no religion in the case of the nonreligious) in which they were raised? Table 4.4 shows that 45 percent of parents think it is very likely that their children will keep their family's religion, 30 percent think it somewhat likely, and 5 percent think it not likely. One in five parents (20 percent) is not sure. So three-quarters of American parents are quite confident that their children will not depart from their own religion.

Table 4.4 also shows that confidence in successful religious transmission to children is positively correlated, as expected, with parents' importance of religious faith, frequency of religious service attendance, and born-again identity. In addition, such confidence varies by religious tradition. Minority non-Christian parents are the most likely to say that it is very likely that their children will keep their faith. Conservative Protestants also express a higher than average expectation that their children will remain conservative Protestant. Jewish parents are much more likely than average to believe both that it is very likely their children will stay Jewish *and* that their staying Jewish is not likely—they tend to gravitate to one of the two poles of expectations. Mormons and mainline Protestants think more than average that it is only somewhat likely that their children will remain in the fold. And, besides the Jewish parents already mentioned, Mormon parents report at twice the national average (10 percent) that their children remaining Mormon is not likely, although that position still represents a definite minority of all Mormon parents. Nonreligious parents who raised their children without religion are relatively quite likely to doubt that their children will remain not

Table 4.4 Likelihood That Children Will Be of the Same Denomination or
Faith Tradition When They Grow Up (Weighted Percentages)

	Not Likely	Not Sure	Somewhat Likely	Very Likely
Religious Importance				
Not very or at all	15	41	29	15
Somewhat	8	18	38	36
Very	2	16	26	56
Religious Attendance				
Never	17	42	33	8
Hardly ever	10	30	37	24
Several times a year	6	21	42	31
Once or twice a month	8	20	30	41
Once a week	2	15	27	55
More than once a week	0	9	17	74
Religious Affiliation				
Mainline Protestant	4	13	48	36
Conservative Protestant	3	21	24	52
Black Protestant	2	21	32	45
Catholic	6	21	34	40
LDS	10	0	50	40
Jewish	30	0	10	60
Other non-Christian	0	13	20	67
Nonreligious	16	30	30	25
Born-again identity	2	13	29	57
Full parent sample (N = 522)	5	20	30	45

Note: Percentages may not add to 100 due to rounding to the nearest whole number.
Source: Faith and Family in America, 2005.

religious. All of these parental expectations are sociologically astute, given what we know about the religious transmission effectiveness of different traditions and the effect of minority/majority differences on religious identity formation.

Whatever parents anticipate about their grown children's religious identities and affiliations, do they think their children will be generally more or less religious than they are? Table 4.5 shows that the most frequently given answer is that they are not sure (48 percent). One-third (32 percent) thinks their children will be about as religious as they are. Fourteen percent

Table 4.5 Do You Think Your Kids Will Be More or Less Religious Than You? (Weighted Percentages)

	Less Religious	As Religious	More Religious	Not Sure
Religious Importance				
Not very or at all	2	8	22	68
Somewhat	10	38	4	48
Very	6	34	17	43
Religious Attendance				
Never	8	25	17	50
Hardly ever	4	23	13	59
Several times a year	10	27	5	58
Once or twice a month	10	31	11	48
Once a week	6	42	9	42
More than once a week	4	35	29	32
Religious Affiliation				
Mainline Protestant	5	41	7	46
Conservative Protestant	6	34	16	44
Black Protestant	9	28	15	49
Catholic	11	32	12	44
LDS	0	20	20	60
Jewish	10	40	10	40
Other non-Christian	4	35	13	48
Nonreligious	3	20	16	61
Born-again identity	6	38	14	42
Full parent sample (N = 522)	7	32	14	48

Note: Percentages may not add to 100 due to rounding to the nearest whole number.

Source: Faith and Family in America, 2005.

think their grown children will be more religious, and 7 percent less religious. Parents who are more likely than the average to be not sure are themselves less religious (on importance of faith and service attendance, being uncertain at 68 and 58–59 percent, respectively), nonreligious (61 percent), and Mormon (60 percent). Those who expect their grown children to be more religious than themselves are both low on religiousness (allowing only an increasing side in which to move) and those who attend religious services more than once a week (29 percent). No great differences stand out for parents who think their children will be just as religious or less religious than they are, other than weekly service attenders and mainline Protestants being somewhat more likely than average to think their children will be as religious as they are.

What about parents' anxieties about the future? Table 4.6 presents the results of our analysis of parents' answers to a question about how much they worry that their children will or will not stay in the same religious denomination or family faith tradition when they grow up. We find that parents are almost perfectly evenly divided. Twenty-seven percent report that they worry a lot, 26 percent worry some, 23 percent worry only a little, and 24 percent

Table 4.6 How Much Do You Worry about Your Child Maintaining Your Family Religious Tradition? (Weighted Percentages)

	Not at All	Only a Little	Some	A Lot
Religious Importance				
Not very or at all	51	31	10	8
Somewhat	24	29	36	11
Very	19	17	24	39
Religious Attendance				
Never	25	33	25	17
Hardly ever	41	23	25	10
Several times a year	32	26	29	13
Once or twice a month	13	33	35	19
Once a week	17	19	28	35
More than once a week	18	14	15	54
Religious Affiliation				
Mainline Protestant	25	20	29	27
Conservative Protestant	19	25	27	29
Black Protestant	32	13	19	36
Catholic	21	24	31	23
LDS	0	10	80	10
Jewish	10	50	10	30
Other non-Christian	30	15	19	37
Nonreligious	39	27	19	16
Born-again identity	18	19	27	37
Full parent sample (N = 522)	24	23	26	27

Note: Percentages may not add to 100 due to rounding to the nearest whole number.

Source: Faith and Family in America, 2005.

worry not at all. One dynamic at work here is that the less parents personally care about and practice religion (as measured by importance of faith and service attendance), the less they worry about their children carrying on a family religious tradition. That makes sense. Conversely, those parents for whom faith is very important and who attend services the most worry a lot at higher rates.

A few notable differences by religious tradition are also evident. Black Protestants (37 percent) and non-Christian minority parents (not including Jews) (37 percent) worry a lot at somewhat higher than average rates. Mormon parents seem to specialize in worrying only some (80 percent). Jewish parents report worrying only a little. And nonreligious parents and black Protestant parents tend somewhat to worry not at all. The results of additional multivariate statistical analyses (not presented here) show that older parents compared to younger parents (perhaps because they can see where their presumably older and more independent children are actually heading religiously) and parents who are more religious (as measured by higher importance of faith and more frequent service attendance) compared to less religious parents are more likely to worry a lot about their children maintaining their family religious tradition.

A related question on a different survey asked American parents about the depth of their fear about the possibility that their children could lose their religious faith. We do not add a separate table with the results of our analysis of that question here, but describe the results, as follows. Seven percent of parents reported that their children losing their faith was "one of their deepest fears." Another 7 percent said that was "a real fear." Eighteen percent answered that it was "a worry but not a fear." The possibility of children losing faith was "only a small concern" for 23 percent of parents. And 44 percent reported that it was not a concern at all. Of the list of 15 possible parental fears offered on the survey, the fear of children losing religious faith ranked 10th, far below kidnapping, sexual exploitation, serious accidents, addictions, lack of ambition, and financial failure, among other concerns; and above their fear of being odd, only average, or homosexual.[9]

Parents may not worry about children leaving their religious tradition or fear their children entirely losing faith for at least two very different reasons. They may not care enough about religious tradition and faith to worry about it. Or they may care, yet be highly confident about their children's religious

---

9. See https://s3.amazonaws.com/iasc-prod/uploads/pdf/4a18126c1a07680e4fbe.pdf.

futures, perhaps because they have invested greatly in their children's religious lives. Such losses may also be a hypothetical future possibility or something parents were confronting at the time of the survey, which could affect their survey answers. So the precise meanings of parents' answers to these last two questions are complex and difficult to interpret. Our additional analysis of parental worries about other concerns (not presented in a table here) revealed that their worrying about children losing their religious faith is positively correlated with their worrying about many other life concerns, including children not learning good values at school, negative influences from other children, paying the bills, violence in the media, and balancing work/family life. That is, parents who tend to worry more about their children's religion also tend to worry more about most everything else. In short, some of them may just be worrying personalities or socially located in worrisome situations. Furthermore, it may seem odd that more parents worry a lot about children not staying in the family religious tradition (27 percent) than are fearful about their losing religious faith altogether (14 percent combining deepest fear + a real fear). But that might be partly because the word "fear" is stronger than the word "worry." And it may be that parents think children are more likely to leave their religious denomination or tradition than to lose their religious faith altogether, which increases the cause for that concern.

What then have we learned here about parents' expectations of their children's religious futures? In short, most American parents do not seem too concerned about major religious "losses" in their children. The majority think it is likely that their children will share their same faith tradition when they grow up; and most of the balance is simply uncertain about it. Most American parents believe that their children will be as religious as they are, or again are simply not sure about it. Of the remainder, twice as many parents suspect that their children will be more religious than less religious than they are. Further, about one-quarter of American parents worry a lot about their children maintaining their family's religious tradition. But half worry only a little or not at all. And only 14 percent fear or worry about their children losing their religious faith. For the rest, that possible loss is only a small concern or not a concern at all. It appears that parents have a lot more troubling dangers to their children to worry about, however unlikely they may be to strike, than their losing their faith. Being nationally representative, let us remember, these numbers reflect the views of many not very religious parents. But even among the more religiously invested and active parents, most do not seem anxious about their children's religious futures, at least as far as survey reports can tell.

Parent–Child Religious Disagreement

Potential conflict with children over religion is a major concern of many American parents, definitely for most religious parents. In another book, one of us (Smith) shows that religious parents are extremely worried about provoking rebellion in their children by "forcing" religion on them.[10] Disagreement and conflict are two different things, yet disagreement is the precondition of conflict. So it is relevant here to examine parents' perceptions of the levels of disagreement with their children about religion. Table 4.7 shows that the vast majority reports little or no disagreement with their children over religion.[11] Three-quarters of parents (76 percent) say they have no disagreements. About one in five (19 percent) report only low-to-moderate disagreement. Only 4 percent say they experience high disagreement with their children over religion. This confirms from parents' perspectives the findings of a previous study of youth that argued that US teenagers very rarely resist or fight against their parents' religion.[12]

Broken down by religious tradition, we see in Table 4.7 that Jewish, other non-Christian, and black Protestant parents report somewhat higher levels of religious disagreement with their children, although those differences are not large. Buddhist and Jewish parents are somewhat more likely to report low-to-moderate disagreement with children. But, with the partial exception of Jewish parents, the vast majority of parents of all religious traditions analyzed here report no religious disagreements with their children. That apparent relative unanimity could mean different things. It could mean simply that most parents and children basically agree about religious matters. It could mean that most parents are so worried about preventing their children from becoming religious rebels that they do not push religion hard enough to provoke any disagreements. For some it might reflect such low levels of religious knowledge and practice that there is not much of religious substance or activities even to disagree about. In any case, the levels of differences between American parents and children over religious matters appear to be minimal.

Furthermore, we find few other significant religious or demographic factors that correlate with greater disagreement (not reported in a table here).

---

10. Smith, Ritz, and Rotolo, *Religious Parenting*.

11. We ought to remember that disagreement need not take the form of highly religious parents dealing with religiously uninterested children; it is theoretically possible and empirically actual, although in probably fewer cases, that disagreement involves children who are more religiously interested or definite and parents who are less so.

12. Smith with Denton, *Soul Searching*.

Table 4.7 Parents' Assessments of the Level of Their Parent–Child Disagreement on Issues of Faith or Religion, by Religious Tradition (Weighted Percentages)

Religious Tradition	Level of Disagreement on Issues of Faith or Religion		
	None	Low to Moderate	High
Catholic	70	24	6
Mainline Protestant	78	20	2
Conservative Protestant	78	18	5
Black Protestant	80	13	8
Mormon	75	22	3
Jewish	58	29	14
Unitarian	77	23	0
Buddhist	70	30	1
Other non-Christian	85	7	8
No religion	80	18	2
Full parent sample (N = 2,904)	76	19	4

Note: Percentages may not add to 100 due to rounding to the nearest whole number.

Source: Culture of American Families Survey, 2012.

Parents who prioritize raising children of strong religious faith report fewer disagreements with children about religion than the average. The same is true for raising children to live according to God's will and purpose. Those whose children attend religious services at least weekly—whether voluntarily or required—report the identical level of no disagreement with children as those whose attend less. Levels of religious disagreement with children also vary little between parental marital statuses, household structure and parent employment situations, different levels of support offered by other spouses or partners, or the religious similarity of the other spouse or partner.

Parental Practices of Religious Transmission

We saw in Chapter 2 that parents talking with children about religious matters was a most important practice for successfully passing on religion to children. What is the prevalence of that practice among American parents? And how might that vary between all parents and those who are more religiously active? The right two columns in Table 4.8 show that one-half of all American parents and more than three-quarters of "devout" parents report talking with

Table 4.8 Faith Transmission Practices Comparing All Parents versus Devout Parents by Parents' Religious Tradition (Weighted Percentages)

	Child Attends Religious Services at Least Weekly		Talk about Faith with Children at Least Weekly	
	All Parents	Devout Parents	All Parents	Devout Parents
Religious Tradition				
Catholic	35	62	43	69
Mainline Protestant	40	64	42	71
Episcopalian	48	81	50	80
Lutheran	32	63	33	62
Methodist	40	62	41	64
Presbyterian	35	66	28	56
Conservative Protestant	59	75	67	82
Baptist	67	81	80	87
Christian only	68	75	71	81
Nondenominational	73	77	78	82
Pentecostal	80	88	73	80
Black Protestant	54	61	75	80
Mormon	93	98	86	89
Jewish	16	27	21	54
Unitarian	18	—	27	—
Buddhist	9	—	15	—
Other non-Christian	35	50	54	79
No religious affiliation	15	35	17	77
Full parent sample (N = 2,904)	42	67	50	77

Note: Percentages are rounded to the nearest whole number. Cells marked with "—" denote insufficient numbers to draw comparisons (fewer than 10 cases).

Source: Culture of American Families Survey, 2012.

their children about religious things at least weekly. (Again, these numbers may be inflated by social desirability bias.) For both categories of parents (all and devout), the numbers are again higher than average for Mormons, black Protestants, and conservative Protestants. Being a "devout" parent of a religious tradition, compared to being "nominal," seems again to make the biggest difference for Catholic and mainline Protestant parents (with 26 and 29 percent increases in reports, respectively), as well as other non-Christian religious parents (25 percent increases) and those with no reported religious affiliation (60 percent increases).

Looking ahead to Table 4.9, we also observe the by-now familiar pattern that parents talking to children about religious matters is highly associated with greater parental importance of faith, weekly or more frequent religious service attendance, born-again identity, and parent histories of religious tradition switching and stability. In addition, we found that mothers compared to fathers; parents with higher incomes compared to those with the lowest incomes; those who enjoy greater parental support from grandparents, personal friends, and fellow religionists; and parents who report being more

Table 4.9 Parents' Faith Transmission Practices by Parents' Religious History and Personal Religiousness (Weighted Percentages)

	Child Attends Services at Least Weekly	Talk about Faith with Children at Least Weekly
Religious Importance		
Most important thing in life	83	93
Very important	56	71
Somewhat important	24	33
Not very or not at all important	11	10
Religious Service Attendance		
Attends services at least weekly	92	86
Attends services less than weekly	15	31
Born-again identity	64	80
Religious Affiliation History		
Never religiously affiliated	18	18
Dropped out	13	17
Stayed in same tradition	44	56
Switched traditions	55	59
Became religiously affiliated	37	43
Full parent sample (N = 2,904)	42	50

Note: Percentages may not add to 100 due to rounding. Coding of religious history is based on answers to the question of what religious tradition parents were raised in compared to the tradition with which they affiliate as adults.

Source: Cultural of American Families Survey, 2012.

likely to seek help from a religious leader are significantly more likely to talk with children about religion at least weekly. Thus, sizeable proportions of American parents (at least say that they) discuss religious matters with their children on at least a weekly basis, a practice that is significantly influenced by a variety of religious and some demographic factors.

Getting children to religious services regularly is another part of religious transmission. Table 4.8 (the left half) also shows that 42 percent of all American parents and 67 percent of "devout" parents report their children attending religious services once a week or more often.[13] (By "devout" we mean parents who report that religious faith is important or the most important thing in their lives and/or who attend religious services at least weekly.) We suspect, again, that these statistics are somewhat inflated by social desirability bias, as is American religious service attendance generally, but they still give us ballpark numbers worth knowing. The percentages are higher for both categories of parents (all and devout) among Mormons, conservative Protestants, and black Protestants; and lower among Catholics, Jews, and members of other religions (and of course no religious affiliation). And being a "devout" parent of a religious tradition, compared to being "nominal," seems to make the biggest difference for Catholic and mainline Protestant parents (with 27 and 24 percent increases in reports from all to devout, respectively). Thus, somewhat less than one-half of all parents and about two-thirds of religiously "devout" parents report (what in most cases means) taking their children to religious services.

Table 4.9 (left column) also shows, unsurprisingly, that parents for whom religion is important and who attend services weekly or more often are much more likely to say that their children attend religious services at least weekly. The same is true of parents who identify as born again. Parents' religious affiliation history is also associated with child attendance differences. Parents who switched religious traditions are more likely (55 percent), those who stayed in the same tradition or became religious are about as likely (44 and 37 percent, respectively), and those who dropped out of religion or were never religiously affiliated are much less likely (13 and 18 percent, respectively) than the average to report having children who attend religious services weekly. Analyzed with multivariate statistical procedures, differences in children attending religious services by all of these variables remained statistically significant after

---

13. Children attending religious services does not automatically mean that parents make their children attend or attend with them, but we know from much previous research that in most cases it does mean that.

accounting for standard demographic control variables. In addition, we found that parents with higher incomes compared to those with the lowest incomes and those who enjoy greater parental support from grandparents, personal friends, and fellow religionists are significantly more likely to have children that attend religious services at least weekly.

Table 4.10 shows parent reports about two more religious practices that are not as important but still relevant for passing on religion to children. One is reading or saying religious devotions with family once a week or

Table 4.10 Family Devotions and Family-Oriented Programs by Religious Variables (Weighted Percentages)

	Read or Say Daily Devotions with Family Weekly+	Participate in Family-Oriented Programs at Place of Worship Monthly+
Religious Importance		
Not very or at all	8	5
Somewhat	22	14
Very	62	39
Religious Service Attendance		
Never	0	7
Hardly ever	15	7
Several times a year	16	5
Once or twice a month	38	24
Once a week	63	43
More than once a week	86	53
Religious Affiliation		
Mainline Protestant	44	27
Conservative Protestant	48	30
Black Protestant	62	38
Catholic	35	19
LDS	50	70
Jewish	50	30
Other non-Christian	54	41
Nonreligious	26	11
Born-again identity	63	37
Full parent sample (N = 522)	44	27

Note: Percentages may not add to 100 due to rounding to the nearest whole number.

Source: Faith and Family in America, 2005.

more often. We see that 44 percent of all American parents report reading or saying daily devotions with their family at least weekly. Black Protestants were especially likely to report doing family devotions weekly or more often. So, predictably, were parents with higher importance of faith, more frequent religious service attendance, and a born-again identity. Examined while controlling for multiple religious and demographic variables, we find five factors that remain statistically significantly associated with reading or saying family devotions: parental importance of faith, religious service attendance, nonwhite race/ethnicity, mothers compared to fathers, and households in which both parents work but one works less than half-time (compared to both working half-time or more). Table 4.10 also shows that 27 percent of parents report participating in family-oriented programs at their places of worship at least monthly. Mormon, black Protestant, and other non-Christian parents were more likely than the average to report participating in such programs. So, again, were parents for whom faith is more important, those who attend religious services more frequently, and those identifying as born again.

Parental Influence or Children's Choice?

Another important issue for the intergenerational transmission of religion is the question of how much parents feel authorized to influence their children to embrace their religion versus providing children the space and encouragement to make their own decisions about religion. One survey asked parents this question: "Now I am going to read to you two statements about children. Please tell me which comes closer to your views. Children should be encouraged to decide their religious views on their own. OR Parents should encourage their children to accept their parents' faith." Parents were then allowed to say whether they somewhat or strongly agreed with the view that most closely matched their own. Table 4.11 shows the results of this survey question by different religion variables. One-quarter (24 percent) of parents strongly agreed that parents should encourage their children to accept their parents' religion. Eleven percent of parents somewhat agreed to the same. Four out of ten parents (42 percent), however, agreed strongly that children should be encouraged to decide their religious views on their own. About one-quarter (23 percent) somewhat agreed with the latter view. In sum, 35 percent of parents thought that parents should lead children to accept their faith, while 65 percent believed children should be led to decide their views about religion on their own.

**Table 4.11 Parental Influence or Autonomous Child Decision?
(Weighted Percentages)**

	Strongly Agree: Children Decide Religion on Their Own	Somewhat Agree: Children Decide Religion on Their Own	Somewhat Agree: Encourage Children to Accept Parents' Faith	Strongly Agree: Encourage Children to Accept Parents' Faith
Religious Importance				
Not very or at all	64	24	5	7
Somewhat	45	27	16	12
Very	35	21	9	35
Religious Service Attendance				
Never	67	25	8	0
Hardly ever	61	21	10	9
Several times a year	41	35	9	15
Once or twice a month	31	28	17	24
Once a week	40	25	11	24
More than once a week	26	11	8	55
Religious Affiliation				
Mainline Protestant	46	21	11	21
Conservative Protestant	35	28	8	29
Black Protestant	51	11	11	28
Catholic	36	27	15	22
LDS	60	20	0	20
Jewish	30	10	10	50
Other non-Christian	35	26	7	31
Nonreligious	61	17	13	9
Born-again identity	37	20	9	34
Full parent sample (N = 522)	42	23	11	24

Note: Percentages may not add to 100 due to rounding to the nearest whole number.
Source: Faith and Family in America, 2005.

These differing parent views about the relative weight of encouragement and choice vary by other religious variables. When it comes to religious tradition, for example, Jewish, other non-Christian, and conservative and black Protestant parents were more likely in this bivariate analysis than average to strongly affirm parents' prerogative to encourage children to adopt their religion (at 50, 31, 29, and 28 percent, respectively). At the same time, nonreligious, Mormon, and black Protestant parents strongly agreed with children being encouraged to decide their religious views on their own (61, 60, and 51 percent, respectively). (Black Protestant parents tend to gravitate to either one strong view or the other.) Parents reporting higher levels of importance of faith and those who attend religious services more frequently also appear more likely to believe that parents should encourage children to embrace their religion. Those religious tradition differences tend to disappear, however, when we controlled for more religious and demographic factors—only frequent religious service attendance remains statistically significant. Of the demographic factors we analyzed in multivariate models, older parents (who in general have more autonomous children) and single parents (who, compared to married parents, generally possess fewer time and energy resources for forming their children religiously) were more likely to say that parents should encourage children to decide their religious views on their own.

Conclusion

The category "American parents" represents immensely diverse types of people, not only socioculturally and economically but also religiously. That diversity shows up when we examine the concerns and activities of parents on questions related to passing on religion to their children. If ever America held a solid middle ground on religion, that era has passed. Substantial minorities of American parents are very religious, practice their faith regularly, and invest in passing on their religion to their children. But another substantial minority of American parents are minimally or not religious, are basically disengaged from religious institutions and practices, and are little concerned that their children grow up to be religious. In between those opposites is another substantial group of parents that is neither highly religious nor nonreligious, but instead prefers to occupy the space of being "somewhat" religious. These positions map onto established religious traditions. Mormonism and conservative and black Protestantism tend to comprise the more highly religious parents. Parents in other religious traditions tend toward more moderation or permissiveness in religiousness and intensity of religious parenting. Interestingly, religious parents from all traditions seem to hold highly similar cultural models about religious parenting (Chapter 1). But they also appear to implement the directives of those cultural models with varying degrees of intensity. All of this points to the need for additional research to understand better the relationship between the cultural models of religious parenting and actual behaviors of religious parents, differences in attitudes and strategies between highly religious and less religious parents, and differences in the cultures and causal mechanisms by which distinct American religious traditions differentially train and deploy their parents to attempt to pass on religion to their children.

5

The New Immigrants and Religious Parenting

Nicolette D. Manglos-Weber

HELENA, A MUSLIM mother of a 17-year-old son, reflects on her experience as a mother:

> I think it's a time of great uncertainty and questioning for Muslim youth. Part of why I decided to cover [my head with a hijab] after my son was born was because of the awareness of myself as a role model. I'm just trying to be a good role model of what it means to be Muslim, from practicing my rituals to being open and not a dogmatic person—that's all been really important to me to demonstrate that, particularly post-9/11. I mean, I think it would've been important to me anyway, but it has a different kind of meaning and importance.

George, who is from Thailand and has three young children with his wife, explains the role of the Buddhist temple in their family's life:

> It's good to have for the Thai community, not just religion, the place that they can meet another Thai, especially the kids. The chance for them to see [it's] not just me in this country, but they have someone like me that's faced the same problem, and if you go there you will learn something. You will be a good person. You come here, you go to class, learn music, learn Thai dance, all those things. So I get them to come naturally, not forcing so much.

Another mother, Luisa, a Catholic from Mexico, talks about her parenting goals and compares her growing-up years to her kids' environment, highlighting both benefits and disadvantages:

> I would like to take my children forward, that they would have a better future, because we didn't get it in Mexico. I would like my children to study, that they would be something in life. I also want them to follow their Catholic faith. To keep them involved in the Church. Right now we are helping in the Church, my children also help, and I would like them to continue forward as well. In my childhood, thank God, we learned to appreciate what is valuable, because, you know, here [in the United States] one sees that the children don't value things.

Expressing similar sentiments, a Hindu father named Abhi talks about parenting his 21-year-old daughter:

> There are at this age a lot of other attractions in life, so we try to inculcate in her that there is a time for everything. She's more restricted, she doesn't stay out, she won't go somewhere else without telling us. As a Hindu family, we try to tell her that this is what we do, not whatever everybody else is doing. That immediately [makes] you a separate person. We don't drink, we don't smoke, it's in all of our scriptures.

These four parents come from very different countries, follow different religions, and have varied concerns for their children. Yet they are all engaged in a similar project: raising children successfully in a new sociocultural environment, while trying to transmit a type of religious faith and practice that differs from what their children see in the media, in schools, in their neighborhoods, and among their peers.

These quotes express certain aspects of their experience: the confusion about identity among youth who see their parents' Islamic faith portrayed as alien and dangerous; the central role that immigrant religious congregations play in families' lives, providing camaraderie and a place to celebrate and pass on their cultural traditions; the ambivalence of upward mobility, when the children of immigrants who receive more material advantages than their parents are also more likely to take valuable things for granted; and the fears of many immigrant parents that their children will adopt the lifestyles of North American youth, engaging in activities that violate the teachings of their faiths.

This chapter describes the cultures of faith transmission operating among immigrant parents, as they seek to pass on their distinct traditions in ways that are also consonant with their children's experiences growing up in America. We focus here on four distinct groups of parents: Muslims, Buddhists, Hindus, and Latino Catholics.[1] The pages that follow address how these religions are practiced in America today, how parents perceive and engage with the American mainstream, and what they do to transmit faith to their children. We begin by setting the larger context, describing where foreign-born parents fit in the current wave of immigration.

A word of caution is necessary here. The situation of foreign-born residents in the United States is ever-evolving, especially since the restrictive policies and enforcement strategies employed by the Trump administration since 2016. The "Muslim ban," the border wall expansions, and the push to dismantle the DACA program (Deferred Action for Childhood Arrivals), are perhaps the most well-known of these policies; but the agenda to discourage both legal and illegal immigration is also pervasive across the U.S. immigration system.

The interviews and analyses reported on in this chapter were conducted in the mid-2010s, so they largely precede the Trump administration's anti-immigration agenda, and the associated sharp declines in new arrivals. In many respects, we are now in a new era of immigration history, one of retrenchment and isolationism. Nonetheless, the seeds of this period of retrenchment were sown in the early 2000s, and are apparent in the stories of the immigrant parents in our study; and the tensions they describe are now likely even more salient, if anything. It thus remains important for our American readers to listen to them describe their parenting strategies, hopes for their children, and religious values, as we collectively decide whether to retain our identity as a nation of immigrants, and ultimately reverse our current political course.

---

1. The best term to use to refer to Spanish-speaking, mixed indigenous and European origin peoples of the Americas is a subject of debate. The more traditional term is Hispanic, and this category is still used in some survey-based studies. The more recent, and now more standard terminology is Latino, with some scholars and representatives preferring the gender-inclusive "Latinx." While recognizing that no label is perfect, here we opt for the term Latino as arguably the most broadly accepted by a range of interest groups, and most commonly used in the sociological research on religion. In participant quotes, however, where they use the term "Hispanic" we leave as is.

The New Immigration

There is no typical immigrant family. In 2014, an estimated 42.2 million people in the United States were born in another country, comprising about 13 percent of the total population. Just over one-quarter come from Mexico, another quarter from other Latin American countries, and another quarter from Southern and Eastern Asia. The top-five sending countries span the globe: Mexico, China, India, the Philippines, and El Salvador. Immigrant groups are also represented at every education level, and in all sectors of the labor force. So immigrant families are a truly global cross-section of races, nationalities, classes, and religions.

Immigration to the United States has occurred in peaks and dips. Today's foreign-born parents migrated as part of the post-1965 immigration wave; which as of the late 2010s, had transitioned into a phase of decline. The late 20th-century influx resulted from a major reform bill enacted in 1965, which dramatically changed the possibilities for legal resettlement by eliminating quotas by nationality, a provision that previously had favored northern and eastern Europeans. The new policy gave priority to the relatives of US citizens and legal residents, as well as professionals with specialized skills. It also allowed for immigrants from Latin America, who had not been included in the earlier quota system, and removed some of the former exclusions on Asian immigration.

At the time, the reform bill was not controversial. The removal of national origins quotas was viewed as an extension of the civil rights movement and a step toward less discriminatory laws. By focusing on family reunification and specialized skills, lawmakers believed the legislation would help maintain the country's ethnic composition while enhancing its professional workforce. Yet because it opened the door to new populations of immigrants from Latin America, Africa, and Asia, just when global flows of people, information, and resources were accelerating, the unexpected consequence was to spark a new surge in immigration, which eventually transformed the ethnic makeup of the immigrant population and the United States itself.[2]

---

2. Timothy Hatton, "United States Immigration Policy: The 1965 Act and Its Consequences," *The Scandinavian Journal of Economics* 117, no. 2 (2015): 347–368; Catherine Lee, "Family Reunification and the Limits of Immigration Reform: Impact and Legacy of the 1965 Immigration Act," *Sociological Forum* 30, Suppl. 1 (2015): 528–548; Aristide Zolberg, "Managing a World on the Move," *Population and Development Review* 33 (2006): 222– 253; David Reimers, "An Unintended Reform: The 1965 Immigration Act and Third World Immigration to the United States," *Journal of American Ethnic History* 3, no. 1 (1983): 9–28;

The social class diversity of this wave of immigration is also much great than in earlier periods. Some new immigrants are rapidly upwardly mobile. They have higher degrees and professional credentials when they arrive and capitalize on them in the US job market. Foreign-born engineers and doctors from South and East Asia are a good example. But for others, assimilation means becoming part of the struggling underclass, with little chance of escaping poverty, even across multiple generations. Manual laborers from Mexico and Puerto Rico, particularly if they are undocumented, uneducated, or have darker skin, often encounter this.

Most foreign-born parents realize that simply getting to America is no guarantee of economic success. The opportunity for upward mobility exists, but the risks of unemployment, underemployment, and stagnant wages do, too. The threat of deportation, which especially falls upon Mexican families, increases economic instability.[3]

Comparing the two largest immigrant groups in the United States today—Mexicans and Filipinos—we observe very different prospects for assimilation. Mexicans in the United States have on average much less education: about 3.5 percent are college graduates, compared to 43 percent of Filipinos. Mexicans' poverty rate is 29.7 percent, while that of Filipinos is 5.9 percent. The approach of the US government toward Mexicans can be seen as downright hostile (increasing border patrols, detainments, and deportations); while its treatment of Filipinos is more neutral. Mexicans, who are mostly working class and concentrate in immigrant neighborhoods, face strong social prejudices; but for Filipinos, prejudice is weaker and their communities are more professional and residentially dispersed. Mexican parents thus often start from a position of disadvantage, which leads to different assimilation pathways and different perspectives on how best to raise their children.

Throughout American history, religion has been a fundamental basis of belonging for immigrants. In past waves of immigration, most groups aligned with some version of European "Judeo-Christianity." But since the 1960s, that has been changing. The unaffiliated and those of non-Christian faiths are the two immigrant groups growing fastest in the 2000s and 2010s. But even Christian groups that are growing owe much to immigration. Hispanics and Latinos now make up 34 percent of US Catholics, and they are also

Charles Keely, "Effects of the Immigration Act of 1965 on Selected Population Characteristics of Immigrants to the United States," *Demography* 8, no. 2 (1971): 157–169.

3. Joanna Dreby, "The Burden of Deportation on Children in Mexican Immigrant Families," *Journal of Marriage and Family* 74, no. 4 (2012): 829–845.

increasingly found in Protestant denominations. Evangelical Protestantism in the United States is ever more multinational, reflecting the expansion of evangelicalism in Latin America, Africa, and Asia—the major sending regions of the new immigration.

As a result of all of this diversity, new immigrants and their children vary widely in how they interact with mainstream American society. Their socioeconomic resources, the broader legal and social context, and the nature of their existing ethnic communities all shape how foreign-born parents and their children adapt to life in America and their chances of economic success.[4]

The Immigrant Parents in Our Study

Just as our study was not designed to perfectly represent all American parents, it cannot represent the full range of immigrant families. We were strategic in selecting foreign-born parents based on what we wanted to learn about intergenerational religious transmission of specific groups. First, Mexican families are overrepresented in our sample, because they are the largest immigrant group in the United States, they are the most threatened by factors that lead to bad assimilation outcomes, and they are simultaneously transforming the nature of American religious institutions, especially the Catholic Church. Second, because we are interested in the relationship between religious cultures and parental religious transmission to children, we gathered numerous comparison points across faith traditions, recruiting quotas of Muslim, Hindu, and Buddhist families. These religions are growing in the United States through immigration from the Middle East, North and West Africa, and South and East Asia. Muslims are estimated to represent 1 percent of the US population, and Hindus and Buddhists each about 0.7 percent.[5]

We interviewed a total of 74 parents who were foreign-born and another 9 whose parents were both foreign-born. Thirty-four parents we interviewed are Hispanic or Latino Catholics; another 34 were Muslim, Hindu, and Buddhist; and the balance of six immigrant parents belonged to other religious

4. Thomas Soehl and Roger Waldinger, "Inheriting the Homeland? Intergenerational Transmission of Cross-Border Ties in Migrant Families," *American Journal of Sociology* 118, no. 3 (2012): 778–813; Alejandro Portes and Ruben Rumbaut, *Legacies: The Story of the Immigrant Second Generation* (Berkeley: University of California Press, 2001); Alejandro Portes and Julia Sensenbrenner, "Embeddedness and Immigration: Notes on the Determinants of Economic Action," *American Journal of Sociology* 98, no. 6 (1993):1320–1350.

5. Pew Research Center, Pew Forum Religious Landscape Survey, 2011, http://www.pewforum.org/religious-landscape-study/.

groups, such as mainline or conservative Protestant churches. They include many of Mexican origin, as well as Vietnam, Thailand, Pakistan, India, Haiti, Belize, and other countries. The parents we interviewed also differ by social class and in their levels of religious commitment. Based on our observations, we classified 40 percent of them as "working/lower" class and 60 percent as "middle" or "upper middle" class. In keeping with our project's focus on religious parents, about 72 percent of our immigrant sample reflect high levels of religious commitment, about 4 percent medium levels, and 24 percent low levels of religious commitment. So, although our sample is not fully representative of the US immigrant population, it does provide a good view into diverse types of foreign-born parents.

This chapter focuses by sections on the four major immigrant religious groups in our sample: Muslims, Buddhists, Hindus, and Latino Catholics. Each section starts with a brief overview of the religion as practiced today in the United States. We then address how our groups of religious parents engage what they see as the American cultural mainstream, followed by a description of how these parents approach passing on their religions to their children.

Muslim Parents
Islam in America

Muslim immigration to "the West" is today a controversial political issue, igniting conflicts about citizenship, inclusivity, and security. Yet the prevailing discourse about floods of Muslim immigrants coming from centers of Islamic extremism obscures two facts about American Muslims. First, although the number of Muslims in the United States is growing, the total is small, roughly only 1 percent of the population. Second, most American Muslims do not come from the Middle East, but from Indonesia, Pakistan, India, Bangladesh, and Nigeria. These facts must shape our image of Muslim parents in the United States trying to pass on Islam to their children.

Muslims in the United States tend to be devout. Sixty-nine percent pray at least daily, 64 percent say religion is very important to their lives, and 45 percent attend religious services at least weekly. They are also educationally and economically diverse, including refugees from poor and politically unstable countries (such as Somalia and Syria) alongside professionals from wealthier countries with strong education systems (like Pakistan and India).[6] Thirty-six percent of the whole have only a high school education or less, but 40 percent

---

6. Pew Forum, Religious Landscape Survey, 2016 (accessed November 17, 2016).

have at least a college education. While 34 percent of Muslims in the United States earn an annual household income of less than $30,000, a substantial 20 percent earn more than $100,000 per year. Finally, to keep our sample in perspective, it is worth knowing that nearly one in five Muslims in the United States (18 percent) is not a recent immigrant, but "third generation or higher." We focus here on immigrant Muslim parents, but we must remember that our sample is not representative of all American Muslims, a group that includes a substantial number of African American Muslims (about 28 percent of US Muslims identify as black).

Muslim teaching and practice centers on the five pillars: the *shahadah*, the profession of faith that there is no god but Allah, and Muhammad is his prophet; *salat*, a directive for ritual prayer five times daily; *zakat*, the giving of alms to the poor and more generally the principle of charity; *sawm*, the month-long fast of Ramadan; and *hajj*, the pilgrimage to Mecca that each capable Muslim is expected to perform once in his or her lifetime. Once a week on Friday, the midday prayer—part of *salat*—is conducted at mosques as a communal gathering. In the United States, mosques have increasingly taken on a congregational model of membership. Called *masjid* in Arabic, mosques in the United States are often community centers, Arabic and Koranic schools, and sacred ritual spaces for Friday prayers all in one. In major urban centers, mosques tend to exhibit distinct national characters. Saudis generally attend the Saudi mosque, Nigerians and Senegalese tend to attend West African mosques, and so on. In small towns, however, mosques more often gather a broad range of ethno-national groups together. For our study, we recruited Muslim parents from a mosque in one large, global-gateway city and from another mosque in a smaller city. The former was primarily Pakistani, the latter highly diverse.

One theological distinction in Islam is important for understanding the situation of Muslim parents in the United States: the division between *Dar al-Islam* ("abode of Islam," the Islamic world) and *Dar al-Harb* ("abode of disbelief," the non-Islamic world). As a religious minority, Muslims in the United States wrestle with the question of whether they are living as semi-permanent "strangers in a strange land" or rather on the frontier of the Islamic World, integrating America into the global geography of their faith. This influences how they view the moral landscape of American culture, as either fundamentally opposed or readily adaptable to Islamic principles. Public fervor over "fundamentalist extremism" assumes that most Muslims in the West take the former view. But close research on immigrant Muslim communities shows the opposite, that most are eager to peacefully integrate their faith and their new nationality, and in the process craft a truly American Islam.[7] Again, these issues bear on our question of how immigrant Muslim parents in the United States approach intergenerational religious transmission.

Engaging the Mainstream

Muslim parents in the United States engage mainstream American society with a variety of concerns in mind. The most challenging are the news media, and their continual depictions of violent Islamic extremism. Muslim parents recognize the very serious problem of religious-based terrorism, but also note a tendency in the media's coverage to focus especially on "bad Muslims." Amina, a mother of three children from Syria living in a small Midwestern town, puts it this way: "When you hear in the media about Islam, the bad Muslims are the ones who are affecting Islam. The media, they always concentrate on the bad people, to make the religion sound bad." She fears being targeted by anti-Islamic activists after the September 11 attacks, because of what she sees in the media. These media messages stand in contrast to her personal interactions with neighbors and coworkers: "The community here, they were wonderful [after 9/11], they were coming to our mosque and comforting us, people from churches, the mayor, everybody was wonderful. But some of the media, I got scared of it, because of the media I thought it's gonna build hatred against Muslims. My kids were young and I got really scared that if they go to school they will be teased or people will hurt them." Others from Amina's mosque report the same: their interpersonal interactions with local non-Muslims are usually positive, and yet the tenor of media coverage of Islam worries them. It negatively shapes their views of their place in American society, even when that contradicts their positive daily experiences.

Often Muslim parents' engagement with the mainstream—and their own experience of difference—depends on whether and how they follow certain religious practices. For women, veiling is a major example of this, because as a public practice it identifies them immediately as an outsider to mainstream culture. So deciding whether to veil and encourage their daughters to veil is difficult. One Egyptian mother named Hebah, who lives in a major city with

---

7. Louise Cainkar, "Learning to Be Muslim—Transnationally," *Religions* 5 (2014): 594–622; Zain Abdullah, *Black Mecca: The African Muslims of Harlem* (New York: Oxford University Press, 2013); Mucahit Bilici, "Homeland Insecurity: How Immigrant Muslims Naturalize America in Islam," *Comparative Studies in Society and History* 53, no. 3 (2011): 595–622; Rhys Williams, "Creating an American Islam: Thoughts on Religion, Identity, and Place," *Sociology of Religion* 72, no. 2 (2011): 127–153.

her husband and three children, described how she chose to wear the veil before the September 11 attacks: "Even though I started to cover my hair before 9/11, that event was a pivotal moment for Muslim women who covered, because you really had to decide if you were gonna stay with it or not. And a lot of women took off their scarves." Helena made the choice to veil as an adult, after she spent most of her later childhood in the United States. She wants her daughter to make the choice on her own, too, and recognizes it is potentially even more difficult now than it was when she was young:

> Post-9/11, it's a different world for Muslims. It is such a different time than when I was growing up. I certainly felt I was different, but there wasn't open bigotry as there is now. It's just so out there now. And I think it's made a lot of [Muslim] kids [reject] their own religious identity, because they don't know what to make of themselves and where they fit into all the political mayhem that's being caused by Muslims right now; and at the same time living in this culture milieu that doesn't really understand Islam.

Helena is aware that the prevailing atmosphere may challenge her children's faith. Nonetheless, she is happy that her daughter, who was 13 at the time of the interview, chooses to wear the veil:

> When my eleven-year-old came to me in the beginning of sixth grade and said, "I want to wear hijab," I was like, "go for it." I could see that she was ready to make that commitment. One of the things I asked her was, "Why? Why do you want to wear it?" She said, "Because I want people to know I'm Muslim." I had a little flutter, I was like "Yay!"

Although she wants to protect her daughter against hostility, Helena is excited that her daughter chose the veil because of the commitment it demonstrates. As a devout woman, she values what this public expression of identity has taught her about her faith: "It formed who I am, increased my confidence level, allowed me to be able to speak up about who I am and what I believe in. And the more confident I felt in my hijab, the more confident I felt in my beliefs as well." Helena believes that veiling strengthened her confidence as a Muslim, and it can do the same for her daughter, who is in the process of crafting her own identity as a religious minority in America. It is a difficult but valuable practice, which she would not force on her daughter, but is very happy to see her choose to adopt.

Other Muslim practices for men and women can put them in a discordant relationship with American norms. Muslim rituals do not fit neatly within North American time-use patterns: working people rarely have Fridays off, the day on which Muslims congregate for worship; employers seldom give breaks during the day, at the times when Muslims are supposed to pray; and few school schedules adapt to accommodate the needs of parents and children observing Ramadan's fast. This last issue is particularly relevant for parents of school-age children, who must explain to skeptical teachers why their children should not eat food during the day for a month. Muslim parents of young children often adjust their sleep schedules to observe the fast—which only applies during daylight hours—so they sleep more during the day and eat at night; but when their children enter school, it is nearly impossible to make those adjustments. Also, as children age and spend more time with their peers, daily prayer rituals can become a potential point of conflict. Aanya, an Indian single mother of a teenage boy, describes her experience around her son's praying:

> I'd like him to pray five times a day and have that be part of his life, but he has to be willing to assert that it's important to him and find a place to pray when he's in school. He says that he's told his friends he has to pray and goes and prays, that when he's playing basketball with them he goes and prays in the park. This is what he tells me, but I never saw it so I don't know. I sometimes have a hard time believing him because I'm aware of my own childhood and how I always tried to sneak and not pray [laughs]. But he says he is, so I have to take his word for it.

Like Helena, Aanya wants her child to be personally invested in establishing his Muslim identity by practicing its most visible teachings. Yet she understands why he might not, remembering her own childhood habits of neglecting Muslim practices that seemed odd to her non-Muslim peers. So she approaches the topic delicately, trusting his word and hoping for the best.

We see then at least three meaningful dimensions in how Muslim parents engage mainstream American culture: media, education, and friendship ties. Of the three, the first is the most troubling, in their experience. Many Muslims in the United States have positive relationships with coworkers, neighbors, and members of their communities. Apart from the logistical challenges of meshing Muslim prayers with school schedules, their relationships with school systems are also fairly positive. Yet the tenor of the dominant public discourse in the media about Islamic extremism is more threatening; and many fear that, if such rhetoric intensifies, it will directly threaten their family's safety and the life trajectories of their children.

Practices of Religious Transmission

The previous section hints at some of the key practices of Muslim parents for passing on their religion to their children. First, they model for their children central practices of prayer, veiling, and fasting, even (or especially) when they mark them as different from the mainstream. Then, as their children grow older, they take a more hands-off, sympathetic strategy, waiting in hope for their children to embrace such rituals themselves. In addition, many Muslim parents seek out Islamic schools of some kind for their kids. As mentioned earlier, mosques in America tend to take on strong congregational qualities, becoming not only places of group prayer but also centers of social activity and instruction. Many mosques in America—and several of those we visited in developing this project—identify formally as "Islamic Community Centers," both to emphasize their diverse activities and avoid any stigma that may be attached to the term "mosque."

Ahmed is a Pakistani father whose children are now grown. He told us how he came to be a lay leader in his local community center:

> When your children are going to public school, they learn other things, all the secular education. But along with that, we always thought that children also need to learn the Islamic education. In Pakistan we have a combined family system, so even if you don't learn from the schools, there are always grandmas and grandpas at home who can teach the values. Here we were missing that. So we taught that it's the parents' responsibility, really. And parents cannot instill any values in children if they are not involved. You can throw them in any [Islamic] school; it won't help if parents are not involved. So we made the decision that every Sunday, we will be with our children and we'll stay in the school the whole day, and we will make sure they don't say their parents leave us and go to the mall and this and that, you know.

His explanation is echoed across the interviews: as a religious minority, most Muslim parents are aware that they cannot take for granted that their children will learn Islam. They also know that, as non-clerical followers, they are not usually qualified to teach their children to read the Koran or answer theological questions on their own. They therefore seek out or build communities where this type of instruction happens as a collective effort. Indeed, when Ahmed moved to the area where he now lives, the community center was a small school and library offering only a few classes. Over time, however, with his investment and that of others, it became a thriving place of worship with a variety of outreach and education programs. As one of the bigger mosques in his wider metropolitan area, it attracts Muslims of various nationalities—though Pakistanis and Indians are the largest groups—who range from conservative to liberal in their views. His mosque has about 1,300 paying members, 30 different committees for various programs and initiatives, a full-time school with a paid staff, and a volunteer board of directors. The weekly Koranic classes for children are 4 hours long, even though, in Ahmed's words, "It's not enough." Investing in such a religious community center is thus one central way that Muslim parents work to transmit their faith to their children.

When it comes to teaching and modeling religion at home, Ahmed has a perspective similar to Amina, Helena, and Aanya. He described many religious practices they did together as a family, including praying on prayer rugs, learning to read the Koran, fasting during Ramadan, then breaking fast each night together during that month. Yet he also says that, as his children grew, he did not force them to practice these things, but rather created an atmosphere in which the practices were modeled by him and his wife, and were integrated into the regular family space and time. In his words, "Every home is a mosque, basically. So we have the material to study, and the children become interested, most of them. They become interested themselves." Ahmed sums up his general approach this way: "With your own children, you cannot teach them; you practice and they will see you. They're like monkeys: they will do what you do. The day you start preaching them, they might go against [it]." In his eyes, his role isn't so much to convey knowledge as to faithfully model the practices of the faith.

Finally, Muslim parents prioritize teaching their children to avoid immoral activities, including drinking alcohol, doing drugs, and engaging in sex outside of marriage. It is common for parents of many religious persuasions to discourage their kids from such behaviors. But Muslim parents talked about this as an explicitly religious issue. Aanya, for example, had gone through a series of sexual relationships in college and later regretted it. Now with her teenage son, she is very explicit about the immorality of sex outside of marriage, as well as the wider dating culture of American teenagers: "There's no premarital sex and there shouldn't be anything that leads up to premarital sex. I have talked to him about how this is not part of our religion and we just don't do this, even though I broke the rules and so he might too, but that's what I've tried to teach him." Although Aanya and her son do not practice Islam as extensively as Ahmed and his family—they do not consistently go to mosque and he doesn't attend an Islamic school—this issue is very important to her. Elsewhere, she said that these instructions are a protection for her son against the problems that often befall typical American teenagers. Ahmed echoes this sentiment. When asked whether the parents at his mosque are worried about their children being "sucked in by mainstream American culture and secularized," he responds: "There is anxiety, not [so much] about melting into American culture but drugs and free sex. We all are worried about that. In fact, I don't know why mainstream Americans are not worried about that." Ahmed recognizes his children will adopt certain aspects of American culture, but he also works hard to keep them from these specific behaviors, which he sees as rampant among US youth.

Hindu Parents
Hinduism in America

Hinduism is growing in the United States, like Islam, but still claims less than 1 percent of the population. Hindus mostly originate from India, Bangladesh, and Sri Lanka. Hinduism is unique in its close relationship to Indian nationality, and its rise in the United States is primarily a result of the recently growing middle class in India and their desire for higher education and professional opportunities. As a result, Hindus in the United States have a more uniform profile than Muslims. A remarkable 48 percent has a postgraduate degree, and another 29 percent has a college education. Thirty-six percent report earning $100,000 a year or more; and 87 percent are first-generation immigrants, so it is a more uniformly foreign-born community.

Religiously, Hindus tend to be less devout by commonly used sociological markers of religious practice and importance of religion: only 18 percent attend religious services once a week or more, 60 percent seldom or never read religious texts, and 26 percent consider religion very important in their lives. But those questions, originally developed to study Christians, do not match well with the basic characteristics of Hindu faith and practice. Most Hindu practices occur in the home or within family units, rather than at congregational worship gatherings. Hindu temples tend to be open spaces where devotees come and go freely to pray when it is convenient for them. Many Hindu homes have their own shrines where family members offer daily prayers to Hindu deities and burn incense. And although Hinduism does have sacred texts, such as the Bhagavad Gita, these are usually collections of stories about Hindu deities, and do not have the same status of divine revelation as the Bible or the Koran. Also, because Hinduism is intimately related to Indian traditional culture, practicing Hindus often have differing perspectives on where "religion" ends and "culture" begins. They may faithfully observe dietary prescriptions, holidays, and family obligations, but they consider these to be more cultural than religious and therefore may be less likely to say on surveys that religion is very important in their lives.

Hinduism in America, however, is not immune to the attraction of congregationalism. Many Hindu temples in the United States function as community centers, as do Muslim mosques. Few have single weekly events for all to attend, in the vein of Christian Sunday worship or Muslim Friday prayers, and memberships tends to be fluid. Yet they often organize community events and classes, and they are run by lay boards of directors. Their religious ministers are usually rotating priests who are professionally trained in India, and contribute little to social and educational program planning. In other words, managerial authority and spiritual expertise reside in separate agents, in contrast to being merged in the pastoral model of Christian congregations.

Hinduism is often thought of as a polytheistic religion, given the host of deities in Hindu texts, homes, and temples. But many Hindus conceive of the gods and goddess as representations of different aspects of a single all-powerful God or spiritual entity, rather than distinct beings. Most of the Hindu parents we interviewed talked about God as one ultimate spiritual entity. This may in part be a result of the influence of American religious culture, where the majority believes in one God in this sense; but our Hindu parents view that belief in God as consonant or easily reconcilable with Hindu tradition. Hindu temples are usually associated with one or several deities; and these are usually depicted in pictures or statues, arranged visually around shrines within the temple prayer rooms. Some large temples are architecturally very impressive, reflecting the investments of Indian doctors, engineers, and other professionals. Hindus often seek out temples based on a connection or devotion to particular deities, although many of the Hindu parents we interviewed were more interested in proximity and programming.

Engaging the Mainstream

The Hindu parents we studied tend to have fewer negative experiences than Muslim parents in engaging with mainstream American culture. Hinduism is not often discussed in the media as a threat, and Hinduism does not prescribe particularly visible or controversial practices, like veiling for women. The growing number of highly educated and well-employed Indians in certain parts of the country—New Jersey, for example, is 3 percent Hindu—means that many Hindu parents live in high-income areas with a critical mass of other Hindu families. This shows up when they talk about their children's experiences at school. One upper-middle-class Hindu mother named Riya, who has two young girls and lives in a major city in the Midwest, says her 7-year-old daughter has always had other Indian classmates, even up to 10 others in her kindergarten class. Another mother named Saanvi, who has a 5-year-old and lives in the Northeast, recalled how different things were for her when she immigrated to the United States as a child, from how her son is growing up now:

> Nowadays everything is different, you know, everybody understands culture more than they did twenty or thirty years ago. [Back then] I was the only Indian student in my class. If you go now, there are fifty, sixty percent of the class Indian. We were teased about being Indian, I would walk to school and you'd have kids shout out remarks, right? So at least my son doesn't have to deal with any of that stuff. I don't think anybody now would dare to say something, everybody appreciates it.

These parents thus tend to feel mostly positive about the mainstream schooling environments where they send their kids. Some of them, like Riya, make it a point to encourage their children to get to know different people: "I have always told [my daughter] that she should not just go with Indians," she says. Many parents speak proudly of how their children play with kids of all kinds of backgrounds in their schools. This reflects their own social universes, in that they tend to have Indian friends but also very positive relationships with native-born white Americans in their neighborhoods, schools, and places of work.

Unlike Muslims, most Hindu parents talked about discrimination in America as a *decreasing* problem since 9/11, as Americans have become more familiar with Indian immigrants. Again, Hindu parents tend to be upper middle class and therefore have choices about where to live and the schools their children attend. They can seek out high-end but diverse communities where their kids can get the best educations and are likely to find other Indian friends and family members. Yet this difference is also about religion itself, not only social class. Many Americans Muslims are also Pakistani and Indian, and thus have similar social-class profiles as Hindu parents. Yet they still perceive the general American attitude toward outsiders very differently. In fact, some of the worst harassment recounted by Hindu parents were times when they were mistaken for Muslims. One Hindu father named Abhijeet, who lives in an upscale suburb of a major metropolitan area, told a story about when his teenage son was in high school: "The Iraq war was fresh in everybody's mind, and my son told me that once he walking down the locker room and another boy said, 'Hey, Saddam.' He laughed, it didn't offend him. I said, 'Look at the level of ignorance, you could have turned around and said you're off by about 4,000 miles, because the country that I come from is India, not Iraq.'" The fact that Abhijeet interprets this event as an isolated and funny incident of ignorance, rather than a sign of threatening hostility toward foreign religious groups, reveals much about the difference in Muslim and Hindu experiences. Muslim parents, even when they are middle- or upper-class Indians, view such interactions through the lens of mounting Islamophobia in the media and the experiences of their fellow Muslims who look more stereotypically Arab and wear the veil. In contrast, Hindu parents view the same hostile acts as the last gasps of a receding general ignorance about minority religions. Most immigrant Hindu parents have stories like this to tell, and most consider them small annoyances rather than real threats.

On the other hand, however, many Hindu parents do express concern about the compromised morality of American youth culture and, like Muslims, consider sexual restraint, self-discipline, and a strong work ethic to be declining values in the United States. Anisha, for example, a single mother of a 10-year-old daughter who lives in close proximity to their extended family in the Northeast, reflects on what is happening among her daughter's cousins and American peers:

I see [my niece and nephew] growing up and feel like, compared to them, my daughter is a bit more religious and more respectful. My nephew, he says, "All of you guys are Indian, I'm the only American in this house." Already he says, "That girl in my class, I think she's cute" and "That's going to be my girlfriend," or they talk about everything which is kind of weird. They know everything. I mean, it's just a pretty different society.

"Does that make you frightened?" we asked. "Very frightened, like they're growing up way too fast. If you don't have proper foundation, then things can go anywhere. Already conversations come up [with my daughter] because they grow up so fast, the conversations my parents had [with me] when

I was fifteen, I'm having them [with her] at nine or ten." The things Anisha wants her daughter to avoid include dating, interacting too freely with boys, body piercings, drug use, drinking alcohol, and neglect of schoolwork. Many native-born American parents share these same concerns. But for Hindu parents like her, these are framed as part of relating to a mainstream culture that is out of line with their religious values. For Anisha, as with many Hindu parents, a "proper foundation" is crucial for withstanding the influences of mainstream American culture, and that foundation has in part to do with passing on Hinduism.

Practices of Transmission

For Hindus in the United States, the home is generally a more important site of religious practice than the temple. When parents talked about religious rituals, they usually mentioned what they practice at home. Only a few said they regularly "attended" the temple, and they thought of temple-going as a family prayer activity performed when it was convenient—stopping by to pray on a weekend or whenever they were in the area—rather than a collective activity with other Hindus. Not one of the parents we interviewed considered the temple as a place to meet like-minded religious people; they often reacted to it as a somewhat odd question when we asked about that.

The home practices of Hindu parents usually involve acts of devotion to certain Hindu deities at the beginning or end of each day, and at certain important festivals or life events, such as weddings. These are called *puja* rituals. One Hindu father named Amit, who raised one daughter, describes the place of such rituals in the daily life of the family in the following way:

> We have our family gods and goddesses [that are] typically in a small shrine in the house. We are middle class, so typically we have our own rooms and then there is always a separate room for the god. Even here in America we have a separate room for our gods where we go and pray, and enter that room if we are clean. That means you always do it after you take a shower and wear clean clothing. Even my daughter being raised here, she will not step into the room if she is not wearing clean clothes. That's how it is inculcated into your brain. So the gods are fed twice a day, because they are not [only] deities, they are as part of the family.

Amit followed this by explaining that such gods are really only aspects of a single divine essence:

> There's only one god, but [these are manifestations], for example, if you are praying for your learning or better wealth or success, you pray to Ganesha. And I pray to Kali, who is a female god, but basically she is a destroyer [who makes] peace of everything. Also, Shiva is another who we pray [to] because it's the supreme god as well. So different manifestations. As I said, I'm not extremely spiritual that I'm going to spend three hours in front of a deity and pray, but I still do believe there is a supreme power.

This perspective is common among Hindu parents. They almost all believe in a supreme power or god, and they teach their children to pray to different deities for different purposes, since such deities manifest different aspects of that one supreme power.

Deities and the legends surrounding them are also used to teach children moral lessons and make sense of life course transitions. Aisha, who is a very devout mother of a 6-year-old son, puts great importance on Hanuman, a monkey deity central in the Hindu epic *Ramayana*. In that legend, Hanuman was a servant of another god, Rama, and was morally notable for humbly denying any particular honor or repayment for his help in fighting a major battle. Aisha was herself taught about Hanuman by her grandfather, who told her he was the "most important god." Now she emphasizes Hanuman to her son, because she wants to teach him humility. Her use of Hanuman is also grounded in the Hindu teaching that there are four stages in adult life, each with its own intention. There is the young adult stage, where the focus is on chastity and education; the middle adult stage, focused on family; the later adult stage, concerned with stepping away from worldly concerns to focus on spiritual matters; and the fourth and final stage, which is the total renunciation of the world. Aisha considers Hanuman an important deity for the first stage focused on learning, because he exemplifies humility and open mindedness instead of arrogance.

This Hindu principle of life stages also helps explain why so many Hindu parents rely heavily on their own parents to teach religion to their children. Grandparents are in a phase of life more suited for spirituality and are thus the natural teachers of children, while parents are in the stage of life be focused on practical matters. This was true of Aisha as well as another woman named Jhumpa, who comes from an upscale family of scientists and who fondly remembers her grandmother as the vehicle of her spiritual and cultural education: "My grandmother lived with us, like typical Hindu families, and would teach me the old epics, like Darmina and Mahabharata. She would lure me to learn the language Bengali by reading half the book and then stopping, and I would ask what happened to the story now? And she would say, 'Well, if you want to finish it, you might start reading this.'" This illustrates a common religious division of labor in a Hindu family, and it shows the intertwining of Hindu culture and religion. The stories taught by the grandparents are tools to teach religious principles but also to teach language and instill a connection to their ethnic identity.

As to parents, their role often involves modeling and teaching practical values of respect, hard work, discipline, restraint, and gratitude. Most of the parents we talked to are happy for their children to learn explicitly religious content from their Hindu tradition, but teaching this is not usually the primary concern in their daily lives. They focus instead on making sure their kids have a "good foundation" and good habits to carry them through life. Because many of these parents are highly educated professionals, it is not surprising that rational dialogue is a cornerstone of their parenting strategies. Aisha and her husband, for instance, have a weekly ritual in the family they call "circle," where as a family they sit on the floor in a ring and anyone can talk about whatever they want. At the age of 6, their son mostly talks about books and interesting animals, but his parents intend it to become an open space where he can converse with them when he has bigger questions or problems. Anisha also describes informal ways to lay a good foundation through discussions about the consequences of certain actions. She explains to her daughter how important it is to work hard and that it is ultimately her responsibility to do well in life. She says they talk about everything, including regular conversations about sex, dating, drugs, alcohol, friendships, and what to do when people misunderstand their religion.

Some Hindu parents do take advantage of educational programs at temples, although these are usually music, dance, or language classes rather than classes focused on Hindu teaching. At several of the Hindu temples we visited for the project, such classes are the primary regular group activities that they host. These are not usually as extensive as the religious programs offered at Muslim mosques, however. In contrast to the 4 hours of weekend Islamic school that takes place at the large Muslim community center described earlier, Hindu temples tend to have hour-long music and language classes, often followed by a vegetarian meal.

Buddhist Parents
Buddhism in America

Buddhism has been a significant minority religion in North America far longer than either Islam or Hinduism. Buddhists from China and Japan lived in Hawaii and on the West Coast since at least the Civil War. When Hawaii became a US state in 1898, nearly half of its residents were from China or Japan. Asian Buddhist explorers and labor migrants were everywhere in California gold rush towns, building temples alongside the Christian churches of westward-moving white settlers.[8] Asian immigrants were not always welcomed. Fear over their growing numbers culminated in the Chinese Exclusion Act of 1882, which suspended immigration from China; and the later Immigration Act of 1923, which banned immigration from all Asian countries. During World War II, conflict with the Empire of Japan resulted in the large-scale internment of Japanese Americans. Certain Buddhist immigrants in US history have thus suffered incredibly harsh political persecution.

Buddhist immigration and the practice of Buddhism in America are quite different today. The Immigration Act of 1965 eliminated the blanket restrictions on immigration from Asian countries. Economic growth in China and Japan, along with the expansion of US higher education, led to new kinds of Asian American immigrants found in highly educated and scientific professions. War refugees from Southeast Asia, notably Thailand, Vietnam, Cambodia, and more recently Burma, also came in large numbers in the latter half of the 20th century. Finally, parts of the 1960s American counterculture embraced Buddhism or adapted parts of its teachings, resulting in a small but culturally significant Anglo-American Buddhism.

Buddhist parents in the United States, therefore, fall into three broad categories: Chinese and Japanese immigrants across first, second, and third or more generations; Southeast Asian immigrants, who tend to be first or second generation; and American converts. Among them, Chinese and Japanese families in the United States tend to be less recently immigrated, and also less religiously observant. Those in the third group, on the other hand, are not immigrants at all. Indeed, of all Buddhists in the United States,

---

8. Maffly-Kipp, Laurie F. "Eastward Ho! American Religion from the Perspective of the Pacific Rim," in *Retelling U.S. Religious History*, edited by Thomas A. Tweed. (Berkeley: University of California Press, 1997), 127–148.

only 26 percent are immigrants and 33 percent identify as Asian.[9] Thus, the Buddhist parents in our study, who are primarily Thai and Vietnamese (although we did interview a few American converts) are a distinct subgroup that do not represent all American Buddhists.

The corpus of Buddhist teachings and philosophy is broad and diverse, but one central prescription is to follow in the footsteps of Guatama Buddha to reach enlightenment. The Buddha is not considered a deity in the sense of the Christian or Muslim God or the pantheon of Hinduism. He is rather a founding figure who discovered the Four Noble Truths: that life is suffering; that suffering comes from the strivings of desire; that the relinquishment of desire will lead to the cessation of suffering; and that by following the path of Buddha the relinquishment of desire is possible. The prescriptions of Buddha for attaining enlightenment by relinquishing desire center on self-discipline and restraint, mindfulness and meditation, and compassion for all living things. Thai Buddhists are usually grouped within a branch of Buddhism called Theravada. The monastic tradition is central in Theravada, and Southeast Asian monks with their signature simple orange robes are a mainstay of temples across Thailand, Myanmar, Cambodia, and Laos, as well as Southeast Asian temples in the United States. Chinese, Vietnamese, and Japanese Buddhists, on the other hand, tend to follow traditions within the Mahayana branch, which includes popular sects such as Zen, Pure Land, and Nichiren Buddhism.

Compared to those of other American religions, Buddhists report more frequent prayer and meditation. They attend religious services less frequently than Muslims and Christians but more frequently than Hindus. Perhaps as a result of the influence of monotheism in the North American context, 68 percent report a belief in God with some certainty, even though most scholarly versions of Buddhism are nontheist.[10] Finally, scholars have identified similar shifts toward congregationalism among North American Buddhists as among Muslims and some Hindus, where temples take on diverse social functions within the immigrant community.

Engaging the Mainstream

Buddhists have a history of discrimination in North America, but today experience it much less. They do not face the same kind of stereotyping and public

---

9. Pew Forum Religious Landscape Study, 2014.

10. Pew Forum Religious Landscapes Study, 2014.

scapegoating as Muslim parents, and therefore they, like Hindu parents, tend to see discrimination as something less problematic for their children than for earlier generations. Yet Buddhist parents' engagement with the American mainstream is not all positive. They feel tensions over how their children engage with peers who do not understand or appreciate their religion; and they see American culture as too focused on materialism and self-fulfillment, which runs counter to Buddhist teaching.

Sandy is a married Thai mother of two girls, ages 7 and 9, living in an outer suburb of a large city. Her family is active at their Buddhist temple, and they enjoy lots of Thai family and friends nearby. Sandy grew up in the area and went to a nearby Catholic school, where she remembers feeling conspicuous as one of two students who were not Catholic. Now her daughters attend a public school, but they still sometimes have negative interactions with their peers over religion:

> When [she] went to kindergarten, she wore a Buddha necklace and one of the kids who was Christian said, "You're gonna go to hell." She just kept taking it off and she wouldn't wear it, and I was like, "What's going on?" She was like, "My friend says I'm gonna go to hell." I said, "Well, do you know what hell is?" and she replied, "No. It just sounded bad so I don't wanna go there." So that gave her a sense of slight segregation with her friend.

Other Buddhist parents shared similar stories of their children being told by peers that they are going to hell. Sandy said later that she tries to explain to her daughters that they just believe something different and their friends should respect that. But it is difficult for young children to understand these concepts and take such challenges in stride.

These threatening experiences do vary, however, between types of schools and how teachers approach diversity in classrooms. Another Thai mother named Anna, who has three children and lives in the same city as Sandy, told a different story about her 10-year-old son, Adam. When Adam was a younger, Anna's mother-in-law passed away and, as part of their tradition, Adam's head was shaved so he could be what they call a "little monk," whose role is to "take grandma to heaven." When it was time for him to return to school afterward, he was nervous: "He didn't want to go to school because his friends are gonna ask [about it], but when I explained to the principal, she said don't worry. And they brought him to explain to all the friends at once, [that his head was shaved so] her could bring grandma to heaven. All the kids said, 'Oh,

Adam, you look handsome. I wanna be like you, you're cool.'" Anna's kids attend a public school like Sandy's, but they live in a diverse area and the school administrators make it a point to be sensitive about religious differences in the classroom, which changes their experience of mainstream schooling.

A more worrisome problem for most Buddhist parents is their children's exposure to certain behaviors and values. Like many immigrant parents from more traditional home cultures, Thai and Vietnamese Buddhist parents see American youth as having less respect for others and less gratitude for their privileges. One Vietnamese mother named Theresa, raising a 14-year-old, an 11-year-old, and a 10-year-old, discussed the problem of disrespect among her children's classmates: "The way we raise our kids is different than others' cultures. We raise our kids to respect people or to do [their] best. But when they go to school they have to deal with others, and they don't treat people right, like the way kids don't respect teachers, or they don't do their homework, or do what they supposed to do." She later drew a direct comparison between her moral education in Thailand and how kids are taught in the United States: "Back in our country, in school they teach us how to respect, how to treat other people, but I don't see that happening here in the United States. And because of that, the kids don't know how to love." Theresa raised these concerns when asked whether she likes her children's schools, suggesting that, for her, the downside of American education is the immoral behavior of the other kids at school. Her daughter even had a big problem with being bullied. Theresa wanted to talk to her teachers about it but her daughter was too embarrassed to let her. Theresa later remarked, "There are a lot of crazy things out there, where people don't believe in good things." She said she brings her children to the Buddhist temple because there they learn to "be respectful" and "care for others," implying that many in US society do not live by such principles.

Practices of Transmission

As the earlier quotes suggest, Buddhist parents emphasize to their children the values of compassion and self-restraint. When asked about the basics of what they believe, most respond by talking about doing good in the world and to others. Theresa, for example, described the teaching of the Buddha as being about "how to love, to be sharing, to care for others, to be respectful, to have a meaningful life for others." George, a devout Vietnamese father of two school-aged children, explained it this way:

Based on what I found in Buddhism, it's not a religion, it's an education system. Because I look clearly and there's proof. You see it, you will observe it. The Buddha said, "When something happen, they call it law and effect. So if you do good, then you know you got a good result."

For this father, Buddhism teaches the truth about the laws and effects of the universe, how to "do good" in order to get a "good result." Later he talked about his experience learning martial arts and compared it to these teachings: "Buddhism you have to practice, too, because it's work. If you want to have a good result, you gotta work." As George parents his children, he applies this principle to issues like proper stewardship, often telling his kids not to waste things like water and food; and thinking very carefully about whether it would be good for them to buy things they want.

Sandy, the mother quoted earlier, similarly defines Buddhism in terms of its ethical teachings:

For me, Buddhism is, do to others like you want done to yourself. We believe in karma. You do good and you'll get good back. Once you give, I feel like the universe has a way to take care of you. Even when I wasn't working, we were fine. I felt like I was giving out to other people and then we were taken care of ourselves.

This description of karma integrates Christianity's Golden Rule—do unto others as you would have them do unto you. At another point in her interview, she explicitly said, "The thing is with religions, a lot of the standard stuff intertwines." For her as a parent, this "standard stuff" is the moral teachings she wants to convey to her children.

This being their core message, the practice of faith transmission for these parents often involves talking their kids through problematic situations with others and encouraging them to be compassionate. When Sandy's daughter was told by friends in kindergarten that she was going to hell, Sandy explained that everyone should respect each other's beliefs. When Theresa's daughter was bullied at school, they talked about how it would make her stronger in dealing with other problems in life, and decided not to talk to school authorities because it might get the bullies in trouble. These moments of teaching Buddhism often occur in situations in which a child realizes that his or her family is different than the neighbors or friends at school. The parents then instill a sense of distinctiveness and pride in being Buddhist. As Sandy said in her interview, she wants her children to have a strong sense of self so that they are equipped to deal with being different from the mainstream. They will be strong enough to keep on wearing Buddhist jewelry, for example, even if that invites negative comments.

Buddhist parents also tend to perform characteristic devotional practices in the home to transmit that sense of distinctiveness. Many have Buddha statues in their homes where each day the family burns incense. George, the father quoted earlier, told us he stands meditating in front of his statue every day, and that his kids often do this with him. Many of the other parents do the same. Sandy also has religious cartoons her children watch that teach about Buddha and dramatize other religious narratives.

Yet sometimes Buddhist parents take the opposite approach, downplaying their "Buddhist-ness" while their children are young and attending school in non-Buddhist environments. Although Anna facilitated a positive experience for her shaved-headed son that would make him seem "cool" and different, with her preschool-aged daughter she does very little to emphasize their religious identity: "I'm still Buddhist and my husband [is] still Buddhist, but we are flexible for our kids. My little one right now is in the preschool [and they] have to go to [a Christian] church and sing a [religious] song. So she just understands God right now, she doesn't get the idea of the Buddhists." With this approach, Anna seems to be balancing the work of transmitting Buddhism as a distinct tradition with helping her daughter adapt to life in her Christian school. Many Buddhist parents either send their kids to Catholic schools or themselves attended Catholic schools, and do not seem particularly bothered by having their kids taught about Christianity's God. In fact, many of them have adopted Christian theism as part of their spiritual repertoire. Many at times attend Christian services and say they would not be bothered if their own children adopted Christianity. What they *would* mind is if they grew up to be immoral. On the whole, then, Buddhist parents care most about transmitting core ethical principles, rather than making sure their children grow up with an exclusive and distinctive Buddhist identity.

Yet, while they are not defensive about the possibility of their children adopting other religions, the Buddhist parents we interviewed are highly proactive when it comes to collectively teaching them certain skills and aesthetic traditions, which cross categories of "cultural" and "religious." According to Sandy: "The thing with Buddhism and Thai culture, it's so closely intertwined that it's hard to say what is part of what. So I hope that they keep some of it, but if they go to church and they are Christian or Catholic, whatever works for them is fine. I just want them to keep some of their traditions." Sandy thinks of herself as a Buddhist who also believes in God and sees the "standard stuff" (i.e., principles of love and compassion) in many religions, so being Buddhist in opposition to other faiths is not something she seeks to convey. But Sandy is also Thai and believes in the importance of traditions and roots. She knows that Thai culture and Buddhism are deeply connected. So in that sense, transmitting Buddhism to her children is very important to her.

For the Thai and Vietnamese Buddhist parents we interviewed, the maintenance of cultural traditions of music, food, language, and art is a central focus of temple activity, and it is a major reason why parents invest in the temple. For example, we visited Sandy and Anna's Thai temple on a Sunday morning, the major temple day. A range of ages was evident, including some young parents who themselves grew up going to the temple. No single collective worship service was offered, as there would be in a church on Sunday morning or a mosque on Friday, but rather a packed schedule of music, language, and art classes for children of all ages. There was also a communal meal of traditional food at lunchtime.

On the Sunday of our visit, the children were preparing for a major Thai cultural festival they were hosting the next weekend. Several members who were nurses were also providing flu shots to the community. Several Buddhist monks resided at this temple, but they are not the primary organizers of weekly activities, a task that falls to long-time members and the board of directors. The monks were sent to the temple from Thailand and do not speak English well; their role is to teach adult meditation and philosophy classes and provide spiritual guidance. This temple also has close ties to the Thai government, hosting a regular flow of Thai exchange students who teach traditional dances and musical instruments. For these Buddhist parents, therefore, the temple is primarily a vehicle for transmitting the expressive and aesthetic culture of their intertwined religious and national heritage. It supports faith transmission in a distinct sense: conveying the traditions of art and culture that reflect and reinforce aspects of Buddhist philosophy. Anna explains: "The Thai temple here is different from the temple in Thailand, because over here it is the place to bring the Thai people together. They have the activity that Thai people do together and so we don't forget that we are Thai."

Anna's contrast of the temple's role in the United States and Thailand reflects the trend toward organizational congregationalism in many immigrant religions, even among religions that traditionally have no congregation-based structure.[11] In Thailand, the temple is a place to meditate, burn incense,

---

11. Fenggang Yang and Helen Rose Ebaugh, "Transformations in New Immigrant Religions and Their Global Implications," *American Sociological Review* 66 (2011): 269–289.

and make offerings to the priests as a way of showing compassion. Thai temples in the United States serve these functions, too—Anna notes, for instance, that her husband often brings food to the priests there—but it also has an additional function as a place of cultural solidarity where children learn to appreciate their heritage. Anna is one of the temple parents who was born and raised in Thailand. Others at this temple, however, were raised in the United States and themselves were temple children before having their own kids. Sandy is one of that group. She fondly remembers the sense of belonging she found with her temple friends in their shared experience being raised by immigrant parents, and she talked about how they have made choices as a group about their own parenting:

> When we grew up at the temple, we were a group of similar kids. So we all hung out together. We were the generation of latchkey kids. We took care of ourselves. Our parents were working. But nowadays, me and my friends, we've decided to kind of raise our kids together. So we all set the same platform, where we choose careers that we could be more flexible in our work [to help make that happen].

These friends she refers to include five other families with young children who were all raised going to temple and who built a close-knit friendship network on that basis. She refers to them as her "core group." As children, they went to Catholic school together and spent their weekends learning dance and music at the temple. As teenagers, they travelled to Thailand with their dance class to perform and study. She notes, "It was what kept you safe as a teenager instead of, you know, going out and doing other things. That's what we did on our weekends, we were at temple."

Sandy also says that as a group they are now very involved in helping each other as parents: "We're almost in constant contact, so if something came up or I have no one to watch my kids, I can go to them. And then if we have any issues or something we can always come to each other, like, 'I heard the girls talking about this—what do you make of it? or have you heard anything from your kid?'" They also decided as a group to raise their children in the temple together. When asked if her daughters ever complain about spending so much time at the temple every Sunday, Sandy laughs and replies: "Oh yeah, it's long, it's boring. But that's why we also decided to do it in a group with the five families, because at least they know they're gonna see their friends. It's easier to have us all go and they can sit with their friends, than just me trying to drag them and they're like, 'I'm bored. I have no one to talk to.'"

For Sandy and her husband, then, a big part of their strategy for religious transmission is connecting it to peer relationships for their daughters, just as it was connected to friendships in her own childhood. The temple provides the space, the routine, the resources, and the history by which to do this. It also makes it easier for her to engage in other areas of her kids' lives and moral training. When asked later about the influence of peers in her children's lives, Sandy notes, "Well, we kind of handpicked them," meaning that she chose their friends by deciding to spend so much time at the temple.

Sandy also notes that most of her friends rarely went to temple after their early years, when they were in their 20s, before having families, because there was little reason for it. The desire to transmit Thai Buddhist culture to their kids was the primary motivation to return as a group. "Buddhism is one of those religions you've always been taught you can practice from everywhere," she explains. "You don't necessarily have to go to temple to give food to the monks to say that you're practicing. However, I have been practicing more as I get older; I'm at temple every Sunday for school." She now directs the summer classes at the temple, which extend Sunday school into every day of the week for 3 months. This role, which she now considers her main form of religious practice, stems directly from her concerns as a parent. The trend toward congregationalism among these Thai Buddhists is thus closely intertwined with the imperative of transmitting religion to their children.

Latino Catholic Parents
Latino Catholicism in America

The largest religion among foreign-born Americans is Catholicism, due to the great numbers migrating from Latin America. Of the top ten immigrant-sending countries, six are predominantly Catholic (Mexico, the Philippines, Cuba, El Salvador, the Dominican Republic, and Guatemala); and of first-generation Americans surveyed by the General Social Survey between 1972 and 2002, 51 percent were Catholic.[12] Thus, although the Catholic Church is losing adherents among the native-born ("white Catholic") population, new immigrants are largely replenishing its numbers.

The Catholic Church is also uniquely organized geographically around the neighborhood parish. As some neighborhoods in cities have been almost

---

12. Alejandro Portes and Ruben Rumbaut, *Legacies: The Story of the Immigrant Second Generation* (Berkeley: University of California Press, 2011).

completely made over by the new immigration, local parishes have also been dramatically changed. Such shifts have not always happened easily or smoothly but have often involved the collision of very different demographic groups and cultures.

One parish we visited for our study, located in a large Midwestern city, provides a good example. The parish was founded and sustained for decades by Polish immigrants who first settled the area as the city expanded in the early 1900s. Then in the 1970s and 1980s immigrants from Mexico and Puerto Rico began arriving. Soon the neighborhood was mostly Latino, but the aging Polish parishioners were reticent to relinquish control of the parish and its associated grammar school. The two groups lived in tension for years, with many Latino parishioners becoming disaffected and travelling to other parishes where they were better represented and accepted.

More recently, two events further changed parish dynamics. First, a new priest came to the parish and started working to repair relationships with local Latino Catholics. Second, the neighborhood started to experience gentrification, with more young urbanites and upper-middle-class families moving in. The parents we interviewed from this parish represented the breadth of this history: some were second-generation Polish, others Mexican or Puerto Rican, and still others white native-born parents in professional occupations. The neighborhood parish and school thus brought together a broad mix of parents that might never have met elsewhere.

Another feature of immigrant Catholicism is its ability to connect immigrants to their homeland, through what Thomas Tweed calls "translocative ritual."[13] For émigrés from predominantly Catholic countries who feel nostalgic for the homes they left behind, Catholic Church ritual serves as a powerful affective force, providing an experience of virtual return to the homeland when physical return is impossible. This is important, because many of these immigrants come from countries suffering social conflict and poverty. Even if they are not explicitly exiles, like the Cubans Tweed studied, many have strong economic and political factors forcing them from their homes. Catholic beliefs and practices thus closely intertwine, rooting ethno-national identities in efforts to preserve memory and a sense of belonging while absent from the homeland.

---

13. Thomas Tweed, *Our Lady of the Exile: Diasporic Religion at a Cuban Catholic Shrine in Miami* (New York: Oxford University Press, 1997).

Engaging the Mainstream

Latinos have become so central to the post-1965 immigration dynamics that it is easy to forget how rapid and recent their growth as an immigrant population actually is. The size of the Mexican-origin population in the United States was 2.2 million in 1980 and 11.5 million in 2013, a more than 400 percent increase in only three decades. That growth is currently slowing, and the proportion of Mexican-origin US residents who are foreign-born is decreasing, but it remains about one-third of the total. Among those aged 30–39, the prime years for parenting young children, 55 percent of Latinos in the United States are foreign-born.[14]

Any new immigration wave of this magnitude will naturally be an issue of public debate. Particularly since the economic recession of 2008, which prompted in many Americans a sense of insecurity about the economic future, the political discussion around Latino immigration has been contentious. Research shows that domestic industries rely heavily on these migrants to fill gaps in the labor market, and that working-class immigrants pay much more into the social safety net than they receive. Yet many Americans still perceive them as stealing jobs from the native-born and taking undue advantage of social welfare services. It is not surprising, therefore, that about half of Mexican-origin Latinos in America report facing discrimination, and about 46 percent see themselves as very different from the typical American.[15]

Unlike the other groups of immigrant parents discussed in this chapter, their religious identity itself is not a major dimension of difference for these Hispanic parents. They belong to a mainstream tradition, Catholicism. But even though they practice a mainstream American religion, they do not necessarily see their religious values as consistent with mainstream American culture. And the ways they engage mainstream culture as immigrants—especially their interactions with the legal system, the foreign language, and interpersonal and systemic racism—shape their strategies for passing on religion to their children. It is impossible to talk about Latino family lives without acknowledging the pressure many face from the criminal justice system. The

14. Pew Research Center, "The Impact of Slowing Immigration: Foreign-born Share Falls among 14 Largest U.S. Hispanic Origin Groups," September 15, 2015, http://www.pewhispanic. org/2015/09/15/the-impact-of-slowing-immigration-foreign-born-share-falls-among-14-largest-us-hispanic-origin-groups/ (accessed December 10, 2016).

15. Pew Research Center, "Hispanics of Mexican Origin in the United States, 2013," September 15, 2015, http://www.pewhispanic.org/2015/09/15/hispanics-of-mexican-origin-in-the-united-states-2013/ (accessed December 10, 2016).

risk of deportation for undocumented migrants has dramatically increased in the past decade, and migrants from Latin America feel the greatest impact of this policy shift. Most Latino immigrant parents have family members who are undocumented in one sense or another—whether that means an overstayed visa, working without a green card, arriving in the country as children, or actually crossing a border illegally. This plays an important role in their lives.

Alanna is from Mexico and has three children in their teens and twenties. She told us about increased immigration status checks by employers, in response to our question about her economic future: "Yes, I feel concerned, and it is normal, because, for example, at work they were going to start checking your immigration status and all that, and it feels as if they were blocking your way." Her situation is complicated because her children were born in Mexico and moved to the United States with her when they were very young, so they did not automatically have legal resident status when they grew into adulthood. Thankfully for Alanna they were able to take advantage of the 2012 Deferred Action for Childhood Arrivals Act (DACA) (which she refers to as the "dreamer's program," mistaking it for the proposed DREAM Act legislation, which as of this writing was not enacted into law), which provides a deferral of deportation and a temporary work permit for children in her situation: "Now I feel blessed and I thank God, give honor and glory to Him, for my children, who were able to qualify for the dreamers program, and the three are working right now and have a good salary." Alanna's gratitude sheds light on the stress of parents who may have entered the country with proper documentation but have not been able to obtain it for their children. Such situations are significant concerns for many immigrant parents, given that 1.7 million Hispanics who arrived in the United States as children appear eligible for DACA; and yet, especially in the recent years of the Trump administration, DACA as a program has been under attack.[16]

Jorge, a father from Columbia, is married to his second wife with whom he has two preteen children. He came to the United States as a preteen himself and lived with his mother after his parents divorced, since his mother wanted to live in the United States and his father refused to do so. Jorge's early years in the United States were difficult:

---

16. Jeffrey Passel and Mark Lopez, "Up to 1.7 Million Unauthorized Immigrant Youth May Benefit from New Deportation Rules," Pew Research Center, August 14, 2012, http://www.pewhispanic.org/2012/08/14/up-to-1-7-million-unauthorized-immigrant-youth-may-benefit-from-new-deportation-rules/ (accessed December 12, 2016).

> I lived with my sister, my mother, and an aunt. I passed [time] alone
> at first, I spent a month locked up in an apartment. My sister went to
> school, my mother worked all day, and I was living alone for a month.
> When school started, I started studying. I found it quite difficult [be-
> cause] I did not speak the [English] language.

The difficulty made Jorge want to return to Columbia to live with his father.
But because he was brought to the United States as a minor, if he left, he
would not be able to return legally, even for visits. So he stayed and worked as
a laborer, as he was when we interviewed him. Later in life, Jorge faced other
challenges as a result of the immigration system. His first marriage was broken
up due to deportation:

> I met a girl who was undocumented. We started a relationship and she
> got pregnant, and then obviously I married her. But there was a small
> problem that she had to leave the country and went to Mexico. She
> took the children, and then I began to send money. Then it turned out
> I had to do all these procedures, and she was there a long time, and our
> relationship really fell [apart]. She met someone else there, and then
> I said, "No, I will not be in [this relationship]."

Because of his wife's deportation, his first two children grew up estranged
from him. They later came to the United States and are now on good terms,
according to Jorge, but it was a difficult experience nonetheless. We see then
that, even if Hispanic immigrants have themselves committed no crime, the
increasingly restrictive legal system—fueled by popular public suspicion of
"lawless" and "desperate" foreigners—can prompt major negative experiences
with mainstream America.

Another major theme is immigrant Latino parents' concern over America's
social ills and a resulting protectiveness of their children. Catholicism
is a mainstream religion in the United States, but they do not tend to see
American society as consistent with their Catholic values. Rather, they often
perceive their neighborhoods and children's schools as threateningly full of
people who do not believe in God and are therefore immoral. Antonio, a
Mexican father of four ranging in age from preteen to early 20s, has lived in
the United States more than 20 years. He echoes the concerns of many immigrant Latino parents with whom we talked about the moral direction of
society:

The truth is that I am very concerned. The truth is we are seeing a time of great decline. Maybe I see it because I have young adults at home. I see how they talk about situations that they see at school or with friends. For me, one of the biggest concerns is the high divorce rates. I explained to my son, in Mexico they always told us that a family is the cell of society. So I would tell him, divorce, it's like a cancer. When the cancer attacks a body organism, it begins with a cell, and then it expands, and it goes and affects more cells, until it destroys the organisms and destroys the body. It's the same in society. With the [high divorce] rate we have here in USA and the world, there is not much attention given to children, parents are thinking about other things. And that brings many [other] problems, such as drugs.

Antonio views one moral issue, divorce, as intimately connected to other moral issues, such as familial neglect and substance abuse. In this, he is far from alone: these problems are seen by many Latino Catholic parents as associated points of concern. According to Antonio, these problems threaten his family through the influence of his children's peers at school and the ubiquity of technology. With regard to school, he wishes he could have sent his kids to Catholic school, which he believes would have been better:

Public schools are a big risk. We have seen that some of [our kids'] attitudes have changed. I saw some expressions that suddenly they began to use here at home, and I [would say]: "Hey, where did you learn all those ugly words." And [there are] drugs at school, and so on.

When asked specifically about the influence of Antonio's children's peers on their religious faith, he replied, "I think, sadly, in most cases, we have seen that they have had very few positive influences in relation to faith. Most of them have been negative. In fact, I can't think of anyone who has been a positive influence, in the matter of friendships." At another point, he— again, representing many of the other parents—linked these problems to the problems of materialism, greed, and privilege:

I believe that, unfortunately, we live by running and running. Materialism consumes us all, right? And sometimes, because we are pursuing the material things, we neglect our children's education. Obviously, there are so many things that are available to them. Right now, with a [cell] phone they have access to the world. So I think there are too many distractions, [and it] makes it harder for us to spend quality time with them, to educate them, to train them.

Later in the interview, Antonio talked about how these issues make him concerned for his children's future: "It worries me that they are not going to [have] any needs. I am also concerned that if they don't graduate, and how the divorces are nowadays, that they [will] marry and then be left alone, how are they going to cope? Like any father, I also worry about drugs and that sort of thing." And still later on, he discussed how this makes him a protective parent:

> We have given them freedoms, but yes, there is always suspicion. There are some things that sometimes I allow, and sometimes not. For example, my oldest daughter wanted to go to California with some friends when she graduated, and I told her no. [She said], "But I'm going to be good and everybody does it, except me." And I told her "Yes. Remember that we live in the USA, but we are Mexicans, and our customs are different, and I want you to keep these customs."

These quotes reveal how concerned these parents are about protecting their children from immoralities they see around them. For many, it is the single biggest focus of their parenting, which they mention even before economic concerns or other ambitions.

Another Mexican mother, Diana, who is raising a 10-year-old daughter alone after being separated from the girl's father, talked about the moral education of her daughter alongside her hopes for financial well-being: "Yes, of course [I want her to have a better economic position], but I don't want my daughter to be ambitious, [thinking that] 'in order to have money, I'll do whatever.' That's one of my fears. The girls, today, in order to have money, they do stupid things, right?" Like Antonio, she told stories of being very protective of her daughter and teaching her to fear the dangers of outside influences:

> As she's already in middle school, there are little boyfriends, boys that she likes. And I know that they offer her drugs and all of that. Those things worry me a lot, because I am a rookie in that. Friends are always going to try to pull her to one side or the other. If she lets them [influence her], she'll go with them. And that is what I tell her even now. She has taught me that she has learned what I have told her, that she has to be afraid of things. It's not that I want to frighten her of everything

she sees, but simply that people can show her things just to catch her, especially the boyfriends. The boyfriend's topic is very delicate. [I tell her], "You can't trust anyone, daughter, you shouldn't trust anyone."

The message that "you can't trust anyone" shows up a lot when these parents described their interactions with their kids. Most of them believe that the world they live in is generally going in a bad direction. Diana says she thinks the world is "crazy," and many others express a similar pessimism. They feel their job as parents is hard, and most outside influences are harmful rather than helpful.

A final and related issue of respect also comes up frequently in their interviews. Even if it is only the loss of "old-fashioned" manners, many Latino Catholic parents see American youth as lacking respect for their parents, teachers, and other superiors. They echo the views of other parents coming from traditional societies like India or Vietnam, where respect for elders is considered very important. An older mother from Mexico named Alberta, who has three girls ages 23, 19, and 14, is working hard to teach her daughters to avoid the dangers of the world outside—like the others, she mentions drugs and sex as relevant threats—and thinks that part of the problem is the way her daughters and their peers interact with their parents: "Today, to be a parent, yes it is difficult, compared to when I was young, because I had a certain fear of my dad. And maybe that fear [would] now [be] identified as 'much respect' for my parents. The environment in which I developed as a youth was very healthy—I did see [tempting] things, but they never caught my attention." Alberta reflects that drugs, sex, and violence were around her, too, in her childhood, but because of her respect and fear of her father they were not real temptations. In her daughters' case, however, the same temptations loom, but the environment discourages respect for parents and so empowers the temptations. The girls are therefore primed to disregard their parents as too strict, and Alberta remembers several occasions when her older daughters directly rebelled against her rules.

Alberta also sees a similar lack of respect in the schools, telling us about an exchange with her youngest daughter that surprised her, when she was thinking about becoming a schoolteacher:

I said, "I will start studying to become a teacher, either a [teacher's assistant] or a substitute teacher." She said, "Mom, do not go to study to work with the children at [my middle] school." I said, "Why?" And she said, "Mom, us children at school are very naughty. We shout at the teacher, do things that [we shouldn't]. I would not like them to do that to you."

In this instance, her daughter wanted to protect Alberta from a level of disrespect that she knew would offend her mother. Alberta finds it shocking but also uses the story to demonstrate how her daughters have learned to see and condemn such disrespect.

Thus, perhaps surprisingly, those immigrant parents who are most religiously similar to mainstream American faiths—Catholics, compared to Muslims, Hindus, and Buddhists—also seem to feel the most alienated and morally dissimilar from mainstream American culture. They are Christians living in a historically Christian country, yet immigrant Latino Catholic parents tend to see most Americans as defying rather than sharing their Christian values. This translates into a sense of struggle, that what they are doing to form their children religiously and morally is difficult, and a fear they may not succeed.

Practices of Transmission

All types of immigrant parents emphasize in our interviews the value of education for their kids. But Latino Catholics are most likely to use the term "education" to refer specifically to moral education in the home, rather than to formal schooling. Transmitting values for right behavior is important to parents generally, but for Latino Catholic parents, this is a serious and difficult task that will make an enormous difference in the life journeys of their children. As working- or middle-class parents who often have little education and live in areas with more crime and poverty, they believe moral restraint can determine whether their children end up on the wrong path of drug addiction, unwanted pregnancy, criminal behavior, dropping out of school, and low-paying work; or on the right path of stable work, a strong marriage, a good family, and moving up into better neighborhoods and schools.

With regard to her three daughters, Alberta hopes that, although their peers are generally negative influences, her daughters can in turn influence others in a positive way: "Friendships do not bother me as long as my daughters do not adopt negative things. Our children have a type of religious and moral education. And I like that they will impact other children, [with] their education, their religion with their morals." Here she means the education that she tries to give her daughters at home, as something parallel to but also different from the education they get in the formal schooling system. Antonio's wife,

Liana, similarly used the word "education" to talk about moral instruction in the home. In her case, she referred to the familial education that she and her husband received as what makes their family different from the surrounding culture. She also notes the tricky balance of transmitting the same education to her children in a changed environment:

> I brought my own education, my own values from my home. And my husband brought his values, his education. It is difficult for us within the USA, that we bring a [different] culture. Here in the house, we live one way, but outside, [our children] also see other ways of living, that we don't know. So it's important to balance what we do at home, as Mexicans, as Hispanics, and what is done outside, because although they live with Mexicans, their lives are outside.

Later on, Liana got more specific about how this influences her approach to moral training:

> We can't force them to think like us, because they don't have our experiences in Mexico; their experiences are here in [the] USA. That doesn't mean that I'm going to [accept] if they [use] marijuana. [We still expect] the values that we have as a family: the values that are not going to take [them] down, that are not going to lead [them] to trip, that are going to make [them] healthy, those values are common. They are the values that we have and want to show them, so they can make their own decisions, and learn to decide [between] what we teach them at home and what they are teaching them in the street.

While she accepts that their children have a different experience, and thus she cannot expect them to think like her on everything, that doesn't mean Liana will accept it if they start behaviors that conflict with her values. She believes "those values are common," meaning they are good for children regardless of where they grow up, and so it is her responsibility to transmit them so that her kids are enabled to make better decisions for their lives.

Alberta, the mother of three daughters quoted earlier, described what moral education involves. At home, it includes many acts of subtly integrating faith into their daily experience. She often plays religious music in the background and goes to see religious films with her daughters occasionally. She encourages conversations about their Christian faith:

They ask me things about Jesus, when they read something. The youngest asks more often because she is going to a Bible study. Why Jesus walked on water, and what did Jesus walk on [in the] water, very scientific things [laughs]. My daughters ask me because they know I'm here, I'm in a Bible study, they see that I read the Bible, they see that I [go on church] retreats, they see that I go to groups where they teach you [about the Bible].

She teaches her daughters how to pray for people when they need support: "About 4 or 5 times my middle girl has had to come to ask me how to pray." And daily she blesses her daughters. "Every day I always do the sign of the cross to bless them. I tell them, 'The Lord protect you, God take you and bring you happiness.'" Alberta attributes her daughters' interest in religion to the visibility of her practices at home and church. She models religious practices extensively, so that naturally they will be interested or at least see her as a resource they can approach when needed. Like many of the other immigrant Latino parents we interviewed, attending Mass is nonnegotiable in Alberta's family. Everyone goes, and her youngest daughter sometimes serves as an "altar girl." Alberta does much more on her own, including Bible classes and spiritual retreats, and her daughters often ask why. She explains that religious devotion is something that must come from a person's heart but can find all of the resources it needs in the Catholic Church:

When they see that I'm really involved they say, "Oh, mom, why so much? Does the church really ask that much of you?" I say "No, it is each person who wants to do it. You see me involved in everything right now because that is my concern, and I can address it. The day that is born in your heart, you'll want to look and you'll see, in your Christian way of life. Do not say, 'In the Catholic Church this is not there, I'm going to another church.' I want you to meet your Church, because everything is here, everything that other churches can tell you."

Alberta is realistic about what she can make her daughters do. Elsewhere she said she knows they will probably be more "liberal in spirit" because of the influences of the surrounding world, which makes her sad. But her strategy now is to work hard modeling religion in order to lay a foundation of Catholic knowledge and practice, so that someday when an interest in faith is "born in their hearts," they will turn toward the Catholic Church and faith.

Alberta is relatively more active among parents at intentionally passing on faith to her kids, but she is also not unique. Many of the other immigrant Latino parents we met similarly combine mandatory church attendance, involvement in other organized church activities, family prayer at home, and conversations about Catholic teaching and morality in a repertoire of faith transmission practices. And many parents of older children reported that they saw their children through all of the sacraments, including baptism, first communion, and confirmation. Jorge, the Colombian father, is not quite as involved in his parish as Alberta, but he also reports a variety of family rituals aimed at transmitting faith:

> I tell them go to church and we will share all together. I am the model, they see that I honestly go to church to live my spirituality. We read the Bible. In fact, I downloaded the Catholic Bible on *Nook* [an e-reading device] and we have read. We pray, but not every day. We bless the food, but not every meal. We listen to religious music and watch movies. We just saw *Noah*, like four days ago.

In Jorge's family, attending weekly Mass is something they simply do. He does not force it, but his children—ages 11 and 13—have also never questioned it. Jorge's wife, Maria, who is from Mexico, provides more insight into the religious atmosphere of their family. Like many parents, she talked at length about the difficulties of raising children in the United States, which she says makes kids "precocious." She says the pervasiveness of technology makes her feel like "There's no control over anything." However, she repeats how they use the *Nook* as a way to link their children's love of technology with an interest in reading the Bible:

> I bought them a *Nook*, so they would read the Bible. I talk to them about the Bible. We don't read it together, but I talk to them about how the Bible is an infinite book, truthfully. Everything that exists in the world, you can find it in the Bible. How? I don't know [laughs]. But it's written there. I would love for them to [read the Bible]. Actually, I've suggested it to them many times. Of course they haven't done it, but I keep on suggesting.

Maria also listens to the Radio Maria Catholic station, which sometimes her children hear because she has it on when she picks them up from school. She says that her oldest has finished confirmation and her youngest is now in confirmation class. Jorge and Maria have their children doing all of the sacraments of the Church, typical of many of the immigrant Latino Catholic parents we studied.

The relation of Latino parents to their larger religious community is different from the other immigrant parents we interviewed: they are deeply committed to the practice of collective worship but often find themselves in local parishes where they feel like semi-outsiders. Devout Buddhist, Hindu, and Muslim parents have usually built their own systems from the ground up, founding mosques, temples, and religious schools for their children as needed. Latino parents, by contrast, come as Catholics looking to the established Church to meet their needs and, given the Catholic parish model, must work with existing local parishes in their neighborhood.

As a result, Latino parents vary widely in how satisfied they are with their churches, although nearly all feel that their parishes could do more to help them pass on their faith to their children. Sometimes the problem is simply that the parish doesn't have many children. Maria says: "Sometimes it's hard, because very few children go to the church that we go to. Basically, the children that do go are my children, who go almost every Sunday, so you don't see other children. If there were more young people, more children, maybe my kids wouldn't see church as so boring." She says this is particularly difficult during Holy Week, when she wants to bring her children to all of the daily services but sees no other families in the parish doing this together.

Liana, the wife of Antonio and mother of four, expresses frustrations more directly aimed at the Church for its lack of programs for her kids:

> It bothers me that in the Catholic Church there is never anything for young people, which is why they are leaving. Here in the USA it is very problematic, because if [someone is] in charge of the youth, [they say] don't intrude. So, even if I see [something is] not helping, I can't intrude, even though I know how to do it, even though I know that the young people follow me, I can't do it, because there is someone who is already in charge, and I'm going to step on their heels. The Pope wants us to think [about] the young people, but the young people will not come because they aren't in church. So then what is the attraction of our Catholic Church for young people?

Her disappointment over the lack of programs for young people in her church, and being excluded from helping to fix the problem, stands in contrast to the immigrant Muslim, Hindu, and Buddhist parents quoted earlier, who also faced a lack of religious activities for their children, were able to build it themselves. Liana brings her family into an existing parish, however, already run by others who supposedly provide those activities. She is left with few options, because leaving the parish to start a new one with better programs is not the Catholic way (this, however, also helps to explain a new trend among Catholic immigrants who are working around the established system by forming "personal parishes" not geographically fixed but developed to serve the particular needs of specific populations).[17]

Not all are so critical. Another mother named Helen, who came from Ecuador when she was 14 and now lives in a city with her two children in their 20s, remembers a more positive experience in her Church when her kids were young: "I remember when my children were in church, there was a lady who would [do activities with] the teenagers to attract the youth, and do other activities outside, like taking them to play volleyball or taking them to watch a movie." She thinks that such activities for teenagers that go beyond simply attending Mass or Bible study—the same ones that Liana does not see in her parish—are very important for getting kids to stay in the Church and avoid getting into trouble.

In sum, immigrant Latino Catholic parents typically view the passing on of religion to their children as a very important yet difficult task. Many devote great time and energy to their children's moral and religious education, and yet see large numbers of them straying from the Church. They then become frustrated over negative influences in the wider culture—the materialism, self-centeredness, self-indulgence, and disrespect—and often their Catholic parishes for not doing more to recognize and address these problems.

Different Problems, Similar Goals

Four groups of immigrant parents—Muslims, Hindus, Buddhists, and Latino Catholics—reflect great ethnic, racial, and socioeconomic diversity. Some of them enjoy advantages that make it relatively easy to engage American mainstream culture and transmit religious faith to their children. Others have limited resources, do not speak English well, struggle to guide their children through schooling and the labor market, and are the targets of public surveillance and hostility—which make the task of passing on religion to children more difficult.

---

17. Tricia Bruce, *Parish & Place: Organizing Diversity in Contemporary American Catholicism* (New York: Oxford University Press, 2017).

To the extent that parents' religious identities correlate with social class, some of the differences in their experiences have as much to do with social positioning as religion. Hindu parents tend to have a lot of social and economic resources, followed by Muslim parents, Buddhist parents (with the exception of Japanese and Chinese groups, which have more), and lastly Latino Catholics. The Hindu parents seem the least concerned about their ability to transmit Hinduism to their children. Their educational and work experiences shape their approach to religion, producing a particular version of Hinduism focused on basic moral principles and cultural and artistic appreciation, which easily integrates with the kind of broad, inclusive, "Golden Rule Christianity" espoused in American culture.[18]

By contrast, parents on the lower end of the social class spectrum—Thai and Vietnamese Buddhist parents and Latino Catholics—tend to have larger concerns about their ability to give their children better lives and to pass on their morality through religion. They often work long hours and cannot spend as much time in religious practice and education as they would like. They tend to send their children to less desirable schools, where drug use, violence, and gang activity may be prevalent. They see themselves walking the tightrope between socioeconomic opportunities and threats of moral decay, and worry that achieving social integration into mainstream American society and maintaining and passing on their faith and morality will prove incompatible.

While Latino Catholics might seem to have a religious advantage in all of this, being part of the mainstream Christian tradition, they are actually the most likely to feel that their religion conflicts with American culture. They value traditional family life and are uncompromising in their desire for their children to remain in the Catholic faith. By contrast—partly because of Buddhism's more open approach to varied religions and philosophies—Thai and Vietnamese parents are less afraid of their children converting to another faith or losing their religion, as long as they grow up to be disciplined, compassionate, respectful, and family-centered.

Many Muslim immigrant parents have the same socioeconomic advantages as Hindus but face a distinct and overwhelming problem, namely, the growing hostility toward Islam in the West. This antagonism defines their experience so much that they often must become active apologists for

---

18. Nancy Ammerman, "Golden Rule Christianity: Lived Religion in the American Mainstream," in *Lived Religion in America*, ed. David Hall (Princeton, NJ: Princeton University Press, 1997), 196–216.

their faith. They often seek to connect their children to supportive religious communities offering supplemental Islamic education or even comprehensive Muslim schooling. They also approach their children strategically, carefully modeling Muslim practices so children learn their value, while remaining sensitive to the cultural pressures on growing children who are developing their own personal identities.

Nonetheless, all of these parents share a similar aim, namely, to raise their children with strong moral and religious foundations within a culture that makes that increasingly difficult. Most of the immigrant parents in our study hold conservative goals for their children: to maintain traditional family life, preserve their particular time-honored cultural rituals, and retain the ageless moral principles of compassion, self-discipline, and respect. And those desires are rooted in what ultimately unites them: they are transnational migrants, building lives in a place very different from their original homes. Despite the differences in their religions, ethnicities, social classes, and life experiences, they all share the experience of bridging two cultures, and struggling with how to raise children well in the new one. That seems to trigger a preservationist reflex. In the face of dramatic change, they look to their religious traditions to teach their children what is more enduring than the transient culture, and what can transcend and hopefully bridge the differences between the places in which they were raised and the place they are raising their children. They find the challenge difficult, but most keep striving forward.

6

How Family Life Shapes
Religious Parenting

THE ROLE OF PARENTS, GRANDPARENTS, SPOUSES,
AND EX-PARTNERS

A WHITE CATHOLIC father explains about his son: "He doesn't have to go [to church] anymore. The last time was just a few weeks ago. And we never have pushed it like my parents dragging me to the car." A Jewish father commented, "Religiously we've tried to promote the same values that I kind of grew up with." And a single African American mother tells us: "I give him a choice [about religion]. My mom gave me that choice so I want to give him that choice."

Most of the parents we interviewed told us that their own experiences as youth growing up have shaped their thinking about how they want to pass on religion to their own children. In some cases, adult children felt very positive about their upbringing and have tried to replicate what their parents did. In other cases, they were unhappy about their experiences and were taking a different approach. This chapter explores the influence of adult children's memories of their experiences of their own parents on how they are trying to transmit religion to their offspring. We also investigate how parents manage differences between themselves and the other parent in the religious faith transmission process. We begin by examining general similarities and differences between adult children and their parents in their childrearing style—focusing on closeness, two-way conversations, and strictness. We then discuss the role of parents' childhood experiences in shaping what they want to pass on to their children, and the extent to which they draw upon childrearing approaches learned from their parents to do so. Next, we assess the often-ignored role of grandparents in shaping adult children's views about religion. Finally, we examine the important role of partners in shaping how parents transmit religious belief, as well as the different processes in which married parents and those who are divorced or single engage.

Intergenerational Transmission

Parents clearly draw upon and evaluate their own experiences in life, including the ways that they were raised by their parents, for deciding how they are going to raise their own children. The power of religious socialization and shared religious experiences means that children often—but not always—develop similar beliefs and practices as their parents.[1] Most young children view their parents as role models. As a result, through imitation, osmosis, and actively seeking out their parents' views, children most often embrace those views actively or by default as they grow up. Parent–child interactions are normally so prolonged, intense, and psychosocially meaningful that, unless something goes wrong, many of the values and attitudes formed during childhood persist into adulthood. About 80 percent of the parents we interviewed told us that they were expressing in their current religious beliefs and practices part of their own experiences of childhood; and nearly 70 percent said that they now follow the same religion as the one in which they were raised.[2]

As part of religious socialization, similarities between adult children and their parents can also result from them sharing similar social-structural positions.[3] Adult children and their parents usually share most of the same demographic characteristics, such as race, ethnicity, and education, resulting

---

1. Vern Bengtson, *Families and Faith: How Religion Is Passed Down across Generations* (New York: Oxford University Press, 2013); Jennifer Glass, Vern Bengtson, and Charlotte Dunham, "Attitude Similarity in Three-Generation Families: Socialization, Status Inheritance, or Reciprocal Influence?," *American Sociological Review* 51, no. 5 (1984): 685–698; M. Kent Jennings, Laura Stoker, and Jake Bowers, "Politics across Generations: Family Transmission Reexamined," *The Journal of Politics* 71, no. 3 (2009): 782–799; Alan Acock and Vern Bengtson, "Socialization and Attribution Processes: Actual versus Perceived Similarity among Parents and Youth," *Journal of Marriage and the Family* 42, no. 3 (1980): 501–515; Albert Bandura, *Social Learning Theory* (Englewood Cliffs, NJ: Prentice-Hall, 1977).

2. About 8 percent of parents told us that there was only some similarity between their religious tradition growing up and what they practice now. About 24 percent of respondents said that they were not practicing the same religion.

3. Glass, Bengtson, and Dunham, "Attitude Similarity in Three-Generation Families"; Alan Acock, "Parents and Their Children: The Study of Inter-Generational Influence," *Sociology & Social Research* 51, no. 5 (1984): 685–698.

in similar experiences, such as attending college or not, or being the target or perpetrator of racial discrimination. These experiences also likely shape attitudes, values, and beliefs, leading to parent–child similarities. The process by which children inherit the same religious affiliations and beliefs as parents also often works through shared religious experiences. For example, many Catholic parents who were confirmed around the age of 8 have children who were also confirmed at a similar age, resulting in a common sacramental experience. Through socialization and shared experiences, many adult children also likely develop somewhat similar childrearing styles (e.g., coldness, empathy, indifference, strictness, etc.).[4] At the same time, some parents choose alternative approaches because they do not like how they were raised or believe that society has changed so much that their parents' style is no longer as relevant. The childrearing approach that they finally adopt also has implications for why and how they transmit religious practices and beliefs to their children.

Using nationally representative data from the 2012 Culture of American Families Survey, Table 6.1 illustrates the intergenerational associations of relational closeness, which is one key aspect of childrearing styles that may be transmitted across generations.[5] Fully 76 percent of parents who reported being very close to their fathers and 67 percent who report the same about their mothers as children say that they are very close with their children now.[6] Only 8 and 9 percent of them, respectively, report that their current relationship with their children is distant.

Virtually all of the parents we interviewed spoke about how they were raised when considering their own parenting styles. Some were clear in explaining the important influence of their parents in shaping how they raised their children. One Catholic mother, for example, remembered:

> When I was a kid, we always ate dinner together. And my Italian grandmother lived across the street, so Sunday lunch and Wednesday

---

4. Toshinori Kitamura et al., "Intergenerational Transmission of Parenting Style and Personality," *Journal of Child and Family Studies* 18, no. 5 (2009): 541–556; Sandra Hofferth, Joseph Pleck, and Colleen Vesely, "The Transmission of Parenting from Fathers to Sons," *Parenting* 12, no. 4 (2012): 282–305.

5. The relationship is stronger for fathers, possibly because children generally report less closeness to them. Leora Lawton, Merril Silverstein, and Vern Bengtson, "Affection, Social Contact, and Geographic Distance between Adult Children and Their Parents," *Journal of Marriage and the Family* 56, no. 1 (1994): 57–68.

6. This includes only parents with at least one child under age 19.

Table 6.1 Percentage Reporting Close or Distant Relationship with Parents by Closeness with Children Now (Weighted Percentages)

| Respondent's feelings toward children now | While growing up: Closeness to *father* | | | |
	Very close	**Close**	**More distant**	**Total**
Very close	76	46	39	46
Close	15	39	38	35
More distant	8	15	22	19

| Respondent's feelings toward children now | While growing up: Closeness to *mother* | | | |
	Very close	**Close**	**More distant**	**Total**
Very close	67	40	36	46
Close	24	41	39	35
More distant	9	19	25	19

Note: Closeness was measured on a 7-point scale ranging from 1 = very close to 7 = distant. The measure was extremely skewed and it was therefore recoded so that 1 = very close, 2 = close, and 3 = more distant.

Source: Culture of American Families Survey, 2012.

dinners we were always at her house. . . . So [today] we do almost everything we can as a family unit. We just feel that it is a very strong part of the upbringing of our faith and what we believe as a family.

Another Catholic father told us how his own father was the disciplinarian, but that "it was rarely physical. And my mom was more the voice of reason, because my dad would at times raise his voice and get mad. That's what I tried to remind myself, and why my wife and I are a great fit, it's like in a weird way we're a lot like my mom and dad."

While most parents connected how they were raised with their own parenting, others saw big differences between themselves and their parents.[7] As

---

7. Of the 235 parents we interviewed, 100 spoke about the extent to which the disciplinary methods they experienced growing up were either similar to or different from what they were doing with their own children. Fifty percent of these said that it was not at all similar, 16 percent said it was somewhat similar, and 24 percent told us that it was very similar. The other

one mother from a black Protestant church explained, "My parents did not have the knowledge or education to direct me in the right direction to be able to do something that I can absolutely say I love it." So it is important to her and her husband that they provide their children with more guidance. Another black Protestant mother reported, "I grew up in the fifth ward, you know, and I've seen a lot, heard a lot. I've seen my mom do things that I don't do. I choose not to do those things with my children." A Jewish parent similarly said,

> I grew up with zero boundaries. Zero. I had no bedtime. Nobody bathed me. Nobody said, "You stink, go take a bath." I just don't know what the hell was happening because we're so attentive [to our children].

Regardless of how positive or negative they felt about their own upbringing, nearly all of the parents we interviewed made clear that they reflected on and evaluated how they were raised. That was one of the dominant themes throughout our interviews.

Research on parental transmission across the generations typically finds a positive correlation between adult children and their parents' attitudes, values, and beliefs. But that is by no means perfect, and it can vary substantially depending on the value or attitude examined. One factor important for the likelihood that parents will successfully transmit their attitudes, values, and beliefs to their children is their level of emotional closeness.[8] The right-hand column of Table 6.2 reports from nationally representative data on the percentage of parents who say that the model of parenting that they experienced as children was either positive, negative, mixed, or irrelevant. The most common answer we see is mixed, with 47 percent of parents (reporting on both relationships with fathers and mothers) saying that they repeat some things from their youth but reject others. Many more parents believe that

---

parents who spoke about this issue fell between not at all similar and somewhat similar or similar and very similar.

8. Annette Roest, Judith Semon Dubas, and Jan Gerris, "Value Transmissions between Fathers, Mothers, and Adolescent and Emerging Adult Children," *Journal of Family Psychology* 23, no. 2 (2009): 146; Joan E. Grusec, Jacqueline Goodnow, and Leon Kuczynski, "New Directions in Analyses of Parenting Contributions to Children's Acquisition of Values," *Child Development* 71, no. 1 (2000): 205–211; Andrea Erzinger and Andrea Steiger, "Intergenerational Transmission of Maternal and Paternal Parenting Beliefs," *European Journal of Developmental Psychology* 11, no. 2 (2014): 177–195.

Table 6.2 Percentage Reporting Close or Distant Relationship with Parents by Likelihood of Emulating Their Parenting (Weighted Percentages)

	While growing up: Closeness to *father*			
	Very close	Close	More distant	Total
The way I was raised is mostly a positive model of parenting, much of which I try to follow with my own children	55	45	29	35
The way I was raised was a mixed bag; I repeat some aspects and reject others with my own children	36	47	50	47
The way I was raised is mostly a negative example that I reject in favor of better approaches	8	4	15	12
The way I was raised is mostly irrelevant; I seldom think about the way I was raised	2	3	7	5

	While growing up: Closeness to *mother*			
	Very close	Close	More distant	Total
The way I was raised is mostly a positive model of parenting, much of which I try to follow with my own children	50	40	24	35
The way I was raised was a mixed bag; I repeat some aspects and reject others with my own children	41	51	49	47
The way I was raised is mostly a negative example that I reject in favor of better approaches	7	6	18	12
The way I was raised is mostly irrelevant; I seldom think about the way I was raised	2	3	8	5

Note: Closeness was measured on a 7-point scale ranging from 1 = very close to 7 = distant. The measure was extremely skewed and it was therefore recoded so that 1 = very close, 2 = close, and 3 = more distant.

Source: Culture of American Families Survey, 2012.

the way they were raised provided them with a positive model (35 percent) rather than a negative one (12 percent). We see that 55 percent of adult children who felt very close to their fathers and 50 percent who felt very close to their mothers also said that they enjoyed a positive approach to parenting, which they are now trying to emulate.

Consistent with these survey findings, our interviews confirmed that adult children who had close and warm relationships with their parents were more inclined to try to pass on similar values, beliefs, and traditions to their children. As one black Protestant mother explained about the closeness she felt with her parents, "So just growing up in that type of [close] family environment and the structuring with God in our household has led me to believe that I am going to do the same for my family."

Changing Historical and Social Contexts

While about half of the adult children we interviewed wanted to emulate their parents' childrearing style and pass on similar values and beliefs, many also noted that the social and historical contexts in which they were raised have changed, providing new challenges. Rather than worrying about the influence of MTV and sex and violence on television, for example, many we interviewed were concerned about the Internet and social media. One Muslim mother explained, "I would like to raise them like my parents raised me. But I know that's not going to happen." While she was growing up, her parents did not let her watch any television, and "Now that I look back I don't know how they did it." But the challenge she is now facing with her own children is not television, but the dominance of the iPad.

Many parents also spoke about how social norms about issues like spanking, attending college, and leaving children unsupervised have changed. Some did not feel comfortable doing things their parents did. A second-generation Buddhist mother, for instance, explained that her parents, along with others in the community, were not around as much when she was growing up. "We were the generation of latchkey kids: we let ourselves in, we let ourselves out, we took care of ourselves. Our parents were working. But, you know, nowadays, I don't know." She said young teenagers spending a lot of time alone at home is a bad idea. A lot of the parents she knows have chosen time-flexible careers so they can spend time with their children in a way that her parents did not. Even adult children who felt positive about how they were raised expressed doubts about engaging in some of the same childrearing practices as their parents, since what might have been appropriate then is different and unworkable today.

Parenting Practices: Two-Way Conversations and Strictness

Two major themes in our discussions with parents was how well or not their parents communicated with them and how strict or not their own parents were when they were growing up. Only about 25 percent of the parents we interviewed said that as children they enjoyed genuine two-way communications with their parents. They were grateful for that and tried to reproduce their happy experience with their children. One Mormon mother, for example, told us that her mother was a real "scholar of the gospel," so "we grew up talking about the gospel all the time." She explained that those engaging discussions left a strong impression on her, and "hopefully I'm leaving the same impression on my children."

At the far extreme, about one-quarter of the parents we interviewed reported little communication at all between them and their parents. The vast majority of them wanted this to be different with their own children. One black Protestant mother, for example, related that she felt more comfortable as a girl talking to her friend's mother than her own, but that things now are different for her kids: "When I say I talk to them [chuckles], I *really* talk to them. I'm listening, not just talking. I'm nosy. I wanna know everything [laughs]." A Muslim father told us that, while his views on religion had not changed, "I have conversations with my kids, as opposed to my parents where [they] just dragged us to the mosque." He said, "I want my kids to think more," and so he purposely talks more with them about religion. A mother who calls herself not religious explained how she regretted the way she was raised: "One of the biggest things I would say my mom did wrong is not even talk to me about any kind of religion, even when I straight asked her the questions." Things are different with her children.

The balance of about one-half of the parents we interviewed said that their parents communicated with them, but mostly in "one-way" conversations in which their parents did most of the talking. A conservative Protestant father, for instance, recalled, "When I say that my dad never spoke to me as a father [clears throat], he spoke more to me as a pastor. The discussion would be, 'Well that's not what Christians believe, so that's wrong.' But for us now, we try to hear what our children have to say." One conservative Protestant mother remembered a time when she asked her mother what a certain curse

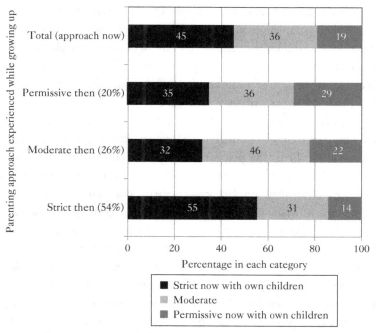

FIGURE 6.1 Parenting approach (permissive, moderate, and strict) used during up-bringing by current parenting approach (weighted percentages).

Note: Question responses range from 1 = very strict to 7 = very permissive. For presentation purposes, the first three, middle one, and last three categories are combined offering a relatively even distribution.

Source: Culture of American Families Survey, 2012.

word meant, because she didn't know. The response: "She flipped out on me, and so I knew, okay, well obviously that's bad. But then I didn't want to ask her [something like that] again. So that's a key thing, I want my kids to be able to come to me and ask."

The other discussion theme related to parenting practices that repeatedly emerged in our interviews was strictness and punishment. Figure 6.1 presents findings from nationally representative data from the 2012 Culture of American Families Survey to show the relationship between adult children's reports of their parents' approach to strictness and their own current parenting approach.[9] About one-half (54 percent) of adult children reported having a strict upbringing, while 20 percent reported a permissive rearing.

9. Also see Erzinger and Steiger, "Intergenerational Transmission of Maternal and Paternal Parenting Beliefs."

Strict parents appear here to be more successful in passing on that parenting approach than permissive ones. Overall, 45 percent of parents say that they are strict now with their own children. Only 29 percent of adult children who grew up with permissive parents are permissive with their own children now. Conversely, 55 percent of adult children who report that their parents were strict say that they are similarly strict today.

An even larger percentage of the parents we interviewed (about 65 percent) told us either explicitly or through anecdotes and stories that their parents had been strict with them (the percent being greater perhaps because ours was a sample of religiously affiliated parents). While some did not mind their strict upbringing and tried to emulate it with their own children, others found it very problematic. Many parents spoke about being hit or spanked as children; some hated it and others said it was a good disciplinary technique. As one black Protestant explained, "I think parents should whoop, not chastise, but whoop a kid! You know people are all, 'Are they abusing them?' But certain, I think that leads them to be a better person." But other parents explained how stifling it was to have overly strict parents. One Jewish mother who as a child was regularly disciplined by her parents by being pinched said, "I was raised with everything so strict, there was no joy in anything. It was all about making sure that it was done correctly, to the strictest letter of law." She and her partner now try to make things more enjoyable for their three sons.

Our interviews revealed much consistency in general childrearing practices across racial and religious groups. But a few differences stood out, most notably the extent to which adult children reported that their parents were strict by race. Among the half of our sample who discussed their parents being lenient or strict, more than 90 percent of the black Protestant respondents described a strict upbringing. By comparison, less than 60 percent of respondents who identified as white or belonging to another non-Hispanic race said that their parents were strict. Among respondents who discussed their upbringing, slightly less than 80 percent of Hispanic adult children described it as strict. We remind our readers that our interview sample is not nationally representative.[10] Still, previous research has found that black parents tend to be stricter

10. While 90 percent of black parents who mentioned their upbringing reported that their parents were strict, only 61 percent of black respondents who talked about disciplining their children said that they currently use physical punishment. The proportion of black parents who said that they currently use corporal punishment is higher than reports from Hispanic (45 percent), white (42 percent), or other non-Hispanic (30 percent) parents. Of all the parents we interviewed, 150 discussed corporal punishment and 112 mentioned their parents'

with their children than parents of other racial groups, so our interview data are not inconsistent with these other findings.[11]

Adult Children and the Role of Their Parents in Religious Transmission

Interviews with parents made clear that the way they were raised by their parents had a big effect on how they approached passing on religion to their children. Many of the parents we interviewed spoke about wanting their children to continue in the same religion in which they were raised. Again, the vast majority of those we interviewed follow the same religion as the religion of their youth, and nearly 80 percent report that they and their parents currently share the same religious tradition. Many expressed an awareness of the importance of their parents' religion influencing their own lives and many spoke about wanting to pass on the same religious tradition to their kids. One Catholic mother, for example, told us: "My personality is loyal, like I've been with this company for 23 years. So that's how I am about my religion. It all goes back to the pleasing thing; I never wanted to let my parents down." She also confesses, however, that "maybe we're not *good* Catholics; we don't follow everything. But I think we follow enough, my kids know enough." When asked whether he had ever considered changing parishes, a Hispanic Catholic father said no, "because it is the belief of my father, my mother, and my town." While most parents wished to pass on their religious tradition, only a few parents felt so strongly about it that they said they would

---

level of strictness. Our black respondents were recruited from a conservative southern state and our sample overrepresents religious respondents, who are more likely to support corporal punishment (see Christopher Ellison and Darren Sherkat, "Conservative Protestantism and Support for Corporal Punishment," *American Sociological Review* 58, no. 1 [1993]: 131–144). Some research has suggested that the relationship between race and corporal punishment, and strict discipline may be conflated with socioeconomic status. We looked at the class distribution of our sample by race. The racial/ethnic group with the lowest average class position was Hispanic, followed by African American, white, and other race. There were no statistically significant class differences between white and African American respondents or between the class mean for African Americans and others in the sample. See Elizabeth Thompson Gershoff, "Corporal Punishment by Parents and Associated Child Behaviors and Experiences: A Meta-Analytic and Theoretical Review," *Psychological Bulletin* 128, no. 4 (2002): 539.

11. Murray Straus and Julie Stewart, "Corporal Punishment by American Parents: National Data on Prevalence, Chronicity, Severity, and Duration, in Relation to Child and Family Characteristics," *Clinical Child and Family Psychology Review* 2, no. 2 (1999): 55–70; Catherine Taylor et al., "Perceived Social Norms, Expectations, and Attitudes toward Corporal Punishment among an Urban Community Sample of Parents," *Journal of Urban Health* 88, no. 2 (2011): 254–269.

end their relationship with their child if someday he or she broke ties with their religion.

Many parents also described specific practices, traditions, and rituals that they experienced as youth and want to pass onto their own children. Chief among them was regular religious service attendance, prayer, and things like singing in the choir. Parents often viewed such activities as part of a larger package providing a foundation of religiously inspired values. As one black Protestant father explained, "You know momma didn't play that, it wasn't like she was forcing us to go [to church], but we just knew it was the right thing and she did teach the value in us and to understand Jesus Christ died for sins and everything like that." He explained that church attendance is important because, "It's just right to have that value instilled in you, because that's something you wanna pass onto the kids." Another black Protestant father told us that he grew up knowing that he would someday be passing on his religious tradition, and it would be bad if "religion wasn't in the household, because we teach our kids to pray, to know right from wrong, and to know the Lord and Jesus Christ." For these parents, religious practices and values form the development of children's moral character, a truth that their parents instilled in them.

How much even religiously affiliated parents encourage their children to participate in religious activities understandably depended a lot on whether they had enjoyed these activities as children. That does not, however, automatically mean trying to develop in them a strong religious faith—especially for parents in strong "ethnic" religions. One Jewish mother, for example, told us about how much she has enjoyed being a part of a Jewish community since her own childhood: "I feel very close with my synagogue and we've tried to give that Jewish connection to our children, but I'm not really a 'spiritual' person." Other parents had negative experiences in their upbringing that caused them to rethink in which rituals and practices to involve their children. One Hindu mother, for instance, recounted that, at one point, her parents took her to all kinds of priests and astrologers and engaged in many rituals and practices (such as fasting) that she did not understand. She concluded that it was "useless, because you don't get things by fasting, you just ruin your metabolism. So I don't believe all that, I don't force all those rituals on her." This mother is careful to select only certain religious practices to pass on to her daughter.

Taking a somewhat different approach, a minority of parents were frustrated by their own parents' disconnect between public religious practices and what they perceived as a lack of personal religious conviction—a contrast that affected their own religion and how they interact with their children.

A Mormon mother, for example, explained that one of the ways she and her husband are different from their parents is that they talk to their kids a lot more about spirituality: "My parents were outwardly spiritual, but although we did things that Mormons do, they didn't talk about their testimonies. That was probably because they were already doubting. I remember as a child feeling like I really want to have Family Home Evening where we all get together and share our feelings about church, cause I remember myself always being very spiritual." Another mother who started living on her own as a teenager, was not raised in any clear tradition, and does not now believe anything religious told us that if she wanted as a child to talk about religion with her mother, "She would be like, it's personal and I don't wanna talk about it. I'm like, wow, [that was] one of the biggest wrongs she's done to me. I think that it's your duty and your responsibility to teach your kids about God and Jesus."

Many of the parents we interviewed had received some formal religious instruction as children, and a minority of them had attended religious schools, although not many discussed being much influenced by them. The few (10 percent) who mentioned it described mixed experiences that seemed to have shaped them in some ways. One single Muslim mother explained to us that during her youth, her religious foundation was laid—her parents provided her with that foundation so now she wants to give that to her son in part by enrolling him in a Muslim school. Other parents described the opposite. One father who was raised Catholic, for instance, but now affiliates with a mainline Protestant church told us that, while he liked some of the things his parents "pushed" on him, "I really wish I didn't go to Catholic school." As a result, his kids are not attending Catholic (or any religious) school. For the most part, however, religious schooling did not figure much in parents' discussions.

Passing on Moderate Religion

Many parents we interviewed were not trying to pass on to their children strong versions of religious faith and practice, but intentionally only moderate levels of religious commitment. For some, this was the kind of religiousness that their parents intended to instill in them. When asked whether she considered sending her daughter to religion classes, for instance, one Hindu mother responded, "No, because I do want her to know the basic core but not really to learn so much depth. For me, my parents never pushed us to learn [through] religion class." A Catholic father said that, similar to his own upbringing, he was not expecting his children to say a lot of prayers or read scripture. Rather, he wanted simply to show them, "This is just how we are." Others, however, were pushing back against what they remember as their strict religious upbringing. As a Catholic mother explained, "We've never said to them, you have to believe. I think part of why I rebelled when I did, as far as the church, was that it was seen as 'You're going to do this, you're going to go to church no matter what.'"

Intentionally transmitting to children a moderated religious commitment was not typical of parents in many religious traditions, however. For example, Mormons, Muslims, and conservative and black Protestants belong to relatively strict religious traditions that tend to generate higher levels of religious commitment. People with strong religious beliefs are more likely to think that their religion is the only true faith,[12] which parents can then reinforce by limiting their children's exposure to other religions and denominations. Relatively few parents in more "strict" religious traditions were trying to transmit only moderate levels of religious belief or were encouraging their children to try different religions. As one black Protestant father explained, "If you grew up believing in Christ and that's all you've been taught all your life, don't let somebody come and influence you to go over to something else."

Osmosis versus Intentional Influences

Regardless of the level of religious commitment parents were attempting to instill, the majority tried to pass on religion through either osmosis or intentional influences. With osmosis, children absorb values and ideas through prolonged passive exposure. With intentional influences, parents are more direct and explicit. Most parents who are intentional religious socializers (60 percent) require their children to participate regularly in religious activities, such as weekly religious services. These parents are direct and intentional, in part, because their parents had been the same with them, and they judged it successful in creating good habits and instilling religion—even if they may not have liked it when they were young. When asked what she would do if her 17-year-old daughter did not want to attend church, one black Catholic mother explained, "Uh, no, she's coming. [laughs] My house, my rules. You're coming

12. Pew Research Center, "Muslim Americans: No Signs of Growth in Alienation or Support for Extremism" (Washington, DC, 2011), https://www.pewresearch.org/politics/wp-content/uploads/sites/4/2011/08/Survey-Report-Muslim-Americans-No-Signs-of-Growth-in-Alienation-or-Support-for-Extremism.pdf; "Views of One's Religion on the One True Faith" (The Pew Forum on Religion and Public Life, 2008), http://assets.pewresearch.org/wp-content/uploads/sites/11/2015/01/comparison-Views-of-Ones-Religion-as-the-One-True-Faith.pdf.

with me: that's how my mom did it, that's how I'm gonna do it." A black Protestant father reported: "When I was young, we had to pray every night. Then we were supposed to pray every morning. And we still do mostly what I was taught to do." Later in the interview he added, "Just like I was drugged [dragged to church], they were drugged." While he did not always like it as a child, this father felt strongly that making his children attend church services was the right thing to do because it instilled strong faith in them.

On the other hand, a substantial minority of parents relied on osmosis to pass on faith to their children, either solely (13 percent) or in conjunction with some more direct approaches (30 percent). Osmosis is a strategy that parents seek subtlety in cultivating religion in their children. More than a few parents recalled how their own parents left an impression on them mostly through osmosis with some intentional intervention. One Hispanic Catholic father, for example, explained:

My parents didn't approach me, but I saw it at my house, I saw the faith of my mother. That faith motivated me to know more. So, also, my children aren't so attached to religion, to go to Mass. But they know. They know that I go to the [Bible] study, I talk to them, sometimes we read the Bible.

Another Catholic father told us that he combined attending Mass with other religious activities. Growing up, one of his favorite memories was "the drive home from church with the Irish radio program on NPR, which I now do with my kids, which is pretty awesome, the exact same one. And then the critique of the sermon [laughs]."

Other parents talked about purposefully creating environments that demonstrated to their children in indirect ways how religious they were or were at least open to discussing religion. Some of these parents seemed to be intentionally using osmosis to transmit religious belief, strategically employing passive absorption rather than direct formation. One black Protestant mother remembered that her father would sit downstairs and read his Bible for hours, "So I want [my son] to see me physically doing that." A Jewish father said he had a laissez faire attitude about religion for his children because his parents never really talked with him about religion. He talked with his kids some, but never proactively: "You kind of learn, kind of let that percolate and you know you'll have another discussion about it two or three months, or two or three years later, and then see where it's come and how it's evolved."

Children Straying and the Dilemma of Demands and Freedoms

Many of the parents we interviewed suspected and sometimes feared that their children would stray from their religion at some point, although most thought that they would eventually return. About 45 percent of parents who talked about children straying thought it was natural or expected, and another 40 percent found it acceptable although not preferred.[13] Many recalled how their own parents handled matters when they strayed, modeling how they hoped to respond. One black Protestant mother, a pastor's kid, said that at various points she would tell her father, "I'm never going back to church. But as you mature and grow older, like the Word says, they may stray but that they will come back to the Word if that foundation is built. It was my ultimate desire that I build a foundation for my kids, because they are going to stray."

A Mormon mother told us that when she was growing up, her family tended not to do certain activities on Sundays, such as to go to the movies. But one Sunday a boy she liked invited her on a date, and her mother told her it was her decision whether or not to go. She went, but it was a miserable date. Years later, she asked her mother about this incident. She said, "I just had to trust you and have faith that the things we'd been trying to instill, you would embrace." She now anticipates similar situations with her teenage son, including the possibility that he strays from the Latter Day Saints faith for some time. She said that, like her mother before her, she is trying to provide a solid religious foundation for her son, so that when the time is right and necessary, she can put the same trust in him, hoping it will lead to a similar good outcome.

More than one-half of the parents we interviewed said that their parents were demanding about attending religious services and classes. The majority also said that it is important for their kids to do the same.[14] For the parents who said they should make their children attend religious services, many had

---

13. Approximately 15 percent of parents thought that their children straying from their religion was unacceptable. Of the 235 parents we interviewed, 91 spoke about the possibility of their children straying.

14. Out of our sample of 235 parents, 105 discussed religious service attendance. Among these, 60 percent (N = 63) said that they required their kids to attend religious services sometimes. About 17 percent (N = 18) said that they did not require them to attend, and the remainder fell in the middle. These calculations do not consider how many parents had children who enjoyed and wanted to attend religious services.

been forced to attend as children and thought it helped to instill religious beliefs in them. As one black Protestant father explained:

> There wasn't a question of going. You *were* going to church. You were going and you didn't have a choice. So I went to church at a very early age and got baptized around age 5 or 6. As far as I can remember we've always been at the church.

Consistent with his upbringing, he now makes his children regularly attend church services. Another black Protestant mother recalled what her dad told her: ' "If you go out on a Saturday, you better be able to get up and go to church on Sunday, cause the car better not back out of the driveway without you in it,' and I feel the same way."

Many parents spoke about how much they resented the way their parents "pushed" religion on them, which some said had a detrimental effect on their faith. One conservative Protestant father related that "It was so much pushed on me as a kid, that's what pushed me away [from religion] at some point." As a result, he soft-pedals religion with his children, and consequently, "I'm not sure they have a grasp on [Christianity] and I feel a little bit like I probably should have been trying to instruct about some of the more specifics of the faith to them." A Catholic father told us that he and his wife never told their kids that they have to believe because, "I think part of why I rebelled when I did, as far as the church, was that it was seen as always, this is what you're going to do, you're going to go to church." And, because of her own strict upbringing, another mother who is not currently religious was cautious when her son approached her about getting confirmed: "I was like, just wait, wait on that till when you're really ready to do it. You'll do it if you really want to. I don't want to shove it down their mouths, like it was shoved down my mouth."

On the other hand, a few parents regretted not following their parents' directive models or taking their advice. A Catholic father whose children were in their late teenage years at the time of our interview, for instance, told us that he was very lenient with them about church attendance because he disliked being forced to attend church as a boy. But now his children are un-interested in religion and he wishes he had been more demanding of them. "I'm sure they would have liked it, and right now they would be thanking me," he thought, "but now they don't because they haven't tried it." This was a definite minority voice, however. Few who had been raised by very strict parents said that they wish they were more strict or demanding with their

own children. And, for the minority of parents who experienced lenient religious upbringings, many were thankful. One Catholic mother, for example,
said that, although she felt religion was very important, "I don't feel like
I should ram it down their throats. I like how my parents did it. It's really,
I give you freedom."

The Influence of Grandparents

The parents we interviewed not only discussed how their parents but also
how their grandparents shaped them. About 10 percent talked about their
grandparents. What role do grandparents have in their grandchildren's lives?
Figure 6.2 presents nationally representative findings about who supports

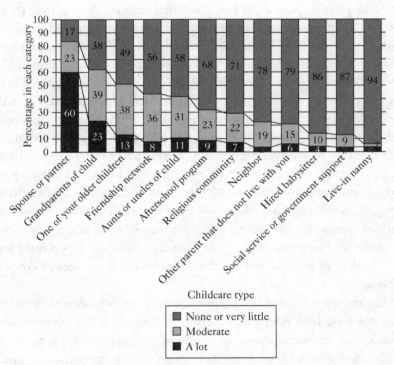

Childcare type

- None or very little
- Moderate
- A lot

FIGURE 6.2 Use of different types of childcare support for parents with at least one
child under age 13 (weighted percentages).

Note: The percentages are very similar for parents who had children under age 13 versus 19.
Question responses range from 1 = no support at all to 7 = a great deal of support. For presentation purposes the first two, middle three, and last two categories are combined, offering a relatively even distribution.

Source: Culture of American Families Survey, 2012.

American parents with childcare—and thus who besides parents has regular opportunities to interact with their children. Besides the 60 percent reporting that their spouse or partner helps with childcare, the next largest category, at 23 percent, was grandparents. This suggests that in some families grandparents enjoy the potential to shape their grandchildren when it comes to religion.[15]

When the parents we interviewed were children, an even greater proportion than that represented in Figure 6.2 very likely spent more time with their grandparents.[16] Notably, in stark contrast to the many parents we interviewed who criticized their strict religious upbringings, none reported their grandparents having a negative religious effect on them. One reason for this is likely that most grandparents do not play the role of "enforcer" that most parents do, so it is easier for them to play happier roles. Still, several studies have found that grandparents can have a positive and meaningful influence on their grandchildren, including on their religious engagement, even after accounting for the influence of parents.[17]

Some parents who talked about their grandparents saw them as part of a long lineage of kin who were transmitting a continuous religious tradition on from previous generations. One black Protestant mother said, "I want to follow in the same footsteps of my mother instilling in me [all] that she got from her parents, so it's like a chain I feel, my mother's mother, and family instilled in her, and then she instilled in me. I feel it's like a tradition thing we have going on." She asks her son, "As far as your religion, are you gonna teach your kids the same things that I taught you?" He responds, "Of course." A black Catholic mother expressed a similar sentiment: "I hear Grandma's

---

15. Casey Copen and Merril Silverstein, "The Transmission of Religious Beliefs across Generations: Do Grandparents Matter?," *Journal of Comparative Family Studies* 39, no. 1 (2007): 497–510.

16. Esme Fuller-Thomson and Meredith Minkler, "American Grandparents Providing Extensive Child Care to Their Grandchildren Prevalence and Profile," *The Gerontologist* 41, no. 2 (2001): 201–209.

17. Lynne Gershenson Hodgson, "Adult Grandchildren and Their Grandparents: The Enduring Bond," *The International Journal of Aging and Human Development* 34, no. 3 (1992): 209–225; Jeremy Yorgason, Laura Padilla-Walker, and Jami Jackson, "Nonresidential Grandparents' Emotional and Financial Involvement in Relation to Early Adolescent Grandchild Outcomes," *Journal of Research on Adolescence* 21, no. 3 (2011): 552–558; Yuli Li et al., "Children's Bonding with Parents and Grandparents and Its Associated Factors," *Child Indicators Research* 9, no. 2 (2016): 551–564; Bernhard Nauck et al., "A Longitudinal Study of the Intergenerational Transmission of Religion," *International Sociology* 24, no. 3 (2009): 325–345; Copen and Silverstein, "Transmission of Religious Beliefs across Generations."

faith and mom's faith and dad's faith, and I'm just wow!" She hopes that her
son will maintain this religious continuity.

The largest number of parents who talked about their grandparents told
about specific rituals and experiences that they taught or encouraged. One
Hispanic Catholic mother explained, for instance, "I remember sitting with
my grandma and my mom doing the rosary in the evening with my dad as
well, and it's funny, it's like a little flashback, and somehow you bring that
up in your own family, so if I do that to her, like they did, maybe she'll do it."
A Hindu father explained, "I tried to teach all the things that I was taught,
especially by my maternal grandmother, who was [the] only person around
when I was growing up. I try to tell her all the verses and all the teachings
that I had." A Jewish mother noted that she was very close to her grandpa,
who taught her some Yiddish, which she recited to us, adding, "And that
is what I've tried to teach my children." Finally a Hispanic Catholic father
explained that parents have an obligation to make sure children are on a religious path, "because as I've told you, my grandmother didn't go, but she sent
me [to church]. Even if I didn't want to go, she sent me." For most of these
respondents, grandparents reinforced rituals, traditions, and habits that they
now want to pass on to their children.

Others talked about how their grandparents taught them religion when
their parents were uninterested or unavailable. For these parents, grandparents
played a surrogate role in instilling religion. As one black Protestant parent related, "My mom didn't sit us down and talk to us about God. I would ask my
grandmother questions. My grandmother was kinda that go-to person when
it came to God." A Hispanic Catholic mother explained that, even though
her entire family is Catholic, "I'm lucky that my grandparents are Catholic
and they passed on that belief to us, because we were five kids, and my dad
died." A Buddhist mother explained that she learned Buddhism from her
grandparents, who founded a temple when they moved to the United States.
She visits the temple now "because I think about my kids' futures."

Differences by Race and Religion

When we analyzed our interviews, we were struck by how many parents from
minority racial groups and religious backgrounds talked about the importance of their nuclear and extended families for their own religious development. Compared to white conservative Protestants, mainline Protestants and
Catholics (the dominant religious traditions in the United States), a higher
proportion of black Protestants, Buddhists, Hindus, Mormons, and Muslims

mentioned the importance of their extended families in cultivating their religious practices, identities, and beliefs.

Some research has found that when the religious tradition of the parents deviates from the majority religion of the surrounding population, parents put more effort into transmitting their family's religion to children.[18] Childhood socialization may matter and require more for adherents of minority faiths since little in the larger culture will be a help. And if the religion of previous generations is going to be transmitted to children, other family members may need to play a greater role. Grandparents may feel more responsibility and likewise minority parents may encourage them to get involved to support their efforts.[19]

African American parents were also more likely than most others to say that their families had an important role in bringing them up in their religion. Many African Americans identify with the traditional black church, which has a long history of political organizing and providing services to the black community.[20] African American parents may view the church as not only offering religious fellowship with fellow believers but also playing an important role in transmitting their political and cultural history.[21] As a result, they may be particularly eager to make sure their children are religiously connected and involved. Black Protestant parents, we have already seen, are more strict and demanding of their children than are white parents. They are also more likely to be confident that their children will return to church if they "stray," compared to many white parents who seemed more inclined to soft-pedal religion out

---

18. Jonathan Kelley and Nan Dirk De Graaf, "National Context, Parental Socialization, and Religious Belief: Results from 15 Nations," *American Sociological Review* 62, no. 4 (1997): 639–659; Sean De Hoon and Frank Van Tubergen, "The Religiosity of Children of Immigrants and Natives in England, Germany, and the Netherlands: The Role of Parents and Peers in Class," *European Sociological Review* 30, no. 2 (2014). Overall, only 7 percent of respondents mentioned their grandparents in discussions about religious faith transmission; however, 3 of the 13 Buddhists (23 percent) we interviewed and 4 of the 14 Hindus (29 percent) mentioned them.

19. Alberto Bisin and Thierry Verdier, "'Beyond the Melting Pot': Cultural Transmission, Marriage, and the Evolution of Ethnic and Religious Traits," *The Quarterly Journal of Economics* 115, no. 3 (2000): 955–988.

20. Neha Sahgal and Greg Smith, "A Religious Portrait of African-Americans," Pew Research Center, January 30, 2009, http://www.pewforum.org/2009/01/30/a-religious-portrait-of-african-americans/; C. Eric Lincoln and Lawrence Mamiya, *The Black Church in the African American Experience* (Durham, NC: Duke University Press, 1990); R. Khari Brown and Ronald Brown, "Faith and Works: Church-Based Social Capital Resources and African American Political Activism," *Social Forces* 82, no. 2 (2003): 617–641.

21. Peter Wielhouwer, "The Impact of Church Activities and Socialization on African-American Religious Commitment," *Social Science Quarterly* 85, no. 3 (2004): 767–792.

of concern to "not shove religion down their kids' throats." African American children no doubt understand their parents' commitments. And we know that these kinds of factors produce a higher level of religiousness among black Protestant youth than whites and Hispanic Catholics.[22]

Religious Similarities and Differences between Parents

Most parents are not raising their children alone, but with a spouse or partner, whose religious experiences were often important for how they approached religion for their children. The parents in our study tended to rate themselves as more similar to their partner in strength of religious belief than different. Many of them had a relatively good relationship with their partner and could recognize the influence of their partner's upbringing in shaping the decisions that they were now making with the religious transmission process. A number of parents mentioned the positive role their spouses and partners played in showing them how to make religion more enjoyable. For instance, one Jewish mother in a same-sex relationship related, "I grew up with this loathing of holidays. Jenny had the opposite experience; even though her family was Orthodox, it was all about family and coming together and this joyousness. That's one area where I did not impose my strong will, and she really set the tone for holidays." Similarly, a Mormon mother told us about how her family now "loves having people from outside their family over on Sundays," which is different from how she was raised. "We've together chosen to raise our kids this way because Timothy wanted to continue that tradition that he had in his family, and I wanted to do the opposite [of my family]." A conservative Protestant mother explained how she used knowledge of her husband's background to convince him to view things differently: "I'm the one who says, 'Come on, understand, Don. You were forced to go to church every Sunday, and you never dared tell your dad 'I don't want to go to church.' Be thankful your children are capable of telling you.'" Coupled parents rarely parent alone, and, whatever influence their experience of their own parents has on the way they pass on religion to their children now, usually their spouses or partners are involved in reinforcing, buffering, or redirecting them.

While many of the parents we interviewed had good relationships with their spouses, differences could be found and conflicts still arouse, even in

---

22. Smith with Denton, *Soul Searching*, 30–71; Smith with Snell, *Souls in Transition*, 103–142.

relatively happy marriages. The major source of religious difference within these relationships tended to center either on the parents having different religions or in differences in their preferred levels of religious engagement. We had some parents who affiliated with two completely different faith traditions like Buddhism and Christianity. But the vast majority (70 percent) of Americans affiliate with a Christian religious tradition.[23] The next largest non-Christian religion is Judaism, which encompasses less than 2 percent of the US population, followed by Muslims (0.9 percent), Hindus (0.7 percent), and Buddhists (0.7 percent). Because the United States is so heavily dominated by Christianity, when parents reported belonging to two different religions, they often meant two different Christian traditions, like Lutheran and Southern Baptist.[24] For some, the different denominations were a real point of contention.[25] As one mainline Protestant father explained to us, "There was something about the church that I found a little bit cold and uninspiring, and then when my wife came over, she went along and she liked it. So we've had endless sorts of tussles over all kinds of things to do with the beliefs and the general atmosphere of the two churches."

While some parents had disagreements that centered on two different religions, denominations, or houses of worship, a larger proportion felt that they differed from their partner in their level of interest in religion and related practices. Religious participation was the major issue about which parents disagreed. As one Mormon mother explained about her husband, "He thinks you don't have to go to church to be like a good person. I don't think you have to for that, but I think church is important because it helps you to focus and you feel the spirit." A Black Protestant father told us about

---

23. An additional 23 percent are unaffiliated. Pew Research Center, "Religion in America: U.S. Religious Data, Demographics and Statistics," *Pew Research Center's Religion & Public Life Project*, 2014 (https://www.pewforum.org/religious-landscape-study/). Accessed August 21, 2019.

24. For those who were married between 2010 and 2014, only about 6 percent of Americans report being in a marriage where there are two completely different religious traditions. About 15 percent report being Christian and having a spouse who belongs to a different Christian tradition. Approximately 18 percent were married to an unaffiliated spouse and 61 percent were married to a spouse of the same religion. See Caryle Murphy, "Interfaith Marriage Is Common in U.S., Particularly among the Recently Wed," *Pew Research Center*, 2015 (https://www.pewresearch.org/fact-tank/2015/06/02/interfaith-marriage/). Accessed August 21, 2019.

25. Some research has found that marriages between people of two different Christian traditions are more durable than those among two completely different religions. See Darren E. Sherkat, "Religious Intermarriage in the United States: Trends, Patterns, and Predictors," *Social Science Research* 33, no. 4 (2004): 606–625.

his frustration in getting his wife to attend religious services with their son, "If you can get your ass up and go to work, why can't you get up and go to church?" While not a point of major disagreement, a Jewish father explained how he differs from his wife in his religious participation. While she will stay at the same shul all day on Yom Kippur, "I do a shul hop. I'll go sit in shul for twenty minutes here, and then I'll walk a mile to a different shul, see what they're doing. I'll spend the whole day going from shul to shul." Parents also differed from each other in how often they preferred to pray, what kind of prayers they said, views about the Bible, religious activities outside of worship services and listening to religious music. As one conservative Protestant husband lamented, "Sharon in her car, [Christian music] that's all she listens to. I just can't get into it."

When parents encountered differences in their religious preferences, how were they addressed? Parents tended to respond in one of two ways. Some of the parents moved forward accepting their partner's position and not trying to change it. If they were married and they wanted their children to have a particular religious upbringing, then they would designate themselves as the primary person for transmitting religion in general or for leading the specific activity with which their partner did not want to be involved. For example, a conservative Protestant mother explained that her husband is a good Christian, but "He just doesn't want to go to church . . . he's not a morning person. And I figure, either eventually he will, or he won't, but the ball is in his court. All I can do is be responsible for myself and my children and he can do what he wants." A mainline Protestant mother explained about her atheist husband, "Pick your battles, talking about religion is not one of the things I choose to battle about. . . . He just knows that religion is my thing just like spanking is his thing." A Jewish mother in a same-sex relationship told us, "I don't need her to be a certain way. I used to want that, like, I wish we were both excited to go to synagogue and do this together. But it's kind of nice that I get the boys to myself."

Some parents came to terms with their spouses' religious differences and moved forward instilling religious beliefs on their own, sometimes with their spouses' blessing. Other parents managed religious differences by compromising their own religious preferences or by either subtly or overtly pushing their spouse to change. For example, a Mormon mother told us about how she will sometimes try to support her more religious husband, "I'm always like 'Go have prayer.' Like, if I'm not there, I'm not doing it. But I do try sometimes to support him." A Buddhist mother explained that her husband does not always want to come to temple because "he has to take care of the house and stuff, but we try to convince him; that's the only day that we can be together—That is our family time." A Hindu mother told us that after her father-in-law died, her husband "started doing certain [Hindu] rituals which are really mandatory and I force him to do [them]. I'm scolding him if he doesn't." Finally, a Jewish father told us that one day his Buddhist wife, said, "'Oh, I want to start going to the Thai Temple.' I was a little bit taken aback. But, I didn't want to fight about it. To me it was more important that my daughter believed in something. And so I just sort of stepped back and we did the Thai temple thing."

So far we have been focused on differences related to parents' religious preferences. A substantial minority of parents also disagreed about how to transmit religion to their children. These differences, which were closely connected to their partner's religious preferences, largely concerned the extent to which parents felt that their children should participate in various religious activities. One Mormon mother told us that "being in the church makes me happy, but he doesn't think our kids, you know should have to go to church if they don't want to, and so that kind of has affected our relationship, too." A mainline Protestant mother described a conversation she had with her ex-husband when they were still married: "I didn't want anything to do with [religion] at that point. He was always saying, 'Well, we need you to take the kids to church.' 'Well what about you?' You know, he was always trying to pass it off onto somebody else."

Differences in parents' religious preferences tended to have repercussions for how parents tried to transmit religion to their children. In some cases, the more religious parent would have their children remain religiously involved, regardless of the spouse's support. A nominally Catholic father who has an Episcopalian wife would have liked his children to be involved with the Catholic Church, but "I had no ground to stand on. I wasn't going to church so what am I going to say? 'No! We gotta do it my way.'" Their children, therefore, attend his wife's Episcopalian Church. In other cases, the more religious parent limited their children's engagement in religious activities and practices to better match that of the less religious spouse. A Jewish mother who sees herself as more religious than her husband explained, "He's not really into attending religious services. And I think that does play out in terms of our activities as a family together. Some things that I would want to participate in or I'd want to go to he would not want to go to."

When parents in intact relationships looked back on the history of their relationship, there tended to be a time point, typically at the beginning, when they had some religion-related disagreements and developed a joint strategy for how they would manage religious transmission. A Hispanic Catholic mother who has a Protestant husband explained that early in their marriage "he wasn't as religious or going to church and I think it was more difficult when our son was first born." Now it was no longer an issue and they have agreed to have their children involved in both churches. A black Protestant mother told us about her formerly Muslim husband: "Now we've gotten to the point where we're more similar, but when we first started dating, he was practicing Islam. I don't have anything against Islam. Believe what you believe, but it's just been that tension. We're closer now as adults." Another Catholic mother noted, "He wasn't very religious when we first got married, and it wasn't until after we had our son Timmy that he started taking interest in going to church . . . now we've worked that out."

In contrast to the parents who seemed to have come to terms with their partners' religious differences, a minority of parents felt that religion remained a point of conflict, which was sometimes related to larger struggles. As one Mormon mother explained about her second husband, "He says he's an atheist, but, you know, deep down, probably not, but that's what he says . . . and those are related to some of our personal issues. We approach life from a different perspective." Another Mormon mother lamented, "I wish that we could do [religious] things that we're supposed to do as a family, and I just kind of feel like we're divided."

Ex-Partners and Religious Faith Transmission

About 63 percent of our sample was in a heterosexual marriage with the parent of their child, another 17 percent were remarried, and 17 percent were single, with the remaining being in same-sex relationships. Previous research has found that compared to people from intact families, young adults who are the product of divorce have substantially lower levels of religious involvement.[26] We compared the parents from intact families to those from single or divorced families in their religious socialization practices. Some key differences emerged in their level of contact and coordination with the other parent.

---

26. Jeremy E. Uecker and Christopher G. Ellison, "Parental Divorce, Parental Religious Characteristics, and Religious Outcomes in Adulthood," *Journal for the Scientific Study of Religion* 51, no. 4 (2012): 777–794. Jiexia Elisa Zhai, Christopher. G. Ellison, Norvall. D. Glenn, and Elizabeth Marquardt, "Parental Divorce and Religious Involvement among Young Adults," *Sociology of Religion* 68, no. 2: 125–144.

Some of the single and divorced parents noted religious differences between them and their former partner. A lot of these differences focused on interactions that they had when they were still coupled. For example, a Catholic divorced mother explained that her ex-husband "didn't really go to church." Because of that experience she now wants "a partner in life. I want someone who will go and do [things] with me, and that includes church." Some parents also mentioned differences in how they perceived the other parent's actions. For example, a divorced Muslim mother whose ex-husband was Christian described his affair as "a sin in all faiths," which has been "very traumatic for the children." While single and divorced parents made some comments about their ex-partner's religious beliefs, they were relatively limited, especially compared to the long discussions we had with married parents about religion-related differences with their current partner.

A primary reason why the discussions about ex-partners' religious beliefs were not extensive was because single and divorced parents had so many fewer interactions with each other, in part, because they were no longer in a romantic relationship. Their more limited involvement in each other's lives shaped the extent to which they were willing and able to coordinate a joint plan for transmitting religion to their children.[27] Often, these parents would hear about something the other parent did after it happened and then work on their own to address or correct it. As a single conservative Protestant mother explained to us, 'There is a lot that we don't coordinate. There's a lot that I won't even know about until it comes out in a major conversation [with my child] . . . I see that Mike is not walking with God and so I can't expect someone who's not walking with God to have beliefs, so I don't try to get him to say a script. I just hope that Sammy has enough of a foundation in his own walk to know what's right." A divorced conservative Protestant father lamented, "My ex-wife gave me a text message saying oh Carol accepted God in her life on her own. When my daughter gets home, I'm speaking to her and she knows nothing about that stuff." He goes on to say that while he is not opposed to her accepting God, he feels like his ex-wife coerced her, "You know, she's five years old. Not saying that she can't understand, but there's certain things that a child won't understand."

---

27. Parents with shared religious beliefs are more likely to stay together, so divorced and single parents may have always been less religiously similar and possibly less willing to coordinate and compromise. See Christopher Ellison, Amy Burdette, and W. Bradford Wilcox, "The Couple That Prays Together: Race and Ethnicity, Religion, and Relationship Quality among Working-Age Adults," *Journal of Marriage and Family* 72, no. 4 (2010): 963–975.

Rather than coordinate and compromise, divorced and single parents tended to work independently to transmit religious belief when they could. If they had access to their children on Sunday and wanted them to attend religious services, then they would take them. A conservative Protestant single mother who regularly takes her son to church explained, "You know we switch back and forth what days we have him, but since he's been born, Sundays I always have him." But if the parent did not have custody on the day of worship, then they had to come to terms with the other parent's decision about whether or not their child would participate in religious activities that day. A Catholic father explained, "When I took them to church on my Sundays that was fine, but she didn't go to church and I was like, 'Well, can I pick the kids up on your Sunday and just take them to church and bring them back?' 'No.' You know that was always a fight."

These parents were not satisfied. But the boundaries around when they had access to their children were so clearly drawn and their interpersonal interactions with each other so limited and strained that they either did not want to or could not coordinate a joint plan for religious transmission. One conservative Protestant mother lamented that her son is now viewing religion in ways that she disapproves, which she attributes to her son's father; "I think he ultimately sees [Christianity] probably how his dad sees it. You can still live your life however you want, sleep with whoever you want, do whatever and still call yourself Christian."

Some currently married parents also had children that were not as religious as they preferred, which they attributed to their less religious spouse. But, in contrast to divorced and single parents, married parents were much more likely to mention their spouse's positive influence, and their willingness to compromise and address religious differences. As this Catholic mother explains about her husband, "We talk about it pretty often where he says if he hadn't married me, he would have been much more rigid and more conservative in his thinking. He says that our conversations have helped him evolve to be a little bit more open with the kids and talk to them."

Our interviews with single and divorced parents offer some insight into why children from these families are significantly less likely to participate in religious services as young adults. Compared to others, divorced and single parents are less likely to discuss their own religious beliefs with their ex-partner and be influenced by him or her. Relatedly, they are less willing or able to compromise and coordinate a joint plan for instilling religious belief in their children.

Conclusion

A variety of factors can shape how religious parents approach passing on religion to their children. In most cases, however, the most important influence is how they themselves were raised religiously by their parents. American parents are not "cultural dopes" who blindly follow their parents' attempts at socialization. People evaluate what is provided to them, sometimes positively, sometimes very negatively. Anyone who wants to explain how and why things operate as they do in one intergenerational link of the chain, between parents and children, needs to go back one generational link and understand the experience of the parents when they were children. In almost all cases, that provides the baseline orientation that everything subsequent may or may not change. Even so, that is not a simple dynamic, as we have seen in this chapter. Parental influences on parents who in turn seek to influence their children are themselves shaped by parenting style, religious tradition, race and ethnicity, the possible presence of grandparents, and the moderating role of spouses and ex-partners. Here we demonstrate the importance of accounting for such factors. Further research is needed to better understand in greater detail the various ways that they work in complex processes to produce different parental approaches to passing on religion to children.

7

Parents' Expectations
of Religious Congregations

THIS CHAPTER EXAMINES how American religious parents think about and engage their religious congregations as part of their task of socializing their children religiously. We begin by examining survey data on the extent of parental and child participation in religious congregations and how that differs across religious traditions. We will see that most parents see themselves, rather than their congregations, as primarily responsible for the religious acculturation of their children. They do so in part because many have chosen their congregations for practical reasons, they have a lot of confidence in their grasp of religion, and they want to be involved in all aspects of their children's lives, including their religious development. The second part of the chapter explores what parents think congregations legitimately contribute to the task. These include providing religious education, helping to make religion fun, and transmitting cultural traditions.

Variation in Children's Engagement
with Congregations

In the United States, many parents attend, and have children who regularly attend, services at religious congregations. Finding from the 2012 Culture of American Families Survey shows that 35 percent of all American parents report attending religious services at least weekly; and 42 percent of all American parents and 67 percent of religiously "devout"[1] parents report that

---

1. Those who say that faith is very important or the most important thing in life and/or who report attending religious services at least weekly.

their children attend religious services weekly (see Table 4.8 in Chapter 4). (We have good reason to believe that these numbers are probably inflated by social desirability bias and other factors, perhaps by as much as 35 percent, in our estimation.[2] Nevertheless, these statistics indicate that at least a substantial minority of US parents and children attend religious services, and that many parents perceive that children attending religious services is [considered to be] a good thing, which itself is a telling fact.)

Research also reveals religious tradition differences in religious service attendance (see Table 4.8 in Chapter 4 for specific statistics). American religions, traditions, and denominations vary in the demands they make on their adherents and their success in winning adherence to their religious prescriptions.[3] These demands may include restrictions on or requirements about food (e.g., not eating pork), dress (e.g., wearing the hijab), social interactions (e.g., not consorting with unrelated members of the opposite sex), and religious service attendance. Rational choice theory makes the argument that while having abundant restrictions can make a religion less desirable for many people, under the right circumstances the exact opposite may occur.[4] Religious adherents may feel that their many sacrifices for their religion provide a special relationship with God, a better life now, a rewarding future, and so on. The adherents of demanding religions tend to find themselves engaged in activities with others who are similar in their religion and relationship with God.[5] These more dedicated followers are likely to reinforce individuals' religious beliefs and provide a community in which to engage in rewarding activities together.[6] Demanding religions also weed out "free

2. C. Kirk Hadaway, Penny Long Marler, and Mark Chaves, "What the Polls Don't Show: A Closer Look at U.S. Church Attendance," *American Sociological Review* 58 (1993): 741–752; Robert Woodberry, "When Surveys Lie and People Tell the Truth: How Surveys Over-Sample Church Attenders," *American Sociological Review* 63 (1998): 119–122; C. Kirk Hadaway, Penny Long Marler, and Mark Chaves, "Overreporting Church Attendance in America: Evidence That Demands the Same Verdict," *American Sociological Review* 63 (1998): 122–130.

3. Laurence R. Iannaccone, "Why Strict Churches Are Strong," *American Journal of Sociology* 99, no. 5 (1994): 1180–1211.

4. Iannaccone, "Why Strict Churches Are Strong"; Rodney Stark, "Why Religious Movements Succeed or Fail: A Revised General Model," *Journal of Contemporary Religion* 11, no. 2 (1996): 133–146.

5. Christopher Scheitle and Amy Adamczyk, "It Takes Two: The Interplay of Individual and Group Theology on Social Embeddedness," *Journal for the Scientific Study of Religion* 48, no. 1 (2009): 16–29.

6. Anna Grzymala-Busse, "Good Clubs and Community Support: Explaining the Growth of Strict Religions," *Journal of Church and State* 56, no. 2 (2014): 269–299.

riders," those who want to benefit from a rich religious community without contributing much to it. These ideas suggest that "strict" religions, those that are more demanding, will have more committed congregants who are particularly concerned about passing on their religion to their children and, as a result, be more likely to bring them to religious activities. This is what the data show.

Mormons and Muslims are typically considered among the strictest religions in the United States, followed by conservative or evangelical Protestants, which include Southern Baptists and Missouri Synod Lutherans.[7] More lenient traditions include Catholicism and mainline Protestantism (e.g., Episcopalian, United Methodist, Presbyterian Church USA). American Jews are a unique group in this framework—many feel "ethnically" strongly connected to their tradition, whether conceived religiously or culturally, but compared to most other faiths, they tend to have lower levels of religious engagement.[8] Among devoted Mormons, 98 percent say that their children attend religious services at least weekly. They are followed by conservative Protestants at 75 percent. Sixty-one percent of devout black Protestants, 62 percent of devout Catholics, and 64 percent of devout mainline Protestants say that their children regularly attend religious services. Jews report the smallest percentage of devout parents reporting that their children regularly attend services, at 27 percent. Compared to parents of other faiths, Mormons and conservative and black Protestants are also more likely to regularly to talk with their children about religion (see Table 4.8 in Chapter 4).[9]

Table 7.1 reports findings from more sophisticated statistical analyses (logistic regression) about whether religious affiliation or parents' religious devotion is more powerfully associated with their children getting regular exposure to religion. Simple bivariate statistics data from the Culture of

---

7. ASARB, *2010 US Religion Census: Religious Congregations & Membership Study: Collected by the Association of Statisticians of American Religious Bodies (ASARB) and Distributed by the Association of Religion Data Archives (www.theARDA.com)* (Association of Statisticians of American Religious Bodies, 2012); Brian Steensland et al., "The Measure of American Religion: Toward Improving the State of the Art," *Social Forces* 79, no. 1 (2000): 291–318.

8. Adam Cohen and Peter Hill, "Religion as Culture: Religious Individualism and Collectivism among American Catholics, Jews, and Protestants," *Journal of Personality* 75, no. 4 (2007): 709–742; Pew Research Center, "A Portrait of Jewish Americans: Findings from a Pew Research Center Survey of U.S. Jews" (Washington, DC, 2013), http://www.pewforum.org/files/2013/10/jewish-american-full-report-for-web.pdf.

9. While our interviews included parents from several non-Christian religious traditions, the survey data presented here do not include them all because the survey sample sizes for some of these groups were too small for reliable analyses.

Table 7.1 Odds Ratios from Logistic Regression Models Predicting Parents' Faith Transmission Practices, by Parents' Religiosity

	Talks about Faith with Child at Least Weekly			Child Attends Religious Services at Least Weekly		
	Religious Tradition Only	With Importance of Faith and Religious Attendance	With All Controls	Religious Tradition Only	With Importance of Faith and Religious Attendance	With All Controls
Religious Tradition						
Mainline Protestant	1.09	1.25	1.12	1.17	1.41	1.5
Conservative Protestant	2.93*	1.36	1.17	2.92*	1.46	1.36
Black Protestant	4.46*	1.71	0.48	2.41*	0.89	0.98
Unitarian	0.38*	1.48	1.21	0.36*	1.08	1.27
Mormon	8.39*	1.72	1.24	36.62	7.4*	7.48*
Jewish	0.49	0.51	0.47	0.45	0.39	0.35
Buddhist	0.25*	0.57	0.43	0.18*	0.52	0.68
Other religion	1.35	1.26	1.19	0.91	0.68	0.82
No religion	0.3*	1.15	0.89	0.33*	1.47	1.76

Reference category = Catholic

Importance of Faith

Very important/most important thing in life	7.61*	7.58*			1.47	2.17*
Somewhat important	3.17*	3.1*			1.15	1.41
Reference category = Not at all/not very important						
Attends religious services at least weekly	3.83*	4.59*			21.17*	23.54*
Considers being persons of faith very important or essential for their children	3.71*	3.83*			2.67*	2.55*
F goodness-of-fit statistic	28.22	23.65	11.56	19.65	9.22	15.56
Number of cases	2822	2822	2822	2822	2822	2822

*p < 0.05 level.

Note: Controls (not shown) include both demographic and marriage/partnership variables. Demographic variables include parent gender, parent age, race/ethnicity, household income, parent educational attainment, and region of residence. Marriage/partnership variables include marital status, degree of parenting support from spouse/partner, religious homogamy of spouse/partner, and household structure/parent employment.

Source: Culture of American Families Survey, 2012.

American Families Survey, 2012, show that Mormons and conservative and black Protestants are more likely than Catholics to talk weekly with their children about religion and have them attend religious services. However, when parental importance of faith and religious service attendance are statistically controlled for in Table 7.1, all of the religious tradition differences disappear, except for the Mormon association with parents talking regularly with children about religion (the odds ratios of statistically significant differences are bolded).[10] What remains most important are parents' own importance of faith (especially for children's service attendance), parents' religious service attendance (especially for regularly talking with children about religion), and parents' belief that it is very important or essential that children be persons of faith.

This does *not* mean that religious traditions do not matter. They do. But the way they matter most, according to these results, is by generating differences in levels of parental religiousness, which is what finally drives children's service attendance and conversations with parents about religious matters. Stated differently, parents of every other religious tradition examined, including Mormonism and conservative Protestantism, if they all shared the same (let's say moderate) levels of importance of faith and religious service attendance, would be no more likely to have children attending religious services weekly or more often than Catholic parents of those same levels of parental religiousness. Religious traditions produce different results with children, but not directly, but rather by more successfully "demanding" that their parents are more highly religious, which in turn shapes child religiousness. If Mormon children attend services more, it is because their parents do so more and hold faith as more important in their lives. If Catholic children attend services less, it is because Catholic parents tend to do those things less. Stated differently yet again, children of highly religious Catholic parents will attend Mass more

---

10. The only religious affiliation that remains significantly different from the others is Latter Day Saints. Mormon parents are more likely than Catholics and almost all of the other groups to regularly have their child attend religious services. Heavy congregational engagement is such a big part of being a Latter Day Saint that it would be difficult for someone to identify as Mormon and not regularly attend. If they stopped engaging, then the Mormon Church may also limit their ties to them. Conversely, many Catholics may attend religious services less than once a year and still consider themselves Catholic and the Catholic Church would still consider them members. See Darren Sherkat, *Changing Faith: The Dynamics and Consequences of Americans' Shifting Religious Identities* (New York: NYU Press, 2014); Melvyn Hammarberg, *The Mormon Quest for Glory: The Religious World of the Latter-Day Saints* (New York: Oxford University Press, 2013).

frequently than children of not-very-religious Mormon parents. In the final analysis, parent religiousness, not religious tradition, is destiny.

Parent Satisfaction with Congregations

How satisfied are religious parents with their religious congregations? According to Figure 7.1, about 70 percent of American Catholic and Protestant parents report that they are satisfied or very satisfied with what their congregations offer youth. Conservative Protestant parents are more likely than Catholic and mainline Protestant parents to say that they are satisfied or very satisfied with the youth services provided—at 79, 64, and 72 percent, respectively. But these differences are not huge and in every case the large majority are satisfied.

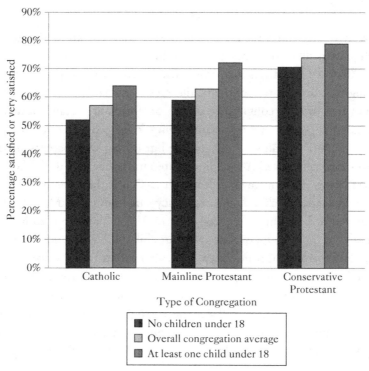

FIGURE 7.1 Percentage satisfied or very satisfied with what their congregation is offering for youth (age 18 and under) (weighted percentages).

Note: There are many more congregants without children under 18, leading to an overall average that is skewed toward this group.

Source: US Congregational Life Survey, Wave 2, 2008/2009, Random Sample Attender Survey.

In our interviews, many parents mentioned their relative happiness with their religious congregations generally and the youth programs and resources offered specifically. A mother from a mainline Protestant congregation, for instance, explained, "Honestly, I don't see myself wanting to go to another church at this point, because that's home to me. I feel if I'm having a bad week and I go there and listen to the sermon and the pastor, I feel at peace." Likewise, a conservative Protestant father said, "I'm happy with where we're going to church and I like our involvement. I think the kids are getting a lot out of it." A black Protestant mother similarly told us, "I love the music. And the preacher, the way he's preaching, the way he gets it out. Because when they say it, the way they say it, the kids' eyes open up." Very few of the parents we interviewed complained or expressed unhappiness with their religious congregations.

"It's My Responsibility, Not My Congregation's"

Given their high approval ratings, we were curious to know the extent to which parents relied on congregations to help transmit religion to their children. What we heard was surprising. The vast majority of parents felt that the religious acculturation of their children was primarily their responsibility and not that of their congregations.[11] As one black Protestant mother said, "I think parents are more important because kids need to see you practicing what you say. They can see other people but if their own parents are doing it, that's more effective." A mainline Protestant father told us, "I feel like it starts at home. At home my kids learned the 'Our Father' prayer; it's not like they learned that in church and then they came home." A Mormon father concurred: "I don't think [the congregation's] sole purpose is to help us as parents. They're not supposed to raise our children." We could provide very many more corroborating interview quotes but will stop here, since we already sounded this theme in Chapter 1 and developed it extensively in a related book.[12] But the brevity of this section does not indicate the central importance of this finding: nearly all American religious parents we interviewed held low expectations of their religious congregations concerning responsibility for socializing their children religiously. That was the job of parents.

11. Catholics were one of the religious groups that had a slightly smaller percentage of parents who reported that they were primarily responsible for religious faith transmission, though the majority still believed, like the others, that they were primarily responsible.

12. Smith, Ritz, and Rotolo, *Religious Parenting*.

The contribution of congregations was always only secondary and supportive. We have already partly theorized in Chapter 2 why parents have become such important players in the process of children's religious socialization. In the following pages we continue our analysis by focusing on related but different kinds of explanations.

Changing Times and Increased Parental Devotion

American families have undergone major changes since the 1960s.[13] Many more parents are divorced or unmarried today compared to a half-century ago, and a much higher proportion of women are employed outside of the home.[14] Single parents of children are likely to be working full-time and have more constraints on their time available to engage in and talk about religious activities. In dual-income households, the time available for parents to spend with their kids and on religious activities would also seem to be more limited. In some ways, many American religious congregations have changed a lot, too. Often, especially moderate and large-sized congregations have youth ministers specifically devoted to pastoring kids. Many offer other programs and activities dedicated for children, like Sunday school classes, Bible study, and parts of the religious service are sometimes set aside for a "children's sermon."[15]

Despite changes in family configuration and drastic increases in the proportion of mothers working outside of the home, extensive social science research has shown that, compared to earlier decades, many parents today are not spending less time with their children.[16] The amount of time that parents spend with their children today rivals the time spent in the 1960s.[17] The continued

---

13. Tamara Hareven, "Historical Changes in the Family and the Life Course: Implications for Child Development," *Monographs of the Society for Research in Child Development* (1985): 8–23.

14. Pew Research Center, "Parenting in America: Outlook, Worries, Aspirations Are Strongly Linked to Financial Situation," 2015, http://www.pewsocialtrends.org/files/2015/12/2015-12-17_parenting-in-america_FINAL.pdf.

15. Mark Chaves, *Congregations in America* (Cambridge, MA: Harvard University Press, 2004).

16. Suzanne Bianchi, "Maternal Employment and Time with Children: Dramatic Change or Surprising Continuity?," *Demography* 37, no. 4 (2000): 401–414; John Sandberg and Sandra Hofferth, "Changes in Children's Time with Parents: United States, 1981–1997," *Demography* 38, no. 3 (2001): 423–436.

17. Liana Sayer, Suzanne Bianchi, and John Robinson, "Are Parents Investing Less in Children? Trends in Mothers' and Fathers' Time with Children 1," *American Journal of Sociology* 110, no. 1 (2004): 1–4.

relatively large amount of time that parents devote to their children offers some insight into why they seem to put so much responsibility on themselves, as opposed to congregations, for transmitting religious beliefs and practices.

Parents today compared to the 1960s also have achieved higher levels of education and are bearing children later in life, leading to changes in child-rearing norms and values. Parents today have greater desire to invest in their children. As a result, they tend to want to spend a lot of time with them and are likely to be child-centric, much more so than in the 1960s.[18] This was reflected in our interviews with parents. As one black Protestant mother explained about being responsible for her child's education:

> They're not supposed to raise our children. You see what I'm saying?
> No, I think you need to be more involved with [your] child. I'm
> sending my child to church, okay, but what are you doing at home out-
> side of church and school? Are you teaching them? Because it starts in
> the home; it doesn't start at church or school.

A mainline Protestant father concurred, "Okay, the responsibility of the parents, first is to remind the children of their obligation, get them ready for church, they have to encourage them, to go to church and go with them, and you have to check with them, you know, what did you learn in church, do you understand?"

Over the last 50 years, the way children spend their time has also changed. In previous generations, it was common for children to spend a lot of unstructured time with other kids. But neighborhoods and norms have changed, limiting opportunities for such causal play.[19] Since the 1960s, there have also been growing concerns about children's safety.[20] Combined, these factors have led to a proliferation of structured extracurricular children's activities.[21] To get to them, parents often have to ferry their children in real or proverbial minivans, resulting in considerable increases in the amount of time parents spend with

---

18. Sayer, Bianchi, and Robinson, "Are Parents Investing Less in Children?"

19. Sanford Gaster, "Urban Children's Access to Their Neighborhood: Changes over Three Generations," *Environment and Behavior* 23, no. 1 (1991): 70–85.

20. Markella Rutherford, "Children's Autonomy and Responsibility: An Analysis of Childrearing Advice," *Qualitative Sociology* 32, no. 4 (2009): 337–353.

21. Sandra Hofferth and John Sandberg, "Changes in American Children's Time, 1981–1997," *Advances in Life Course Research* 6 (2001): 193–229; Demie Kurz, "Work–Family Issues of Mothers of Teenage Children," *Qualitative Sociology* 23, no. 4 (2000): 435–451.

their children commuting. We do not have data on how often parents spoke with their children about religion in earlier decades. But evidence suggests that today the amount of time parents spend talking with them about religion is not inconsiderable, with more than 50 percent claiming to do that at least once a week (see Table 4.8 in Chapter 4).

Parents have also become more emotionally invested in their children in recent decades, so the pressure to devote a lot of time and energy to providing them a good childhood has likewise increased.[22] For example, homeschooling, a highly labor-intensive form of parenting, has substantially increased over the last two decades.[23] While much responsibility for children's development still lies with mothers, fathers are also expected to devote a lot of time to helping their children develop.[24] So, when asked if he wants to shoulder the responsibility of passing on religious faith to his children, one conservative Protestant father replied:

Yes, yeah. I want to. I believe I hold responsibility and I have to hold responsibility for the knowledge of God that my children have. If the church is replacing that because I'm lax in my job, so be it. Can they do it? Yes, they can be the sole provider of spiritual information and spiritual insight. But I don't think as a parent that is their responsibility. I believe that's my responsibility.

Most Parents Are Comfortable Representing Their Religion

In addition to changing social institutions, norms, and values, our interviews suggested some other factors for why parents depend more on themselves than their congregation for transmitting religion to their children. Many American religious parents who we interviewed actually felt moderately comfortable discussing religion with their offspring and engaging with them in a variety of religious activities and rituals, ranging from talking about morality

---

22. Viviana Zelizer, *Pricing the Priceless Child: The Changing Social Value of Children* (Princeton, NJ: Princeton University Press, 1994).

23. Mitchell Stevens, *Kingdom of Children: Culture and Controversy in the Homeschooling Movement* (Princeton, NJ: Princeton University Press, 2009).

24. Anita Ilta Garey, *Weaving Work and Motherhood* (Philadelphia: Temple University Press, 1999); Anna Dienhart, "Make Room for Daddy: The Pragmatic Potentials of a Tag-Team Structure for Sharing Parenting," *Journal of Family Issues* 22, no. 8 (2001): 973–999.

to cooking Shabbat dinner to explaining what happens to the body and soul after death. As a single black Protestant mother noted, "We're very open about talking about what happens to the body, to be absent from the body is to be present with God, so they understand that because I've talked to them for so long about repenting." A Jewish mother told us that around Passover, "I really clean the house. And I do that also to transmit it to my children. They see it and we talk about it." Another black Protestant mother said that she "purposely" studies the Bible in public parts of the house where her son can see her, as opposed to in her bedroom.

Later in this chapter we explain that one of the things congregations provide for children is an opportunity to learn about religious scriptures and how they apply to life. Many parents think this role is valuable, yet many also feel quite comfortable talking to their children about religion themselves (for nationally representative quantitative data on these practices, see Chapter 4). To be qualified to guide and answer their children's questions, a lot of parents (typically the more devout) said that it was their responsibility to regularly read religious texts. As one conservative Protestant father explained, "If they got questions, we should have the ability to answer, or to say 'I don't have an answer now, I gotta do some research and ask around and get back to you.'" Another black Protestant father said that he regularly reads and "refers back to the Bible for knowledge, use it as a guide. I think that's very important." A Mormon father explained, "And every day, we read the scriptures, we don't go a day without reading the scriptures. Before we read the scriptures, we'll sing a little hymn. And then we'll say a prayer." And a black Protestant mother told us, "I teach my kids about the Lord. They can talk about the Word. We have little quizzes, little Bible studies."

This does not mean that all parents endorsed all that their religions teach. Some parents thought it was important that they themselves be theologically informed and the overwhelming majority felt comfortable talking with their children about religion. But some parents also said that they thought their religion was too legalistic or taught rules that were difficult to reconcile. For example, one Jewish mother told us, "I'm very logical and linear, and if things don't make sense, I have a very hard time with them. And there were just certain things that just didn't work for me [in Judaism] about rules and structure that didn't make sense." Other parents noted that, although they were comfortable introducing their children to their religion, they still harbored some doubts about them. One Mormon mother, for example, confessed:

I just don't see, how do I say that? It's like a contradiction. I see where organized religion is good, especially when you're raising children, you have a set of values it's like following a syllabus, you know what you're supposed to do. But, when I look at it individually, I don't feel like I necessarily need organized religion.

Possibly because of their own struggles, some parents were hesitant to rely heavily on congregations for training their kids, especially in a culture where parents are expected to devote so much time and energy to raising their children. Parents who were not religious were particularly leery about the role of congregations in transmitting religion to children.

These findings about parents' sense of self-competence and responsibility surprised us somewhat. That is because of our familiarity with a common stereotype among and sometimes complaint from congregational youth ministers and some clergy that parents often back away from taking responsibility for the religious raising of their children, claiming ignorance and incompetence in the matter. That stereotype must have some basis in fact. But it did not show up much in our interviews. The parents with whom we conversed are admittedly all formally affiliated with some religious congregation, so that must make them more competent to socialize their children than most nominally religious parents. But we also intentionally sampled both more and less active congregation members, so we did not only talk with congregational "superstar" parents. Perhaps what parents project to congregational staff and what the latter interpret from parents' behaviors or from what their children (not purely objectively) report differs considerably for some reason from what parents told us. We cannot say based on our data. (Few youth ministers, let us note, are unbiased observers and actors in the larger youth formation and family interaction process.) We merely report here what we heard from parents, which must be taken seriously. Any discrepancy between our findings and stereotypes to the contrary merits further research.

Congregational Proximity and Realistic Expectations

Another factor that may help explain parents' limited expectations of congregations concerns a constraint on their realistic options: geographic proximity. A few families commute long distances to their congregations. But most want shorter drives from home. Once the constraint of religious tradition is added to the equation, many parents face somewhat limited choices of congregations. It appears to us that they select the most viable option they have and adjust their expectations accordingly. Better, the logic goes, to attend a congregation that is accessible if not ideal than one that is perfect but very far away. And part of those trade-offs involves setting realistic expectancies about what the more convenient options might provide. That, too, likely contributes to many parents' readiness to take on the primary responsibility to raise their children religiously and not demand too much from or invest too much in their religious congregations.

The US Congregational Life Survey conducted in 2008 and 2009 asked how many minutes it took respondents to commute to their religious congregations. We present the results for parents in the three largest religious traditions in Figure 7.2. Here we see that the majority of parents in these traditions drive only 15 minutes or less to their churches. One in five lives within a 5-minute drive from their church. Only small minorities drive more than 20 minutes to church. Conservative Protestant parents—who are more inclined to "church shop" to find a congregation that meets their "spiritual needs"—were the most likely to drive longer distances to church than mainline Protestants and Catholics, although those differences are not enormous.

This choice for geographical proximity showed up in our interviews. One conservative Protestant father told us that, because they were previously driving 45 minutes to church each way, "distance was an issue" and "we found ourselves missing more than going," so they "decided it was time to find a church that was local." A Catholic mother explained that her family initially chose their church because of "proximity," but "once we got in there we really liked it." Another conservative Protestant father recounted that when his family first moved, "we had no idea where we were going to go to church. So we found our new church on a website and to us it didn't seem that far. It's about twenty-five minutes."

Previous research has found that distance is one factor in congregation choice.[25] Those in religious traditions with geographical parish models (e.g., Catholics, Mormons, Orthodox Jews) or stronger denominational loyalties (e.g., Missouri Synod Lutherans) are expected to attend designated congregations, and typically do. As one Catholic father told us, his family attends their particular parish because "it's the one we're technically in. You know, they try to split up [i.e., assign the boundaries of] these parishes for a

---

25. William Swatos and Peter Kivisto, "Parish by McKinney," in *Encyclopedia of Religion and Society* (Walnut Creek, CA: Rowman Altamira, 1998); Ram Cnaan and Daniel Curtis, "Religious Congregations as Voluntary Associations: An Overview," *Nonprofit and Voluntary Sector Quarterly* 42, no. 1 (2013): 7–33; Jill Witmer Sinha et al., "Proximity Matters: Exploring Relationships among Neighborhoods, Congregations, and the Residential Patterns of Members," *Journal for the Scientific Study of Religion* 46, no. 2 (2007): 245–260. But see William D'Antonio, *Laity, American and Catholic: Transforming the Church* (xxx: Rowman & Littlefield, 1996).

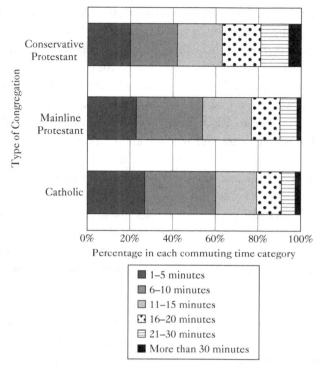

FIGURE 7.2 Commuting time from home to congregation for parents with children age 18 and under (weighted percentages).

Source: US Congregational Life Survey, Wave 2, 2008/2009, Random Sample Attender Survey.

reason, so unless it's a big problem, you should just go to your own parish." Organizational change for congregational choice is afoot, however, even in those traditions.[26] Traditions that are naturally amenable to a "free market" approach (e.g., conservative Protestantism) provide greater choice among congregational options offering variety in worship styles, clergy personalities, and programming.[27] Some scholars argue that this helps to explain their relatively stronger religious vitality.[28]

---

26. See, for example, Tricia Colleen Bruce, *Parish and Place: Making Room for Diversity in the American Catholic Church* (New York: Oxford University Press, 2017).

27. Nancy T. Ammerman, "Organized Religion in a Voluntaristic Society," *Sociology of Religion* 58, no. 3 (1997): 203–215.

28. Roger Finke and Rodney Stark, *The Churching of America, 1776-2005: Winners and Losers in Our Religious Economy* (Brunswick, NJ: Rutgers University Press, 2005); Rodney Stark and Roger Finke, *Acts of Faith: Explaining the Human Side of Religion* (Berkeley: University of California Press, 2000). In this way conservative Protestant parents are similar to parents

Immigration, race, and ethnicity also matter. Many first- and second-generation immigrants we interviewed mentioned driving further to attend a congregation that would help their children feel more at home and learn more about their culture. When asked how they chose their temple, one Buddhist mother replied, "I go there because I want my daughter to meet the Thai people, because around here we don't have many Thai." Some parents want a service in their native language, even if that means a longer drive. One Hispanic Catholic mother said that the church they like "is far away from us, about 40 minutes from here." Still, "for all the years we've been living in the USA, we continue to enjoy the Mass in Spanish more, and that is what we seek."

African American parents were also less likely to mention proximity as a factor in choosing their churches, and more likely to attend their family or spouse's "home" church. As one African American Catholic mother said, "I've been going there since I was born. I like the people there because it's a small church so everybody knows each other." A black Protestant father explained, "I have quite a few family members here, you know, cousins, aunts, uncles. I'm here, everybody knows me, it's kind of like being in your neighborhood for a while." Most congregations in America are racially and ethnically segregated, and our interviews suggested that parents are willing to commute further so their children can be in a congregation with an ethnic and racial profile they prefer.[29] Findings from the US Congregation Life Survey indicate that about 12 percent of African Americans report commuting more than 30 minutes to church, compared to only 3 percent of the rest of the sample.

Such differences are worth noting, but they are not the main story. Most American religious parents seem concerned about having a reasonable commute. Few are prepared to drive long distances to attend "the perfect" church,

---

who are particularly concerned about their children's education and thus move to an area with better schools, whose children commute longer distances to better schools, or who invest time and energy into home schooling. See Jennifer Jellison Holme, "Buying Homes, Buying Schools: School Choice and the Social Construction of School Quality," *Harvard Educational Review* 72, no. 2 (2002): 177–206; Amanda M. Fairbanks, "The Trip to Bronx Science: A Long Ride to a Choice School," *New York Times*, February 12, 2008, http://www.nytimes.com/2008/02/12/nyregion/12bus.html; Stevens, *Kingdom of Children*.

29. Michael Emerson and Christian Smith, *Divided by Faith: Evangelical Religion and the Problem of Race in America* (New York: Oxford University Press, 2000); Michael Lipka, "Many U.S. Congregations Are Still Racially Segregated, but Things Are Changing," *Pew Research Center* (blog), December 8, 2014, http://www.pewresearch.org/fact-tank/2014/12/08/many-u-s-congregations-are-still-racially-segregated-but-things-are-changing-2/; also see Omar McRoberts, *Streets of Glory: Church and Community in a Black Urban Neighborhood* (Chicago: University of Chicago Press, 2005).

mosque, synagogue, or temple, even if such an ideal option exists. And that inevitably limits their choices. Being, in our experience, largely realistic and reasonable people, most parents seem to adjust the expectations they hold of the religious congregations they choose to modest levels that will not lead to disappointment. And that too fits with their larger belief that they and not their congregations are primarily responsible for the religious socialization of their children.

What Do Parents Want and Value in Religious Congregations?

Our discussion so far has focused on how and why most American religious parents feel primarily responsible for socializing their children religiously. The vast majority said that responsibility rests largely with them. Still, most also agreed that religious congregations do provide supportive resources and benefits for raising children. Here we describe the things parents like about their congregations, how parents use them, and what that suggests about the role of religious congregations in intergenerational religious transmission.

Formal Religious Education

When we asked parents what congregations provide for their children, one of the most frequent responses was religious education. Most religious parents do want their children involved in formal religious activities, send them to religious services, and express appreciation for the teachings their children receive there. As one black Protestant mother said, "It's a place for them to get an extended lesson on God, a professional lesson on God." A conservative Protestant mother reported: "I like what the church is doing up to this point with Sunday school and instruction. I might not sit down with the Catechism and do memorization, [so] I like that they're getting that background." What parents appreciated about congregations was the formal and systematic education it offered, like studying the Ten Commandments or passages from the Koran. One conservative Protestant mother praised her church's "curriculum where the kids understand what the trinity is" and "that God has always been here, that Christ didn't just come in the New Testament, he's all through the Old Testament so they get more of the big picture." One Muslim mother explained, "I'm looking for old-school, hard core, where my children can take Koran lessons, like at the local Islamic center. The Sheikh, the person who teaches the Koran, is an immigrant from Egypt. He's got that old school style of recitation, that beautiful way of saying it."

The 2012 Congregation Life Survey asked what respondents most value about their religious congregations. Figure 7.3 reports the results. People with and without young children felt that the Holy Communion, Eucharist, or Lord's Supper were the most important, followed by sermons. While the survey results show a lot of similarities for people with and without children under age 18 for these two most popular categories, we see a big difference for the third category, children and youth ministry. Thirty-two percent of parents with children under age 18 reported that the congregation's children's and youth ministry was one of the top-three things that they valued. Only 10 percent of congregants without young children or teenagers agreed.

These survey findings were reflected in our personal interviews. Many parents commented on how their congregation's services and educational classes helped them to engage their children on religion. One mainline Protestant father explained that on Sundays, "we'll sit down, and I will say, 'What did you do in Sunday school?,' and then I'll maybe tell them what happened with me" in "a sort of debrief of that kind." A black Protestant mother said that "even after service we have a habit of asking our son, 'Well, what did you learn?'" Another conservative Protestant father concurred: "I'll

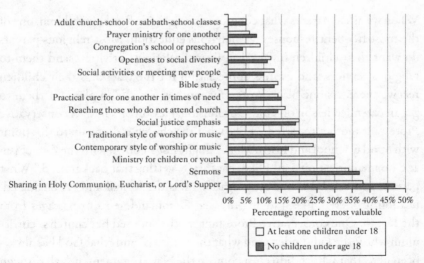

FIGURE 7.3 Most valuable aspects of the congregation for congregants with and without children under 18 (weighted percentages).

Note: Congregants could select up to three items as being most valuable.

Source: US Congregational Life Survey, Wave 2, 2008/2009, Random Sample Attender Survey.

ask them, 'Tell me what you learned.' You know, 'I want to know what you learned when you come out.'" Religious classes and sermons offer parents an opportunity to test their child's religious knowledge, to elaborate on the teachings given, and to talk more generally with them about religious matters. Congregations thus provide part of children's religious education, but most parents remain quite actively involved, following up afterward and in some cases warning children beforehand that they will need to report back on what they are learning. That too reflects their belief that they remain the primary religious agents in their children's lives.

Moral Instruction

The primary purpose of the religious education that American parents want for their children is to instill a sense of moral right and wrong so they can become "good people." The overwhelming majority of parents say that what is important about religion is morality.[30] A mainline Protestant father, for instance, told us that, if his child did not believe in God, he would be "lost in the sense that, God the almighty is our creator, and unless you believe in God, there is no way you are going to behave yourself. Most people are placed in situations where we have to make decisions, like they want to steal or do something bad, and you sit there and say, 'No. I cannot do this because the God almighty will not be happy.'" A Muslim mother told her children what to report to others about their religion: "I would just say we want to be good people, we want to be compassionate, we want to not hurt our neighbors." A Hispanic Catholic father said, "We try to do the best we can for our children, so they become good men in the future." And when responding to our question about the consequences of religion being removed from his family's life, a black Protestant father answered, "I think it would be tragic, like maybe my kids wouldn't be on the right track because there are so many temptations."

One of the (we presume unintended) consequences of parents prioritizing basic morality over, say, continual theological education or lifelong personal growth in the faith is that it ends up defining the most important feature of religion as of primary relevance for children. Religion is ultimately child's stuff. For most parents, congregations were useful because they helped children develop good moral compasses, learn to be nice to others, to be able to distinguish right from wrong, and to make "good decisions." But once those

---

30. This theme is developed in Smith with Denton, *Soul Searching*.

basics are learned by the late teenage or early emerging adult years, so the obvious logic runs, religious moral teachings and the congregations that offer them are not particularly necessary. By analogy, once one has learned in part through required, formal driving school how to drive, why would anyone keep attending driving school classes? One has one's license, is competent to drive, so no longer needs those classes. The same with religious congregations. Why keep learning about the Ten Commandments or how to make good choices when one learned that well enough back in elementary school?[31]

This outlook, that religious congregations are more important for children's education than adults', is corroborated by other findings in Figure 7.3. For instance, only 13 percent said that one of the three most valuable services their congregations provide was Bible study, and only 5 percent said that adult church or Sabbath classes were important. Apparently grownups have much less need to learn than children—which makes total sense when the learning is thought to be about basic moral education rather than, say, the fullness of life shaped by a religious tradition. Even when formal religious education is not primarily about foundational ethics and good decisions, but basic doctrinal beliefs, it is still usually approached with a "graduation model" operating in the background. So, for instance, one Hispanic Catholic mother said about her daughter's completing the sacrament of Confirmation, "I know that even though she doesn't come to Mass every Sunday, at least she has that in her already."

Enjoyable Religious Activities

Most of the parents we interviewed are successful in getting their (especially younger) children to attend religious services and other activities. In many cases, that seems not too difficult. More than half of the parents we interviewed told us that their children enjoyed religious functions. A black Protestant mother said, "They understand going to church, because they

---

31. See Smith with Snell, *Souls in Transition*. There we saw that, consistent with the responses of the parents we interviewed, many of the young people explained that their congregation had helped them develop a solid moral foundation. Weekly classes like Sunday school, Catechism, and Bible Study, which are often geared toward children and adolescents, provided their religious training. However, now that they were emerging adults, many assumed that their congregation had a lesser or no role to play in life. Just as they had graduated from high school, they had also finished their religious education. If in the future they ever had children, they might become more involved with a congregation again in order to help lay their children's moral foundation.

ask, 'Are we going to Bible study? Are we going to Wednesday nights?' Yes, we're going. So they're real cooperative, they're not like, 'Ohhh I don't wanna go!'" A Hispanic Catholic mother told us that her little girl likes helping her Godmother, who is in charge of the children during church services: "She likes to be with her a lot; she likes going to church." And a Mormon mother said that their daughter is "a thoughtful Christian and very, very committed. She goes every morning by her own volition to early morning seminary, at 6:00 in the morning!" These reports are consistent with the findings of other studies. The first wave of the National Study of Youth and Religion (NSYR), which focused on adolescents, ages 13–17, showed that 45 percent of youth report that if it was totally up to them they would attend religious services once a week or more; and the vast majority (75 percent) said that their congregation was a warm and welcoming place for them.[32] The NSYR survey also found that 62 percent of US teenagers said that their religious congregation's environment made them think about important things; only 15 percent said that it is boring.

Nonetheless, some parents admitted that their children and sometimes they themselves did not attend religious activities regularly. The most common reason for skipping weekly religious activities was not because their child did not want to go, but rather the demands of active involvement in other extracurricular activities, especially sports. As one mainline Protestant father explained, "Sports take place on Sunday mornings sometimes. So you have conflicts and then it's just harder to pull them along." A Catholic mother explained that attending Mass "doesn't fit my lifestyle all the time and because of how busy my daughter is with sports. It's so hard because she travels, she does travel softball and travel volleyball and we're gone every weekend." A Mormon mother told us that her oldest daughter is very musically talented and plays in the local orchestra, which practices on Sundays, so her daughter is unable to attend religious services.

Earlier in this chapter we said that, since the 1960s, the number and variety of extracurricular activities for youth have proliferated, requiring parents to expend large amounts of energy and resources to help their children participate.[33] For a minority of parents, the consequences have included limiting their involvement in religion-related activities. Still, the majority of parents

---

32. Smith with Denton, *Soul Searching*, 61–62.

33. Hofferth and Sandberg, "Changes in American Children's Time, 1981–1997"; Kurz, "Work–Family Issues of Mothers of Teenage Children."

we interviewed said that religious activities were important for passing on religion to children and prioritized their children's religious involvements. As one black Protestant mother explained, "No, they going to church. You can give me a little attitude if you have it, but surprisingly they like it." In fact, confirming the NSYR findings just mentioned, only a minority of parents had children who strongly resisted religious involvements. Recall the black Protestant father who said, "just like I was drugged [dragged], they were drugged." A Catholic mother reported, "There's no question, they're not allowed not to [stop going]. They complain about it. 'Oh we're tired. We stayed up till whenever.' Blah blah blah." Such parents face the greatest difficulty in balancing their influence with their children's self-direction— especially given the widespread fear among parents of teenage rebellion against religion, which they see as more damaging than simply skipping religious services.[34] One way or another, parents muddle or glide through. But having religious congregations that offer more rather than less enjoyable programs and activities makes their lives easier.

Friends

Many religious congregations offer activities for children and teenagers besides formal weekly services and Sunday school, such as youth groups, volunteer days, mission and service trips, and summer camp. Parents expect congregations to provide such opportunities for kids, and most parents were at least somewhat satisfied with the offerings of their congregations. However, the parents we interviewed did not focus heavily on them. Much more important to parents was whether their children had friends in their congregations and how that affected their interest in participating in various religious activities. One Jewish mother explained the value of her daughter having close friends at their synagogue: "If she didn't have that little group of five, it would be a totally different situation. But the fact that those kids are there week after week with her, it turns religion into a social gathering." A Catholic mother confessed that she found it "kind of amazing" that her teenagers were willing

---

34. A belief that has basis in fact. Using survey and interview data from four generations of families, Vern Bengtson analyzed the factors that shaped religious transmission across generations, finding that, not only parents having a warm relationship with their children increased their likelihood of success in transmitting religion, but also that parents who forced their children to be involved with religion tended to be less successful than those who did not force it (Bengtson, *Families and Faith: How Religion Is Passed Down across Generations* (New York: Oxford University Press, 2013).

to attend Mass without her, but then added, "I think it's because they were hoping to see their friends." A Buddhist father said that he felt it was important that their children start attending temple "at the age of two, because that's when they develop their friends, their friendships, their bonds. There are a lot of people that don't bring their kids until they're five or six, and by then it's harder." Parents wanted their kids to enjoy religious activities, and they believe their having friends there plays the key role in attracting them.

The negative is also true. Parents told us how much more positive the experience for their child would be if they had friends in their congregations. The same Jewish parent who mentioned her daughter's five close friends also lamented her son not having any friends there: "So that's missing for Donald. If he had friends in the synagogue, it would be a much more positive experience." A mainline Protestant mother said it was hard for her sons to build connections at church because "none of the kids that go to their school go to their church" and "it is hard for them to make friends with the kids at church." One Mormon parent, extending beyond friendship to romance, lamented the lack of girls for her son to meet in their church:

> It's like, where do you meet girls? Because our church doesn't really have girls his age. Most of them are in college or in Utah or someplace else. We just don't have a lot of girls his age. I'm like, well obviously you could join a different church group, and they [my fellow congregants] look at me like I'm absolutely insane. But that's where the other people may be.

A conservative Protestant mother told us that she intentionally chose a church that was "just packed with cool young people," hoping that her son might connect with them and "see that there is a community, that you're not here all by yourself doing this."[35]

---

35. Some research has advanced a "channeling hypothesis" that parents may use resources like congregations to channel their children into desirable peer groups that will help them make better religious and life decisions (e.g., Marie Cornwall, "The Influence of Three Agents of Religious Socialization: Family, Church, and Peers," *The Religion and Family Connection: Social Science Perspectives* 16, no. 2 (1988): 207–231; Harold Himmelfarb, "The Study of American Jewish Identification: How It Is Defined, Measured, Obtained, Sustained and Lost," *Journal for the Scientific Study of Religion* 19, no. 1 (1980): 48–60; Todd Martin, James White, and Daniel Perlman, "Religious Socialization: A Test of the Channeling Hypothesis of Parental Influence on Adolescent Faith Maturity," *Journal of Adolescent Research* 18, no. 2 (2003): 169–187). However, we interviewed only a few parents who were consciously using congregations to channel their children into friendships or romantic relationships; that does not rule out the possibility, however, that parents may be unaware that they are channeling their children.

Community

The last factor parents said was particularly important about congregations was "community." Parents described the importance of the congregational community as being different from school and other extracurricular activities. Congregations were seen as offering larger associations with people—not only age-similar friends—who cared strongly for them and their children, providing safe havens where they could go if they needed help. One single conservative Protestant mother, for example, explained, "It gives my girl that safe, secure home. She is so comfortable there and she makes good safe connections." A Muslim father explained that it was good for his kids to connect with the Muslim congregation, "so that they have peer groups and other adults from that faith community who can be a support network for the kids." Numerous parents described their congregations as families, including this black Protestant mother who values her church "because this is my extended family, because I have been here so long and I've watched people grow."

In addition to enjoying community support from congregations, some parents also explained that they wanted their children to learn their contributing role in their congregation. One Jewish mother explained that she did not want necessarily to spend her day going to synagogue, but she did want to show her kids that if they want "to be a part of the community, you have to step up and be involved." Likewise, a conservative Protestant father told us about the importance of a church "where kids are being influenced and are being part of this community where the children feel responsible to the congregation."

Another aspect of congregational community that was important to parents was providing a setting where their children could meet and observe others, not just their friends, like themselves. A Muslim mother explained that it's important for her kids to see other Muslims "just like them. They live the same life, practice the same religion. It's very important for the kids to see everybody else in the mosque, that they're doing the same thing that we do. It's not like they are a weird minority." This concern with feeling like an odd minority was particularly prevalent among Buddhists, Muslims, and conservative Protestants. Fewer than 1 percent of Americans identify as Muslim (0.6 percent) or Buddhist (0.7 percent).[36] While numerically plentiful in the

---

36. Pew Research Center, "America's Changing Religious Landscape," Pew Research Center on Religion & Public Life, May 12, 2015, http://religions.pewforum.org/reports. Different surveys find somewhat different numbers, but the point remains.

United States, many conservative Protestants feel marginalized in the United States and so are concerned about their children feeling "out of place." As this conservative Protestant father explained, church is important "especially for teenagers where there's such safety in that community, because then you're not the oddball where the nightmare for a teenager is to be different."

Finally, many Muslim, Buddhist, and Hindu parents felt that their mosques, Islamic centers, and temples were important for providing opportunities for their children to learn about their native cultures, be they Pakistani, Tibetan, Indian, or something else. These congregations tended to provide many cultural services, including language lessons, ethnic food, and interactions with others who share the same national or ethnic background. As one Hindu mother explained, "we want my son to have a similar cultural group so he feels comfortable talking in the language and understands what we are, because it's a big challenge for him to grow up because he doesn't want to eat the [Indian food]." Seeing other kids and parents eating it, however, makes him more at home with that difference.

Conclusion

American religion has historically been centered on voluntary congregational participation. Even the geography-based parish system of American Catholicism and the household-centered piety of some new immigrant religions have been profoundly influenced by the dominant institutional model of Protestant congregationalism. The American experience tends to "denominate" nearly every expression of religion into discreet organizations that can be listed in the yellow pages. However, we have seen that, when it comes to the crucial question of the socialization of the next generation of young people into religious practice and belief, the people who have the most say-so over children, their parents, do not expect much from or depend heavily upon their religious congregations. Instead, they view themselves as primarily responsible for the religious acculturation of their children. Religious congregations, they believe, should play a secondary and supportive, not a leading, role.

This approach of parents is not because most of them are disappointed with or alienated from their congregations. The vast majority are quite satisfied, in fact. This is rather, we suggest, the result of broader social and cultural transformations in family life and norms, as we explained earlier, that intensify parental investments in children. It also reflects, we think, a long-term transformation of life in the American religious field—per our argument in Chapter 3—from religion being a "communal solidarity project" to becoming a "personal identity accessory." If so, the implications for both families and congregations are big. Furthermore, American parents value and seek very specific things in their religious congregations, some of which (age-similar friends for their children, a supportive community, instruction in basic morality and values, a supply of enjoyable activities) do not directly concern specifically liturgical or doctrinal aspects of religion. Potential exists for a mismatch between the "demand" of parents and "supply" offered by congregational leaders concerning the goods they seek and offer—although it seems that in most cases an adequate match is being negotiated.

If there is a large body of religious parents in the United States who feel disenfranchised from their parental responsibilities to actively raise their children to understand, appreciate, and practice their religious traditions, we did not find them in our research. Stereotypes of parents who drop their children off for Sunday school and drive away to another activity until it is time to pick them up later do not ring true with our findings. Such parents must exist, or else the stereotype would never have arisen and taken hold. Perhaps these "religion is not my area" type of parents were more common in previous decades but have since faded away. Perhaps such "do as I say and not as I do" parents remain common today among those with weaker ties to religious congregations than the more connected parents we studied. Both explanations are plausible. But we are confident based on our religiously diverse sample of parents who are involved in different levels in their congregations that those stereotypes do not represent the vast majority of congregationally affiliated religious parents. Nearly all of them want to own the religious formation of their children. Parents should play the leading role. Congregations should perform the supporting acts.

Conclusion

THIS BOOK EXAMINES American religious parents as the key agents in passing on religious faith and practice to their children. We began with the simple descriptive fact, well-established by previous research, that parents are indeed the crucial players in intergenerational religious transmission. Yet we noted that little research has been conducted that explores beyond that mere fact to better understand parents' own perspectives, approaches, and experiences in passing on religion to their offspring. The combination of this known fact with our lack of deeper knowledge about it motivated our inquiry.

One of the larger takeaways from our study concerns the complex of multiple levels and types of influences that shape parents' religious engagement with their children. The cultural models that inform parents' efforts at religious socialization matter, but so too do macro-cultural transformations and definitions of religion and family. The present practices of specific families matter, as do the past experiences of parents' religious upbringing, as well as parents' desires and fearful anticipated future scenarios involving their children. And the specific religious traditions to which families belong make a difference in the likelihood that their children will remain religious, but so also do the parenting styles of those parents, which are not religiously determined. No simple factor or formula explains or predicts how or why intergenerational religious transmission operates or succeeds. As with all things humanly social, the processes are complex, contingent, and multileveled.

This we learned as our investigation unfolded. At the level of specific cultural vision of religious parentings, for example, we found that American religious parents across a wide range of religious traditions, social classes, races and ethnicities, and family structures share an underlying set of "cultural models" explaining why passing on religion to their children matters and how they ought to do it. Parents did not differ much in their fundamental background assumptions about why and how to raise their children religiously, whether they were Christian, Muslim, Buddhist, or Jewish. The particularities of their religious beliefs and practices vary. Parents largely shared the basic cultural ideas informing their approaches, despite major religious and social differences that otherwise distinguish them. At the same time, we also learned that parents in different religious traditions do vary in how successful they actually are at passing on their religion to their children. Mormon, black Protestant, and conservative Protestant parents are relatively more successful—measured as children's greater importance of faith and religious service attendance in their later 20s—while mainline Protestant, Catholic, and Jewish parents fare significantly less well. The research provided here offers insight into some of the differences that distinguish the practices of parents from relatively "strict" religions. Whereas parents from mainline Protestant and Catholic faiths wanted to pass on only moderate levels of religiosity, in general, Mormon, black Protestant, and conservative Protestant parents were deliberate in trying to transmit strong religious belief.

Yet, we also saw, intergenerational religious transmission is also influenced by the particular parenting styles of parents, completely separately from their religious tradition. Authoritative parenting—compared to the alternatives—exerts a direct, independent effect on children's greater subsequent religious commitments, even when other factors like parent religiousness are statistically removed. Moreover, we see this pattern not only for explaining high levels of religious importance and engagement but also in predicting lower levels for the offspring of parents who were not religious. Put differently, authoritative parents who are less religious are also successful at passing on lower levels of religious belief and engagement. And no one religious tradition has a monopoly on any given parenting style, as the four parenting styles are distributed fairly evenly across all the religious traditions we examined. So simply being a highly religious parent trying to pass on that religion to kids is not the only significant factor in children's religious outcomes. Parents' general styles of parenting—how much they expect and demand from their children and how warm and communicative they are with them—is also important. Moreover, the influence of parenting styles also interacts synergistically with parent religiousness, such that parents who are both authoritative in their parenting style and more highly religious receive an extra "boost" in effective religious transmission to children. The variables that matter do so independently as well as in combinations.

Those findings focus on the individual level of parents and children. Yet the particular experiences of American religious parents trying to raise their children religiously must also be understood, we argue, within the larger macro-cultural frameworks that profoundly affect them. Understood from that perspective, we see that the cultural and institutional meanings and experiences of religion and family have transformed over the last century, in ways that redefine the place of parents in raising their children. The religious field itself has become socially constituted today as a "personal identity accessory," rather than the "community solidarity project" it was in the past. This has not only changed the character of the "religion" that religious parents are seeking to transmit, but it has also altered the locations, influences, and processes that stand any chance of succeeding. Meanwhile, "the family" has morphed from being a community-embedded social institution to a model of home-centered companionate relations during the mid-twentieth century, and then to a set of individual identity and lifestyle choices more recently. This has simultaneously weakened the position of parents to socialize their children as they wish and also placed on them greater responsibilities to inculcate their children with the skills of self-reflexivity (as we discussed in Chapter 3). That helps to explain why most religious parents are keen to see their children embrace their religion as adults, yet also very anxious not to "shove religion down their throats" and provoke rebellion. Such a larger cultural situation requires, in parents' common experience, that for many years they carefully step forward in a precarious balancing act across a soaring high wire, which they fear may have no safety net below.

It gets even more complicated. America's religious parents also act within the demographic context of a total population of parents who are less invested in religion or reproducing religion in their children than they were before the 1970s. Our analysis of nationally representative survey data shows that in general about one-third of American parents (a number also likely inflated by social desirability bias) report being truly invested in having their children carry on their religion. But for the majority of parents it seems that religion matters less, as other values and priorities take precedence.[1] Our interviews revealed that the more religiously committed parents were surrounded by others who do not firmly share and reinforce their priorities. So when it comes simply to arranging and coordinating the rhythms and features of daily

---

1. See Pew Research Center, "Teaching the Children: Sharp Ideological Differences, Some Common Ground—Wide Gaps over Teaching Faith, Tolerance, Obedience" (Washington, DC: Pew Research Center, 2014). On nonreligious parenting, see Cristel Manning, *Losing Our Religion: How Unaffiliated Parents Are Raising Their Children* (New York: New York University Press, 2015); Dale McGowan, *Parenting beyond Belief: On Raising Ethical, Caring Kids without Religion* (New York: Amacom, 2007).

life with, say, the parents of their children's school or neighborhood friends, the more highly religious parents cannot count on others to see, evaluate, and prioritize things—such as sports schedules or screening movies or computer activities—in the ways they would prefer. That then forces the more highly religious parents into a dilemma. They can either reluctantly lower their preferred standards and expectations for their children in a way that might feel secularizing, or else they can reconstruct family social relations in tighter networks of like-minded co-religionists in ways that might feel sectarian. Additionally, parents in the same households sometimes do not agree about religion or the preferred level of engagement, which complicates the intergenerational transmission of religion.[2]

Adding yet another wrinkle, all of these dynamics tend to play out differently within various immigrant subcultures, which together comprise increasingly larger proportions of the overall American religious population. The experience of belonging to a minority religion or a minority ethnicity in a majority religion, of negotiating the Americanization of one's children, of the oftentimes inextricable interweaving of one's religion and nationality, and of being viewed as exotic or dangerous by the surrounding society adds additional complexity to the process of religious socialization for most immigrant parents. They, too, share the underlying cultural models that inform most American religious parents on the question of intergenerational religious transmission. But the particular cultural and institutional opportunities and constraints they face as immigrant parents shape the ways they can and do deploy their efforts to transmit religion to their children.

Our research here has also revealed influences operating at different temporal phases of parents' lives. For instance, how parents approach religious socialization is profoundly shaped, in addition to all of the other factors examined here, by their own experiences as children growing up. Diverse religious traditions can select, train, and deploy parents in different ways and with different resources to pass on religion to children. But those tradition-level influences are inflected through the earlier personal experiences of parents growing up. Different parents experienced their family's religions variously as youth. Some appreciated and embraced their parents' religion. Others resisted and rejected them. Yet others felt negatively about the ways they were raised to practice religion, but nonetheless stayed with the religion,

---

2. Pew Research Center, "One-in-Five U.S. Adults Were Raised in Interfaith Homes," October 26 (Washington, DC, 2016).

modifying their relationships with the traditions and practices. Still others were raised without religious influences and later became religious. And each of those experiences colors the ways parents, regardless of their religious tradition, engage and try to form their children religiously. More generally, this fact highlights yet another factor that sociologists of childhood have emphasized in recent decades—namely, that children are not passive and receptive objects of, but rather active, evaluating participants in their own socialization.[3] So religious parents today represent one link in an ongoing, interactive chain of social reproduction and transformation in which all participants involved are the recipients, evaluators, and agents of transmission. The paths and trajectories that such a process can take are dynamic and layered.

Parents' partners also play an important role. Regardless of how they might ideally want to transmit religion to their children, parents have to consider their partners' religious preferences. Parents who have a partner from a different religion or prefer a different level of religious engagement have to make strategic decisions about how much they want to influence their partner's religious participation, which has implications for how they transmit religion to their children. Some parents work hard to compromise, even if that means not doing some of the things that they think would help instill religious belief in their children. Other parents operate independently from their partners, engaging in rituals and activities with their children while their partners are absent. Since most divorced and single parents do not have much in-depth contact with the other parent, there are fewer religion-related disagreements. Child custody arrangements tend to shape their children's level of formal religious engagement. If they happen to have custody on a religious holiday, then their children can participate. But if they don't, they often lose that opportunity. The greater level of discussion and willingness to coordinate among married parents offers some insight into why their children tend to have higher levels of religious engagement than those from divorced or single parent families.[4]

---

3. William Corsaro, *The Sociology of Childhood* (Thousand Oaks, CA: Pine Forge Press, 1997); Leon Kuczynski and Melanie Parkin, "Agency and Bidirectionality in Socialization," in *Handbook of Socialization: Theory and Research*, ed. Joan Grusec and Paul Hastings (New York: Guilford, 2007), 259–283; Lynda Ashvourne, "Reconceptualizing Parent-Adolescent Relationships: A Dialogic Model," *Journal of Family Theory and Review* 1 (2009): 211–222; Gerald Handel, Spencer Cahill, and Frederick Elkin, *Children and Society: The Sociology of Children and Childhood Socialization* (New York: Oxford University Press, 2007).

4. J. E. Zhai, C. G. Ellison, N. D. Glenn, and E. Marquardt, "Parental Divorce and Religious Involvement among Young Adults," *Sociology of Religion* 68, no. 2 (2007): 125–144.

What American religious parents expect of and how they relate to their local religious congregations affects their approaches to religiously socializing their children as well. Conventional wisdom has it that many parents want to push off the job of religious education onto religious experts in their congregations. That may be true of more religiously disconnected parents. But we found that the vast majority of parents who affiliate with religious congregations actually hold modest expectations of their churches, temples, synagogues, and mosques. They view themselves as the primary agents of their children's religious formation. They tend to see their congregations as secondary resources only supporting and reinforcing their tasks as parents. Furthermore, what most religious parents are looking to get from their congregations are not primarily religious content—the theology, liturgical experience, formal religious instruction, or formation in scripture or spirituality—but the more general goods of warm and friendly atmospheres and inviting and rewarding activities and relationships for their children. If congregations can provide those limited goods, then most parents are satisfied with them for their community support in backing up parents' primary work of socializing their children religiously. The more congregational leaders are aware of the actual preferences of parents, then, the less incentive they have to highlight the one feature that makes them distinctive, namely, their *religious* character. And the more those leaders must recognize their own back-seat role in the formation of their congregations' youth, since parents are the ones who determine what and how religion will be transmitted. That is simply the reality of life for religious organizations under the macro-cultural regime of religion constituted as a personal identity accessory.

Stepping back from religious parenting in particular and surveying the larger landscape of American parenting broadly, we find a much contested terrain. Many psychology, pediatric, and religious "experts" have over the decades pulled American parents through various, often inconsistent, and sometimes contradictory programs and fads instructing them on how to practice good parenting.[5] Parents have been variously taught to exercise firm authority to demand obedience, to be permissive and warm, to provide children with firm boundaries, to allow children to clarify their own values, to teach children to just say "no," to allow children to experiment and learn for themselves, to "dare to discipline," to insist that "true love waits," to make children

---

5. Ann Hulbert, *Raising America: Experts, Parents, and a Century of Advice about Children* (New York: Knopf, 2003).

"kiss dating goodbye," and then somehow to recurrently back-pedal when such directives are later retracted.[6] Current experts stress the need for parents to "be the parents" and treat children as children, not as little adults. The physician, psychologist, and popular author, Leonard Sax, for instance, argues in his 2016 book, *The Collapse of Parenting: How We Hurt Our Kids When We Treat Them Like Grown Ups,* that too many American parents suffer "role confusion" and so are afraid of being dictatorial.[7] They therefore abdicate authority over children to a "culture of disrespect" promoted by peers and the media. That, Sax observes, has resulted in dramatic declines in the achievement and psychological and physical health of American children. Parents, he insists, need to reestablish the parent–child relationship and exercise healthy parental authority, including "educating children's desires," for children's own well-being. Sax recognizes that "parents today shoulder a greater burden than parents in previous generations but have fewer resources to do their job."[8] Still, parents need to step up and do their jobs if we want to save America's children.

Sax may very well be right. We are not unsympathetic to his critique and recommendations. But when it comes to *religious* parenting in particular, the situation that parents face is extra challenging. It is one thing to limit the playing of video games, to make sure the homework and piano practice happen, and to enforce lights out at bedtime. It is quite another thing to inculcate strong religious beliefs and establish firm religious habits, especially for teenagers. Somehow, things like schoolwork, sports, chores, basic civility, and the regulation of risk and health behaviors are more legitimately enforceable than religious things. The latter nearly everyone considers too personal, too subjective, too voluntary for parents simply to make happen. Parents may be culturally authorized to insist that band practice and homework get done. But the same approach to, say, children's prayer or scripture reading is impossible. That would be "shoving religion down their throats." To understand why, we have to see, again, that the character of the American religious field

---

6. See, for example, Ruth Graham, "Hello Goodbye: The Author of a Best-Selling Abstinence Manifesto Is Reconsidering the Lessons He Taught to Millions," *Slate,* August 23, 2016. https://slate.com/human-interest/2016/08/i-kissed-dating-goodbye-author-is-maybe-kind-of-sorry.html; https://joshharris.com/statement/; https://www.npr.org/2016/07/10/485432485/former-evangelical-pastor-rethinks-his-approach-to-courtship.

7. Leonard Sax, *The Collapse of Parenting* (New York: Basic Books, 2016).

8. Sax, *The Collapse of Parenting,* 20.

has transformed in recent generations. What most Americans consider religion even to *be* has changed. So has the significance of religious congregations and the authority of religious traditions. The American family itself has also altered and, along with it, the position and authority of parents vis-à-vis children. More broadly, the very notion of what a human "self" *is*, and the associated vision of what makes for a "good life," have transformed to prioritize individual autonomy, choice, and acquisition of the resources needed to consume both material goods and stimulating and fulfilling experiences. Bad grades in school and failures to fulfill commitments threaten to compromise the likelihood of children living good lives, as American culture defines that. A lack of interest in religious devotion, by comparison, poses much less of a threat. How then in such an environment are committed religious parents supposed to transmit to their children anything like coherent religious worldviews, authoritative religious traditions, and formative religious practices?

The majority of American religious parents decide that their most promising strategy is simply to model religious values and practices naturally for their children in their own lives, and then to look for "teaching moments" to talk with their children about religion. A minority of parents do not even try or actually have reservations about passing on their religion to their children, and so instead merely "expose" their children to their religion or many religions and then let them decide for themselves which option is "right for them." Yet even parents who take a more direct approach pay careful attention to not overdo the religious socialization, so as not to incite pushback and rejection. In the end, it turns out, the children are in the driver's seat when it comes to religion, so parents have no choice but to finesse more subtle approaches and hope they succeed in due time. Some definitely do. But others, as trend data on the religiousness of young Americans show, increasingly do not.

What are the implications of our findings for religious parents and communities of faith? This is obviously not a how-to book. But some practical implications stand out for those who are interested. Religious parents, communities, and institutions that are invested in the next generation carrying on their religious practices and beliefs have evidence-based reasons to take note of the following. Parents are crucial. Above and beyond any other effect on children's religion is the influence of their parents. Rarely do or can other factors—congregations, youth groups, religious schools, mission or service trips—override the formative power of parents. The more aware and intentional religious parents are about this, the more effectively they should be able to shape their children religiously. Most religious parents do seem to understand that their children will pay more attention to what they do religiously than what they say. Contradictions and hypocrisy are not effective means of socialization. However, strong evidence also shows that parents *talking to* their children about their religion, and not simply quietly role-modeling it for them, is a powerfully important practice. If there were only one practical take-away from our research, it would be this: parents need not only to "walk the walk" but also regularly to *talk* with their children about their walk, what it means, why it matters, why they care.

Religious parents might also work to reflect critically about the "cultural models" that run in the background of and govern their beliefs and feelings about religion and their children. How invested in religious transmission are they and why? How well do their motives match up with the teachings and expectations of their own religious traditions? What is the intended purpose or goal of all the religious doings anyway? The more thoughtful about these questions parents are, the less the defaults of life will simply happen to them and their children. And the more potential there will be for fruitful discussions among parents and within their religious communities about what they are trying to do, what their actual motivations are for doing it, and how effective (or not) the kinds of means they are employing seem to be. In particular, parents and clergy could benefit from candid discussions about expectations and desires regarding the role of religious congregations in intergenerational religious transmission.

Another clear implication of our findings is that general parenting styles matter. Parents who want their children to carry on their religious traditions should practice a general authoritative parenting style. Combining clear and implemented life standards and expectations for their children with expressive emotional warmth and relational bonding with their children fosters relationships that most enhance effective religious transmission to children. Comparatively, independent of other religious factors that also matter, parents who are more permissive, disengaged, and authoritarian are simply less successful in passing on their religion to their offspring.

Our findings suggest other implications than simply parents being more attentive and deliberate. Sociology also demonstrates the powerful effects of broader social relationships, cultural movements, and social statuses. We have seen, for example, that familial factors, such as how religious parents were raised religiously as children themselves, whether parents are married, single, divorced, or something else, how the other parent fits into the religious equation, and whether grandparents are involved in their children's lives, also make a difference in the parents' own attitudes, opportunities, and support in religious transmission. Faith transmission processes unfold within complex networks of influential social relationships, not between autonomous individuals. More broadly, we have seen that parenting for religious transmission to children is also powerfully shaped by factors like immigrant status, race and ethnicity, background nationality, and religious tradition itself (for example, the Muslim parents who bend over backwards to avoid being tagged as "extremist," or the Jewish parents who wrestle with the fact that Judaism is often more than just a religion). In such ways, what seems at first like private concerns limited to families and local religious congregations turns out to be much influenced by social statuses and experiences of migration, globalization, and geopolitical history (such as the Holocaust and September 11). At an even bigger level, religiously interested people would do well, we think, to consider how massive, macro-cultural transformations—such as religion's reconstitution as a "personal identity accessory" instead of a "community solidarity project"—have revolutionized the challenge of intergenerational religious transmission. The key underlying question is: how can a religious community carry on a distinct *tradition* without either capitulating to cultural conditions alien to itself or ossifying into inert irrelevance?

Having said all this, the sociology of religion's job is not to judge, make recommendations to, or influence religious worlds, but rather to understand and explain those worlds for all who are interested in them. In the end, they need to figure out the implications for their own situations. Human beings, especially in the twenty-first century, are environment-monitoring and self-reflexive creatures. We want to know what is happening around us and how it influences what is happening to and within us, so that we can better understand ourselves in relation to the social and natural worlds in which we live. Religion is a massively important part of the world. And the elementary question of how religions are reproduced and transformed from one generation to the next in various social contexts is consequential not only for religious people and traditions, but it is also descriptively, analytically, and theoretically important for the discipline of sociology. To shed light on one aspect of that basic process in one particular time and place has been our purpose here, which we hope provides valuable knowledge, insight, and understanding.

Research Methodology

with Heather Price and Sara Skiles

Interview Data Collection Methods

The findings of this study are based significantly on in-depth, personal interviews and observations with 235 coupled and single parents living in the United States that we conducted in more than 150 households. We purposively selected these parents from religious congregations to represent different religious traditions, regions around the country, racial and ethnic backgrounds, social classes, family structures, and other factors, based on their theoretical importance. Religious traditions represented included white evangelicals, white mainline Protestants, black Protestants, white Catholics, Hispanic Catholics, Mormons, Conservative Jews, Muslims, Buddhists, and Hindus. We also interviewed a sample of nonreligious parents for comparative purposes. Our study included an oversample of Catholic households, including 25 parents who spoke Spanish at home. Each household study involved in-depth interviews with parent couples, single parents, or parent figures living in residence. We did not interview children in the household. We and our research team took extensive field notes on the household's physical appearance, family interactions, material possessions, neighborhood locations, and so on. When granted permission, we also took photographs of households—particularly of religious objects—and neighborhoods as visual supplementary data. In some cases, we also visited worship services or other activity at the religious congregation or spent other time outside of interviews with parents in a family activity, such as eating a meal with the family or tagging along in a recreational activity. This research design produced richer data than simple one-shot interviews would have offered, but thinner data than what a full-fledged field ethnography would have yielded.

The religious parents we sampled to participate in this study we purposively selected from membership lists of religious congregations. We collaborated with clergy and pastoral and administrative staff to select appropriate parents to study. Because this study is focused on the parental transmission of religious faith to children, the study design chose to focus on parents who had some membership connection to a religious congregation. This tilts the sample in the direction of parents who are more religious than the national average, but for the purposes of this study, that is an advantage, not a weakness. Our sampling of parents from congregations worked to obtain both high-involvement and low-involvement parents. We wanted to be able to compare families who were more involved in their congregations with those who were marginally involved. Our sampling of religious parents from congregations also strove to obtain variance when possible on families' social class and family structure. Some of our sample's nonreligious and "spiritual but not religious" parents—which we intended for more informal comparisons— also emerged from our selection of low-involvement parents formally tied to religious congregations. Most of our nonreligious parents, however, were sampled using convenience methods relying on the weak social ties of interviewers. These parents had to have not been raised religious and not married to a religious spouse in order to fit our nonreligious American parent type.

We sampled households through a stratified sampling process. First, major regional areas of the United States were selected from which to collect data. Combinations of religious traditions most appropriate for those areas we then identified (e.g., black Protestants in the South, Conservative Jews in New York and Chicago). Specific locations in regions we then selected based on access to the researchers. Specific religious congregations in those locations from which to sample households we next identified, in part randomly and in part based on convenience, depending on possible insider contacts or "local knowledge" that we may have had. Once we selected specific religious congregations, we contacted the relevant clergy or other leaders, explained the nature of the research project, and secured their cooperation to study a set of parents in the congregation. Using congregational membership lists and the sampling-type criteria described later, we worked with congregational leaders or administrators to identify potential subjects to participate in the study. We then contacted the parents of these households directly, explained the nature of the study, and asked them to participate. All sampled households we provided FAQ documents describing the study and were offered financial incentives to compensate for their time and effort participating in our research. The few sampled households that refused participation we replaced by a second-ballot household from the same congregation that was highly similar to them, and we repeated the process of contact, explaining, and gaining cooperation. We sampled regions, religious tradition types, and household demographic types and collected data from them until all of the sample types of cells were filled. We made careful efforts to guarantee the accuracy of types of households needed to make the valid analytical comparisons built into the study's basic design, as described next.

Our study intentionally wanted to be able to make numerous analytical comparisons among kinds of households and parents we studied. We did not wish to produce a study of basically white, middle-class, suburban Christians. Based on sociological criteria, we drew our study sample from a purposive, stratified method in order to make empirically grounded analytical comparisons on the following key dimensions:

- *Religious Tradition*: White and Hispanic Catholic, white evangelical and mainline Protestant, black Protestant, Conservative Jew, Mormon/Latter Day Saints, Muslim, Hindu, Buddhist, and nonreligious households
- *Social Class*: Middle/upper-middle versus working class/lower
- *Race and Ethnicity*: Hispanic, white, black, and other race/ethnicities
- *Family Structure and Type*: Two biological parents, remarried/mixed household types, single-parent households; heterosexual versus same-sex parents
- *Religious Commitment*: Higher and lower religious commitments in parents/ families in the same congregations
- *Region of the United States*: The American Midwest, Northeast, and South, Southwestern, and Western regions
- *Urban-Suburban-Rural*: Type of population of residential contexts

With the central, qualitative part of this study we were not interested in and did not seek to construct a truly nationally representative, probability sample. Our purpose with this study was not primarily to make claims about nationally representative statistics— secondary analysis of existing survey datasets, which we also conducted accomplishes that. Rather, the purpose of this kind of qualitative household field study is to understand, in greater depth than surveys can, things like the cultural assumptions, priorities, meanings, routine practices, aspirations and fears, relational dynamics, histories, rituals, material and visual household objects, and social and institutional contexts that shape different kinds of religious faith transmission from parents to children. We found little extant research prior to this study that accessed and described the life narratives, emotional associations, cultural meanings, and causal mechanisms involved in the intergenerational transmission of religious faith comparing across different kinds of households. Our research design was thus dictated by the specific purposes of this project. We also proceeded on the belief that not every last possible sample cell representing every theoretical combination of features needed to be filled by empirical cases for our study. It was not necessary, for example, to find and interview Hispanic families who belong to black Protestant churches or lower-class Conservative Jews. The most socially important sample cells designed to achieve the most relevant analytical comparison are more limited in number.

Table A.1 indicates the specific distribution of numbers of types of parents that our research project sampled and studied (column F shows the oversample of Catholic cases). There we see, for example, that the study samples and researches 12 conservative Protestant (evangelical) households, half of which were middle class and half working class or poor, and then each of those types representing different kinds of family structures and levels

Table A.1 Final Stratified Quota Sample Distributions of Parent Interviewees

Religion	Social Class	Family Type	Religious Commitment High	Religious Commitment Low
White Catholic (N = 38)	Middle/Upper Mid	Two-Parent Biological	14	10
		Blended		2
		Single Parent		
	Working/Low Income	Two-Parent Biological	3	4
		Blended		
		Single Parent	2	3
Black Catholic (N = 4)	Middle/Upper Mid	Two-Parent Biological	1	
		Blended		2
	Working/Low Income	Single Parent	1	
Hispanic Catholic (N = 32)	Middle/Upper Mid	Two-Parent Biological	4	1
		Single Parent	1	
	Working/Low Income	Two-Parent Biological	13	1
		Blended	1	
		Single Parent	7	4
Conservative Protestant (N = 29)	Middle/Upper Mid	Two-Parent Biological	11	1
		Blended	4	
		Single Parent	2	1
	Working/Low Income	Two-Parent Biological	4	
		Blended	2	2
		Single Parent	1	1
Mainline Protestant (N = 23)	Middle/Upper Mid	Two-Parent Biological	4	8
		Same Sex	1	1
	Working/Low Income	Two-Parent Biological	3	1
		Blended	2	
		Single Parent	2	1

Table A.1 Continued

Religion	Social Class	Family Type	Religious Commitment High	Religious Commitment Low
Black Protestant (N = 24)	Middle/Upper Mid	Two-Parent Biological	6	1
		Blended	6	
		Single Parent	1	
	Working/Low Income	Blended	4	2
		Single Parent	3	1
Conservative Jewish (N = 15)	Middle/Upper Mid	Two-Parent Biological	7	3
		Same Sex	2	
		Single Parent	3	
Mormon (N = 10)	Middle/Upper Mid	Two-Parent Biological	5	
		Blended	2	1
	Working/Low Income	Two-Parent Biological		1
		Blended		1
Muslim (N = 13)	Middle/Upper Mid	Two-Parent Biological	9	1
		Single Parent	2	
		Blended	1	
Hindu (N = 14)	Middle/Upper Mid	Two-Parent Biological	1	10
		Single Parent	1	
	Working/Low Income	Two-Parent Biological	2	
Buddhist (N = 13)	Middle/Upper Mid	Two-Parent Biological	6	3
		Blended		
	Working/Low Income	Blended	2	
		Two-Parent Biological	2	
Non-Religious (N = 20)	Middle/Upper Mid	Two-Parent Biological		9
		Blended		3
	Working/Low Income	Blended		4
		Single Parent		4
Total (N = 235)			148	87

of religious commitment. Majority type religious traditions in the United States receive roughly proportionately most of the sample cases. Minority religious traditions, at the same time, we oversampled to provide enough data on them to be able to make meaningful comparisons. Mormons received the least attention here, because we already know a great deal from previous research about their expectations and practices, which, relative to most other groups, tend to be highly prescribed and standardized. Our sample also included 20 nonreligious parents and four same-sex-parent households.

A team of 12 experienced, trained interviewers conducted interviews with parents for this study. Nine of the 12 interviewers were (at the time) faculty, graduate students, and research associates in the Center for the Study of Religion and Society at the University of Notre Dame. The remaining three interviewers were two academic faculty and one research assistant from Rice University (Houston, TX) and John Jay College of Criminal Justice (New York City). This book's authors (Smith and Adamczyk) personally conducted 65 interviews; Manglos-Weber (coauthor of Chapter 5) conducted an additional 25 interviews. Most of the personal interviews conducted for this study we completed in the homes of the parents being interviewed. If a parent preferred otherwise, we also conducted interviews in restaurants, coffee shops, work offices, and the buildings of their religious congregations. We always took steps in all contexts to insure the privacy of our interview conversations, so parents were able to speak freely and confidentially. Initially, we were concerned that parents would defensively feel as if they were being investigated or judged by researchers. That concern passed quickly, however, as most parents proved to be very open and frank in the interviews. After the initial greetings and required paperwork for informed consent were completed, we conducted and digitally recorded the interviews. We paid incentives to interview respondents upon completion of the interviews. Our interviews with parents averaged a mean of 2.0 hours in length, with a range from 41 minutes to 4.2 hours, depending on the family structure, size of the household sampled, and the verbosity of the parent interviewed. As noted earlier, we also visited a subsample of the parents' congregations for worship services or other meetings.

The interview questionnaire for this project (provided later) asked comparatively broad questions, especially at the beginning, relative to those asked in many other interview-based studies that closely follow predetermined scripts, intending to invite long, self-directed answers from parents. Our strategy was to set a context of inquiry that focused on our interests but allowed plenty of leeway for parents to narrate their own stories, make their own crucial points, and provide their own examples. we asked all of the interviewed parents to address the same set of shared questions and speak to the same kinds of issues as all others, but we allowed room for both interviewers and those we interviewed to approach their discussions in ways that seemed to best suit the specifically sampled parents and households. This approach followed the method of many cognitive cultural sociologists and cognitive-psychological anthropologists, which commends not being too directive in interviews, but rather allowing for much open-ended talk to take place; and conducting many levels and types of analysis of the transcripts, not merely "hearing" what is said "on the surface."[1] This approach improves the chances that the research uncovers whatever reality is operative in households, rather than being too agenda-setting or leading in fixed questions and thus risking finding results that the study itself presupposed and to which it led. Only near the end of interviews, in cases when interview respondents had not addressed important questions of concern, did we more directly probe for answers.

Our approach to interviews thus facilitated a complex, multileveled analysis of interviewee's talk, enabling us to pull apart different aspects of assumptions, claims, feelings, and judgments of those we studied. Allison Pugh puts it this way:

> Interpretive, in-depth interviewing enables access to four kinds of information—
> "the honorable," "the schematic," "the visceral" and "meta-feelings." ... Although
> people surely evince different cultural schemas to explain away particular
> problems, they have a sense for what counts as honorable behavior in their cultural
> world, which may or may not mesh with their innermost predilections.
> Their meta-feelings are a demonstration of the degree to which they are cultural
> migrants, a measure of the distances they have traveled from their early social
> contexts shaping the meanings of their early experiences, to the strictures of the
> cultural milieu in which they find themselves today.[2]

Intentionally conducting this kind of analysis helps us better understand not only what is "on the surface" of the content of what parents say, but other levels of complexity, meaning, ambivalence, emotions, and evaluations that often come out when people are asked to talk at length about topics, rather than asked pointed questions that evoke short answers.

After the interviews were completed, all of the interviewers met together for a two-day debriefing on our experiences, to share our notes and initial reflections on the interviews, and to begin to identify dominant themes and subsample differences in the interview conversations we had. The discussions both relied upon and helped to develop initial "sensitizing concepts" that informed the coding process described later, so that our analysis did not attempt pure, "tabula rasa" induction. The project PI (Smith) took notes on the debriefing meeting discussions, which helped inform the initial phase of the data analysis process.

Our preparation of the collected data for analysis involved four steps: transcribing the digitally recorded English interviews into text, transcribing and translating Spanish interviews into English text, coding the transcribed texts for themes and subthemes of theoretical interest, and developing a supplemental quantitative dataset. A team of three dozen undergraduate and graduate students and contract employees worked to transcribe the nearly 500 audio hours of interview recordings, and as an extra measure of

---

1. For example, Naomi Quinn, *Finding Culture in Talk* (New York: Palgrave Macmillan, 2005); Allison Pugh, "What Good Are Interviews for Thinking about Culture?: Demystifying Interpretive Analysis." *American Journal of Cultural Sociology* 1 (2013): 42–68.

2. Pugh, "What Good Are Interviews for Thinking about Culture?," 64.

quality control, each transcript was thoroughly checked for accuracy. The 25 interviews conducted in Spanish were transcribed by a project researcher who is fluent in Spanish, and those Spanish transcripts were translated into English by 10 Spanish-speaking undergraduate and graduate students. Those transcripts were then prepared for analysis and imported into the analytic software platform.

We coded interviews over a 10-month period, between late 2015 and the summer of 2016, with the help of a team of two dozen highly trained and closely supervised University of Notre Dame graduate and undergraduate student research assistants using the qualitative data analysis software, MAXQDA. We held an initial coding-methods workshop with members of the coding team, to train them on the goals of the project, the purpose of and process for data coding, proper storage of interview data, interrater reliability, and the use of the MAXQDA software interface. After an initial foray into coding, we tested interrating reliability and adjusted coding protocols and rules for consistency of coding. The coding team then performed two stages of coding: (1) a first-order coding of passages in the transcribed interviews and (2) a second-order coding of the coded passages.[3] First-order coding involved the direct selection of phrases and passages in the interview transcripts that provide qualitative evidence of the presence or absence of a particular idea, action, attitude, perception, intent, or other quality or disposition in the respondent, relating directly or indirectly to their transmission of faith to their children. Two dozen main themes were coded, including:

- Parents' role of religion in their own lives

- Parents' assumptions and understandings about religion

- Parents' connection between religion/religious practice and belief and happiness/future happiness

- Approaches to passing on religious faith, belief, and practices to children

- Practices and behaviors of children

- Gender division in teaching children about faith and beliefs

- Motivations for passing on religious faith and practice (or not)

- Parents' influence in thinking about passing on religion and faith— own experiences in church, influence from parents and other family, life experiences, etc.

- Choice of congregation

---

3. See Heather Price and Christian Smith, "Procedures for Reliable Cultural Model Analysis Using Semi-Structured Interviews," *Field Methods* 33, no. 2 (2021).

- Parents' importance of particular beliefs and practices vs. general values or morals

- Importance/priority given to passing on religious faith to children

- Parenting style

- Discipline of child

- Particularly emotional passages

- Career-household parent division in teaching children about faith and beliefs

- Disagreements between parents about what/how/ when/ why to teach children about faith and beliefs

- Parenting influence

- Challenges to parenting

- Childhood demographics

- Role of congregations: fellow congregants, ministers, the general influence of the congregation and programs

- Youth group, youth programs, youth ministers

- Primary/secondary parent role division

- Trauma to parent: during any part of parent's life

- Demographics

The coding team followed a systematic process to code each interview, first developing and continuing to refine the decision rules that determine the scope of their assigned theme. These decision rules guided the coding process and defined which data to include and exclude from the parameters of the themes being coded. Each coder followed a coding method whereby the interview was skimmed for organization, passages related to main themes and subthemes were highlighted, keyword searches were used to increase reliability and reduce coder fatigue error, brief summaries for each interview were written, and codes were reviewed by a supervisor before being submitted and integrated into the larger dataset. After 7 months of coding, the first-order coding process was completed.

To test for reliability, eliminate the chance of single-coder biases occurring, and reach near-consensus of method, we paired coders and assigned them themes. These pairs separately coded identical interviews, from which we calculated interrater reliability (IRR) statistics. Each themed pair was also assigned an external senior coder in relation to whom an additional round of IRR testing was performed. Coders met with their coding supervisors to have their topic explained to them, to review the associated decision rules, and to discuss the scope of their assigned theme. After completing a limited amount of coding, the pairs of coders met in IRR sessions to discuss their working assumptions and revise their decision rules to achieve shared understandings of the themes. IRR sessions repeated during coding until consensus of a minimum of 80 percent of coded passages was achieved,[4] meaning that passages highlighted and marked by two different coders overlapped 80 percent of the time. Once coders met this minimum threshold, we judged consensus to have been reached and the pairs of coders proceeded to code the interviews.

Second-order coding works to code the first-order selected passages and the summary documents to further identify types within themes and underlying commonalities and differences across themes within interviews. In this phase of data preparation, coders did not use the primary transcript documents, but rather coded in greater detail the first-order coded themes. Within themes, coders looked for clustering of ideas and the presence or absence of common elements within the theme. We then used these interpretations to organize subsequent data analysis. For example, coders reviewed all of the passages about motivations of parents to transmit their faith and outlined the common ideas expressed by parents, such as the importance of keeping a heritage alive, reproducing fond memories from parents' childhood, or commitment to develop strong values within a secular society. The coders' interview summaries were also collated and analyzed for emergent themes across first-order themes. These cross-theme patterns we categorized and coded across all of the interviews.

From the clustering of characteristics of themes, we built a supplemental quantitative dataset from the coded interview transcripts' dataset. By interview ID, we identified columns of variables based on the types, patterns, and characteristics for the first-order and second-order themes. For example, religious practices would be quantified into a series of categorical variables, such as "prayer frequency," "religious service attendance," and "volunteering type," where the coder, for instance, interpreted one respondent's interview data to input "daily," "weekly," and "church committee," respectively. These quantified themes produced one comprehensive dataset for all the topics across all coded interview transcripts data. This allows quantitative cross-theme pattern analysis, as well as provides a filtering mechanism to identify subpopulations within the interview pool.

The Interview Questionnaire

Our parent interviews followed the interview guide of questions, while allowing interviewers and interviewed parents the flexibility to explore promising questions and discussions not specified here:

"Intergenerational Transmission of Religious Faith"
Interview Questionnaire

Introduction: "Thank you again for agreeing to do these interviews. Remember that all of your answers are totally <u>confidential</u>, so you can speak freely here. Also, you may <u>skip</u> any question you prefer not to answer."

---

4. As suggested by Matthew Miles and Michael Huberman, *Qualitative Data Analysis: An Expanded Sourcebook* (Thousand Oaks, CA: Sage, 1994).

Current Life Big Picture

Overview: So my goal here is to learn about you, your family, and your experience as a parent—especially as it relates to passing on (or not) of your religious or spiritual faith and practice to CHILD.

Q: First, can you start off just telling me about the big picture of your life now? What's your situation when it comes to family, work, living, schools, friends, or whatever I need to get a context for you and your family?

Q: What sorts of things do you hope to <u>accomplish</u> in the next 10 years of your life?

Q: Do you feel like your life is generally on the <u>right track</u>? Tell me about why and how.

Background

Q: Stepping back, can you tell me about your <u>family situation growing up</u>, about your parents and other family members. How were you raised? And how has that shaped you into the person you became?
  – Social class, education, region/state, neighborhood, values, religion?
  – Happy times? Traumas? Difficulties? Highlights?
  – Childhood friends, school, play, interest, aspirations?
  – What kind of approach did your parents take in parenting you as a child and youth?
  – What about your teenage years?—Work or college experience?—Crucial moments/experiences? Turning points?

View of Life

Q: So back to today, can you tell me more about you <u>yourself as a person</u>? What are you like, your personality, values, interests, etc.?

Q: Can you tell me some about <u>yourself religiously</u>? Are you a religious person?
  – What <u>kind</u> of religion? Tradition? Denomination? [Does particular denomination matter to you?]
  – What do you <u>believe</u> religiously? Probe.
    • particular beliefs about or relationship toward <u>God</u> (or spiritual forces? Or?)? How do you view God? What do you think God might be like, if anything?
  – Regular religious <u>practices</u>?
  – <u>Importance</u> of religious faith and practice?—[IF] <u>Why</u> is religion <u>important</u> (or not important) to you in life?

- How did you learn your religion or spiritual life?—Did it change religiously over time or not? Why? How?
- Doubts or confusions about religious or spiritual matters?
- [If involved at a place of worship] What are the benefits of organized religion in your life? Any drawbacks or problems or liabilities of your being religious?

[*IF R THINKS SOMETHING WRONG WITH WORLD/LIFE*] Q: What do you think is the cause or source of what is wrong with the world, humans, life? [trying to get at any notion of "sin"]

Q: How is religious faith or spiritual life expressed especially in ordinary, everyday life? Beyond possible formal, official CHURCH expressions of religion, are there any other ways faith or spiritual practices show up in your "everyday" living? (e.g., religious meanings of "secular" things, personal spiritual practices, private prayers) [looking for "everyday religion" here]

Q: What about PARTNER? Is religious, which, how, why? How similar/different is PARTNER?

Q: How would family would be different if you removed religion or spiritual life from it? How? Why?

Family Formation & Becoming a Parent *[if single, PARTNER = "the father/mother of your children"]*

Q: How did you and PARTNER meet or get together? What is your story there?

Q: What has your experience with PARTNER been like over the years? Probe.

Q: [*If not repetitive*] Can you tell me the specific story of having CHILD?

Q: Did becoming a parent change you in any particular ways? Change your relationship with PARTNER?

Q: Has becoming a parent changed your views about religion, God, religion, or spirituality in any way?

Q: Tell me about your CHILDREN [1, 2, 3]. What is he/she/they like?

Q: What is your relationship with him/her/them like? Has that changed over time? Close or distant?

Q: How is CHILD doing in life? Getting along with others? School? Attitude? Maturity?

Q: [IF SCHOOL AGE] What sort of school does CHILD attend? How did you decide where to send CHILD to school?

[*IF ALTERNATIVE/PRIVATE*] How did you decide you wanted that kind of school for CHILD?

[*IF PUBLIC*] Do you ever wish you could send CHILD to alternative or private schooling? Why?

Q: [IF PRESCHOOL] What are your thoughts or plans about schooling for CHILD when he/she is older?

Family Description [*IF NOT REPETITIVE*]

Q: So how would you <u>describe your family</u> in general terms?
   - What words or ideas best tell someone what your family is like, what you are all about?
Q: What do members of your family do with <u>free time</u>? Hobbies? Recreation?
   - Time family/CHILD spends watching TV, using computer, or other visual technology?
Q: What sorts of organized or informal <u>activities</u> outside the home is CHILD engaged in?
   - Sports? Music? Drama? Games? Playgroups? Scouts? Religious?
Q: How actively <u>involved</u> are <u>you</u> in these activities (e.g., going to games, seeing performances)?
Q: Does anyone in your family engage in any <u>volunteer</u> work? Is CHILD involved? Why or why not?
Q: [*IF NOT REPETITIVE*] Tell me more specifically about <u>religion</u> and your <u>family</u>—not just you, but your <u>whole family</u>. Very religious? What does that mean? How is religion or faith or CHURCH in your family?
Q: Who is more of the "<u>leader</u>" or "<u>point person</u>" in <u>religious matters</u> in the family?
Q: <u>Why</u> are you <u>part of</u> a CHURCH? How important is that? What does it do or mean for your family?
Q: What specifically do you <u>look for</u> in a CHURCH/place of worship? What are the most important things to you in deciding where to attend?—*music?*—*location?*—*style of service?*—*size?*—*children/youth programs?*
Q: What specifically, if anything, do you <u>look to CHURCH to provide w/re to CHILD</u> in religious influence, teaching, support, or whatever?
   - What has been your <u>experience</u> (re CHILD) with things like religious education classes, Sunday school, youth groups, religious travel, missions trips, etc.?
   - Do you feel <u>cooperation</u> and shared purpose at CHURCH in the spiritual formation of CHILD? Or are there any <u>tensions</u> or people working at <u>cross-purposes</u>? Or?

Aspirations and Challenges

Q: What are your <u>hopes and goals and dreams</u> for CHILD? What do you want to see him/her become or experience or achieve or enjoy in their life, w/re school, money, romance, sports, marriage, religion, etc.?

Q: What are the biggest <u>challenges or difficulties</u> for parents today? What makes parenting hard?

Q: Has CHILD been <u>easy or difficult to guide</u> in a positive direction? How so? Any particular <u>concerns about the well-being or development</u> of CHILD?

Q: What is your experience trying to manage or <u>negotiate the different demands</u> of various parts of CHILD's life—how do <u>you prioritize or coordinate</u> (or not) between different demands and activities?

Q: What do you think is <u>your influence as a parent</u> in CHILD's life <u>compared to other influences</u>, such as their friends and peer groups, the media, school influences, other adults, other institutions?

Q: Are any <u>groups or organizations or programs or institutions particularly supportive</u> of or helpful to you as a parent—like extended family, friends, neighbors, school or community groups, religious, recreation or sports leagues, support groups, play groups?

Q: Some parents we interview see <u>problems in the national and global economy</u> and they <u>worry</u> about whether or not their children will be [as] <u>financially secure/stable</u>; other parents do <u>not</u> seem to see a cause for concern here. Do you ever worry about your child about financial security? Why or why not? [IF SO] What do you do to alleviate that?

Parenting Style

Q: What kind of <u>general style or approach</u> do you take to parenting?—Strict or lenient?
- Boundaries or limits or rules set?
- Freedoms and self-directions you allow?
- Punishments or disciplines? (did ever spank?)
- How much can trust CHILD with independence, or need for oversight?
- Feel responsible to protect, versus allowing CHILD to take risks?
- Relate as friend of or authority over CHILD?—explain things, or just say how it's gonna be?

Q: Is CHILD <u>required</u> to go to [RELIGIOUS ACTIVITIES] or is that up to them?

Q: How <u>well</u> do you think your overall parenting style <u>works</u>? Has it <u>changed</u>? Why, how?

Q: Do you and PARTNER ever <u>disagree</u> about parenting styles/approaches? How do you handle that?

Importance of (Religious) Reproduction

Q: Generally, how important is it to you that CHILD ends up sharing most of your personal general beliefs, values, and lifestyle?

Q: How would you feel if CHILD grew up to look, believe, live very differently from you in lifestyle?—re: family, social class, sex, religion, politics, work, possessions, financial security, cars, vacations, entertainment, etc.

Q: How important is it to you that CHILD grow up believing and practicing the same religious faith as you? [NR = "beliefs about religion"]

Q: Why [IF] do you want CHILD to grow up to be a religious or spiritual person?

Q: What, if any, are the essential spiritual beliefs or practices that you hope CHILD will adopt?

Q: How religiously different from you could CHILD grow up to be before it would bother you?

Q: Do you think CHILD should marry someone of the same religion as you are, assuming they get married, or not necessarily? [NR = "someone not religious"] Why?

Q: How much would it bother you if your grandchildren grew up being non-religious? Of a totally different religion? Why? [NR = "very religious"]

Q: Some youth drop out of religion as teenagers until their earlier 30s, when they have their own children. Would it be okay with you or it would bother you if CHILD did that?

Conversations and Confidence

Q: Do you and CHILD have conversations about significant things? How easy or hard is that?
  – Topics? Dealing with hard moral questions? Topics avoided? Why?

Q: Have you had any conversations with CHILD about God, spiritual matters or religion? How did that come up and go?

Q: Has CHILD ever asked you questions about God, religion, or spirituality that you've found difficult to answer? How? Why?

Q: Do you ever feel you don't understand your own religious tradition/faith well enough to convey it effectively to CHILD? If so, how do you deal with that? (*Probe*: Q: Some parents feel generally confident and secure in shaping their children's religious and spiritual lives; others feel uncertain, hesitant, or insecure. How do you personally feel? [IF UNCERTAIN] Areas that are particularly challenging for you? Why?)

Q: Some parents we talk to seem to feel the need to "outsource" the religious training of children to "specialists," like CHURCH, youth ministers, religious camps. Have you ever felt that? [IF SO] Why?

Q: Has CHILD ever known someone who <u>died</u>, or ever been to a <u>funeral</u> that provided the occasion to talk with CHILD about <u>death</u>? Describe.

Q: Do you ever talk with CHILD about <u>your</u> or <u>their</u> religious <u>doubts</u>, confusions, disbelief, etc.?

Q: Has talking with CHILD <u>influenced you</u>, your own religious beliefs or knowledge or practices?

Relation to Religious Communities

Q: Does CHILD generally <u>like CHURCH</u> or not? Why or why not?
- Do you ever have to negotiate or argue <u>about going to CHURCH</u>? What is your approach?

Q: What <u>role does CHURCH</u> play (or not) <u>in shaping</u> CHILD religiously or spiritually? Or otherwise?

Q: Who, if anyone, at CHURCH has been <u>helpful</u> to you as a parent or has <u>most influenced</u> CHILD?

Q: Have you had any <u>disagreements</u> or <u>conflicts</u> with anyone at CHURCH about the approach to the religious or spiritual formation of CHILD or other children at CHURCH?

Q: How helpful or not is your CHURCH in <u>equipping or supporting you as a parent</u> for the job of passing on your religious faith and practice to your children? Describe/explain.

Q: Is there <u>anything</u> your CHURCH <u>could do better</u> to equip or support you in this way? What? How?

Religious Transmission

Q: What role do you think that *parents* <u>ought</u> to play in helping to <u>form</u> the religious faith and practices of their children? That is . . .
- Do parents have the <u>right</u> or <u>obligation</u> to influence children to accept and practice their own faith?
- Or should they *just expose* children to different religious options and leave choosing up to them?

Q: Are parents or CHURCH more *responsible* for passing on religious faith and practice to children? Why?

Q: What are the most important things, if any, that you as a parent <u>have intentionally done in the past or do now</u> to try to pass on religious faith and practices to CHILD?
Probe:
- Reading scripture or other religious texts together?
- Praying together at meals?

- Family devotions or prayers apart from meals?
- Play spiritual/religious music/talk radio in home?
- Watching religiously oriented TV shows or movies together?
- Enrolling CHILD in catechism class/confirmation/other sacramental prep programs?

Q: Is CHILD interested in religious things, or not? What do [WOULD] you do if/when CHILD expresses <u>resistance</u> to religious activities inside or outside of the home?

Q: Is there anything you have decided definitely <u>not</u> to do as a parent in passing on your religious faith or practices to CHILD? Anything you <u>avoid</u>? What and why?

Q: Are there other people <u>outside</u> of your family <u>who have significantly influenced</u> CHILD's <u>*religious formation*</u>, of beliefs, identity, practices, etc.? Describe.

Q: What about CHILD's friends and <u>peers</u>? Are they a <u>positive or negative influence</u> on CHILD's <u>religious</u> faith or practices?

Q: Does your church have a <u>youth group</u>? [IF SO] Does CHILD participate in it? Do they like it? What kind of influence do you think it might have on them?

Q: Do you and PARTNER <u>agree</u> or ever <u>disagree</u> on what sorts of spiritual beliefs or practices you would like CHILD to adopt? [IF SO] How do you handle those disagreements?

Q: [IF *INTERFAITH* HH] Do you try to pass on both your own *and* PARTNER'S religious tradition? Or just one or the other? How does that work?

Q: Are there <u>other adults</u> beyond your immediate family who play a role in the formation of CHILD's religious faith (i.e. grandparents, family friends, school teachers, etc.)? What do they do?

Q: Do you have any <u>visual or material religious objects</u> in your home (e.g., pictures, statues, icons, candles, wall hangings, etc.)?

Q: Do you have religiously oriented <u>media</u> (playing) in your house (or car), like magazines, TV, CDs, radio, literature? If so, what role does that play?

Q: If you had to make your best guess, what do you think CHILD will look like religiously or spiritually at age 30 or 35?

[IF CHILD IS OLDER] Q: Looking back, do you <u>wish you would have done anything differently</u> in raising CHILD, either generally or religiously?

<u>Last Opportunity</u>: Okay, so I have asked a lot of questions and we've discussed a lot in depth. Are there any other ideas we have not already discussed that you'd like to share before we stop? Anything that did not come up in our talking so far that is worth adding?

[**CODES**: CHILD = name of child if only one, "children" if 2+ children. CHURCH = "church" for Christians & LDS, "synagogue" or "temple" for Jews, "mosque" or "prayer center" for Muslims, "temple" for Hindus and Buddhists.]

Survey Datasets Quantitatively Analyzed

Descriptions of the survey datasets that we analyzed for this book and their background methodologies can be found at their associated website links:

- The "Culture of American Families" survey of the Institute for the Advanced Study of Culture at the University of Virginia: https://s3.amazonaws.com/iasc-prod/uploads/pdf/4a18126c1a0768oe4fbe.pdf.
- The "Faith and Family in America" survey of *Religion and Ethics Newsweekly*: https://www.pbs.org/wnet/religionandethics/2005/10/19/october-19-2005-faith-and-family-in-america/11465/ and https://www-tc.pbs.org/wnet/religionandethics/files/2005/10/ReligionAndFamily_Methodology.pdf.
- The National Study of Youth and Religion (NSYR) first and fourth wave surveys: https://youthandreligion.nd.edu/research-design/, https://youthandreligion.nd.edu/assets/102496/master_just_methods_11_12_2008.pdf, https://youthandreligion.nd.edu/assets/102499/survey.pdf, and https://youthandreligion.nd.edu/assets/140961/w4_survey_instrument.pdf.
- The US Congregational Life Survey (2008–2009): http://www.thearda.com/Archive/Files/Descriptions/CLS08LS.asp.

Index